Illinois Central College
Learning Resources Center

CHARLIE
CHAPLIN

BY JOHN McCABE

Charlie Chaplin
The Comedy World of Stan Laurel
George M. Cohan: The Man Who Owned Broadway
Mr. Laurel and Mr. Hardy
Proclaiming the Word (with G. B. Harrison)
Laurel & Hardy (with Al Kilgore and Richard W. Bann)

CHARLIE CHAPLIN

John McCabe

DOUBLEDAY & COMPANY, INC. GARDEN CITY, NEW YORK 1978

ISBN: 0-385-11445-1
Library of Congress Catalog Card Number: 77-11771

Copyright © 1978 by John McCabe
ALL RIGHTS RESERVED
PRINTED IN THE UNITED STATES OF AMERICA
FIRST EDITION

For
VIJA

Manai sirds mīļai sievai

CONTENTS

INTRODUCTION

When my publishers suggested a Chaplin biography I reacted as I think most film historians would: enough. Surely no man in film history has been more written about, more documented. It must all have been done. Mostly it has, excepting the memoirs Mrs. Chaplin will surely favor us with one day.

But Doubleday was right, I am now sure, to commission an omnibus biography because, despite the extensive Chaplin bibliography, much of it is to be found only in rather obscure journals or books long out of print. Moreover, the only full-scale biography, Theodore Huff's *Charlie Chaplin*, although still available, was written over twenty-five years ago. My principal task, as I see it, is to update and amplify Huff in view of recent scholarship, and to draw from some remote corners a fuller overview of Chaplin as man and artist than anything yet published—all of this without unduly emphasizing the analytical.

For the dreary fact is that no artist in the history of modern culture has been more overassessed. I have succeeded (if that is the word) in reading virtually every book and magazine article published about Chaplin in English and French. The French material, on the whole, did not contribute much. Chaplin is almost sainted in France and understandably that kind of reverence is largely unjudicial. But no matter the country, many of these exegeses make depressing reading. Some of them are metaphysical posturings that find in Chaplin's art every nuance of existence,

and others too frequently crush an obvious entertainment device
into a vapory metaphor pertinent only to the writer's psychological enthrallments. It is always a temptation, says Robert Sherwood, to soar into symbolism when considering a Chaplin film.

Within these pages, "Charlie" is the word used for the boy, the
young man, the son of Hannah and the brother of Sydney as well
as The Tramp; "Chaplin" is the public figure, the professional,
the adult. "Charlie" and "Chaplin" are at times bewilderingly
different people. In these pages I have tried to give the essential flavor of Chaplin's principal films, not detailing the action ex-
haustively by any means but seeking rather to convey the films'
uniqueness and character as best I may. I must say this is the
most difficult thing for film historians to do. Telling others of a
singular visual experience ("You really should have seen it!") can
never be fully satisfactory. It is not unlike a beer lover's describing
to a teetotaler the warm rushing glow when the first dollop of ale
hits the stomach. Nonetheless if such visualization as I can sum
up stimulates readers to see some of these films for themselves,
that will be reward enough for me.

Inevitably for my purposes Chaplin's My Autobiography
(1964) must stand as final word on many matters although it
sometimes errs on dates and contains a number of small inaccuracies, the results surely of an aging memory looking back over
an unusually full life. I have also made very judicious use of an
early Chaplin autobiography, Charlie Chaplin's Own Story
(1916), some of which is melodramatic fiction concocted by his
ghostwriter. Stan Laurel gave me his annotated copy of that
book; common sense and Stan's marginalia have, I believe, steered
me away from dubious matter there. Other vital biographical material has come from even earlier Chaplin autobiographies, sparse
though they tend to be. "Charlie Chaplin's Story—As Narrated by
Mr. Chaplin Himself" (1915) is one, as published in the then rep-
utable Photoplay magazine; others are Chaplin's My Trip Abroad
(1922) and a later biographical memoir, "A Comedian Sees the
World" (Woman's Home Companion, 1933). Chaplin also gave
numerous interviews throughout his life and, although contradictory in some details, these help make the general flux of his life
and career more visible. Two former Chaplin press agents, Jim
Tully and Carlyle Robinson, have written with eloquent and

somewhat puzzled affection about their ex-boss; and two close
friends of Chaplin, Konrad Bercovici and Max Eastman, have left
valuable personal insights into his unique character. As Stan
Laurel told me, Charlie Chaplin never answers letters so I have
been denied the opportunity of personal encounter with my subject. But I believe I am not greatly disadvantaged thereby. His
work speaks for itself, and in respect to his life presumably his autobiography and his recent *My Life in Pictures* (1974) give all he
wishes to say publicly about his work and himself.

Twenty years ago when I was researching my book, *Mr. Laurel
and Mr. Hardy*, Stan Laurel spoke to me at length about his
much-loved former colleague and roommate. He spoke indeed so
lengthily that I was a little offput. I was more interested at the
time in matters close at hand. But every comment Stan made
about Chaplin I dutifully included in my notes and set them
apart. Commencing work on this book, I went gratefully to those
notes and found them illuminating the personality of Charlie
Chaplin in striking terms. With them in mind I began work in a
spirit of cool objectivity until, through the courtesy of Blackhawk
Films, Davenport, Iowa, rbc films of Los Angeles, and a few
friends, I was able to see virtually all of Chaplin's films, some important ones among them, for the first time. My cool objectivity
changed to warm objectivity.

Until just recently some key Chaplin films have been generally
unavailable. Like many film buffs, I own copies of some good
early Chaplins, *Easy Street*, *The Cure*, and a few others, but also
like most film buffs, I had not had the opportunity to see the mature Chaplin extensively, particularly the films of his middle
period—those coming after the great Mutual two-reelers and before
the classic feature films of later years. When in the course of six
months I saw all of Chaplin plain, I was moved (in several
senses) to discover again what so few people are able to these days
—that Chaplin is one of the choice and master spirits of our age.
When one looks at what passes for comedy presently on television
and film, one sees so much more vividly the colossus Chaplin truly
is. In his own creative period (1915–57) he was also a giant but
one had no trouble finding him. His ideogram of derby, cane, and
splayfoot shoes was the universal icon of great film comedy. To
some extent he persists so in our consciousness but immediate,

particularized memories of him are not now so readily available. Hence this book, which tries to see him in the context not only of his times but of our own as well.

Stan Laurel informally set forth for me this major biographical premise which he firmly believed: Charlie Chaplin, given his background, personal and professional, was an inevitable eccentric, deeply shy yet heartily gregarious, a childlike romantic, a non-intellectual, who husbanded his genius carefully to become the greatest comedian-actor of this century. That hypothesis I believe the best evidence verifies.

                              J. McC.
                              Mackinac Island, Michigan

CHARLIE CHAPLIN

THE BITTER BOYHOOD

If, as is likely, one never gets over one's childhood, Charlie Chaplin's was the true shaping force of his personality and to large degree of his talent. In his very old age he was still capable of flushing hot with anger, striking the arm of his chair, and saying vehemently, "Victorian England was a cruel, damnably cruel place. It was a pitiless time!" It was certainly pitiless to him.

Chaplin's almost terrifying indignation at the circumstances of his youth was deeply justified. The South London neighborhoods of his youth, Walworth and Lambeth, are even today depressed areas. But when Chaplin was born on the evening of April 16, 1889, in a flat on East Lane, Walworth, the mean streets surrounding his birthplace were Cruikshankian in their squalor. In later years before he was able to confront the memories of his cruel upbringing, Chaplin told at least two interviewers that he was born in Fontainebleau, France. Later he admitted to birth in London but engagingly allowed that he had been "conceived" at Fontainebleau. This romanticizing was an urgent attempt to blot out the festering recollections of his childhood.

Shortly after Charlie's birth his mother moved her little family —Charlie and his half brother Sydney—to West Square and St. George's Road in nearby Lambeth. The three rooms they occupied there were comfortably furnished and gave no hint of the poverty-drenched atmosphere just outside its windows. Hannah Chaplin was a resolute and charming woman. Her daintiness consorted well with her impeccable performing talents as a comedy soubrette, usually in roles of the clever maid or the cheery confidante of the heroine. It was in just such a role that Hannah first attracted Charlie Chaplin's father when the two were featured players in G. H. Jessop's romantic comic opera, *Shamus O'Brien*. Charles Chaplin and Hannah were married in 1886 and not long after Charlie's birth separated. At the time of this breakup Charles had attained considerable reputation as a music hall singer and comedian. Quiet and easygoing when sober, as his alcoholism took ascendancy he flamed into ungovernable rages and he became, in the words of one friend, "more than a bloody handful." Hannah's innate coolness toward him on these increasingly frequent occasions during their marriage was usually touched with humor. When his temper caused her to flee temporarily for refuge in Brighton, he wired, "What are you up to?" "Balls, parties and picnics, darling!" was the reply.

Hannah Chaplin was tenacious of will, a family trait. Her father, Charles Hill, was an Irish revolutionary of considerable mental resilience and staying power. He fled English oppression in Ireland to find refuge paradoxically enough in the heart of England. His work as a cobbler fascinated Charlie, who watched his grandfather in rare moments of anger or frustration overcome them simply by taking pieces of leather and working without cease through the night to fashion a shoe. Then the old man would hold up the shoe without a word, looking at it appreciatively as if to say, "I made that, that whole shoe; no one can take that creative act from me. I am satisfied." This perseverance of Grandfather Hill was not the least of the characteristics Charlie inherited from him. Hill was also a gentle person.

Grandfather Hill's wife was half Spanish, half Gypsy, the latter blood a well-kept secret; Charlie did not reveal the fact until his middle age. The knowledge delighted him as it would almost any artist. Grandmother Hill was also reputed to be part Jewish but on that the differences of opinion are curious indeed. As nearly as can be determined, Charlie Chaplin is virtually part Jewish almost most of the time. If that statement confuses, it is clarity itself compared to the contradictory evidence prompting it, particularly the evidence coming from Chaplin himself. Of that, more anon.

Charles Chaplin, Sr., derived from Huguenot blood. "Chaplin" stems from the French word *capeline*, a mailed hood. Chaplin's ancestors emigrated to the Suffolk coast of England as refugees following the St. Bartholomew's Day massacre. One of five brothers (three of whom settled in South Africa), Charles, Sr., had a rollicking baritone voice and a gift for writing popular songs that made him a favorite in London music halls of the 1880s. He later traveled briefly to the United States, appearing at Tony Pastor's Music Hall in 1898. His favorite place of resort in London was his brother Spencer's pub where he delighted patrons with popular ballads in his repertoire like "Oui! Tray Bong!" and "Eh! Boys?" Out of affection for his brother, Charles, Sr., named his son Charles Spencer Chaplin.

Charles and Hannah Chaplin together were rather well off. Hannah, alternating the stage names of Lily Harley and Lily Chaplin, made a good salary which augmented her husband's considerable if sporadic income and gave the couple a comfortable living. Charlie's earliest memories went back to this time at West Square in the house where he almost died. He kept a little box of childish treasures as youngsters frequently do, and among his collection were a few coins. His brother Sydney had been attempting to impress Charlie with a few magic tricks, the most spectacular of which was a quite creditable pretense at swallowing a coin and bringing it up again through his nose. Not to be outdone, Charlie promptly swallowed a halfpenny and began choking to death. His mother held him upside down, slapped and pummeled him until the offending coin was dislodged.

It was shortly after this that Charlie made what his mother always called his comedy debut. He was playing on the floor of the West Square house when he noticed for the first time under his mother's long skirts the outlines of her anklebone. He had never seen her anklebone before. Like halfpennies, he had connected bones with swallowing; it was, it seemed to him, what dogs always gulped down. After being told by Hannah what her anklebone was, Charlie said, "You must have swallowed a big one to have it stick out like that." Hannah told that story all her life, instancing it as her son's first contribution to comedy.

As her husband's visits to Spencer's pub grew more and more protracted, Hannah had a difficult time of it financially. She received little help from her husband or from her former husband, Sydney Hawkes, a self-styled British aristocrat and father of her other son, Sydney. In the days when Charles, Sr., lived with Hannah he was much taken with bright-eyed young Sydney and insisted the boy bear his surname. In later years Sydney remembered little of his stepfather. He was born March 17, 1885, in Cape Town, South Africa, where his mother had eloped with Hawkes a year before. Hawkes convinced Hannah that he was a member of the House of Lords; it was a great disillusionment to her a few months later to find that he was a not particularly successful bookmaker. Tiring of the occasionally affluent but uneventful life of Cape Town, Hannah divorced Hawkes and returned to England where she married Chaplin. Oddly, her son Sydney very much resembled his stepfather and a number of family friends said he looked more like Charles Chaplin than Charlie did. Sydney and Charlie were one in more than looks, name, and blood. They formed through the years a brotherly compound of comedic talent, business acuity, and deep affection that was to take them to very great heights. Charlie without Sydney would have gone far but not as far as he did eventually and certainly not as easily.

When Charlie was two, at a time when his father and mother were separated, Hannah fell in love with a personable music hall singer, Leo Dryden. From that romance came two other half brothers for Charlie: Guy Dryden, born in 1901, and Wheeler Dryden, born a year later. Leo Dryden took his sons to Canada where they were raised. Wheeler came to visit his mother and Charlie in the mid-1920s and remained as a minor functionary and actor in the Chaplin studio until his death in 1957.

When Charles, Sr., began to come home less and less it became clear that he was constitutionally improvident. Hannah left him and concentrated on her career. For some months she was able to provide adequately for her boys until her voice, never strong, weakened under a strenuous regimen of music hall performances. She fell prey more and more to laryngitis. Her husband's improvidence grew; he ultimately terminated the support money for the boys he had been sending her. Hannah sued him but unavailingly, and she continued to strain her voice in her now urgent need to work in music halls. At times her voice would break sharply onstage and the audience's rude reaction was another enervating tension.

One evening, singing in Aldershot at a theatre frequented mainly by uninhibited soldiers, Hannah's voice failed her in mid-song, the howling laughter driving her from the stage. Charlie had been brought to the theatre that night and the stage manager, who had seen the little boy entertain Hannah's friends, led him onstage and explained his presence to the startled audience. Confident little Charlie announced that he would sing "Jack Jones," an old coster song his father had taught him, and the boy began forthrightly as the orchestra sought to find his key.

> "Jack Jones well and known to everybody
> Round about the market, don't yer see,
> I've no fault to find with Jack at all,
> Not when 'e's as 'e used to be.
> But since 'e's had the bullion left him
> 'E has altered for the worst."

There was a roar of appreciation from the crowd that Charlie could not comprehend. He suddenly felt a sharp sting on his cheek and thought for a terrified second that they were hurling things at him. And so they were—thick pennies and shillings, not easy to come by in 1894. "Oh, wait, wait!" Charlie shouted to the orchestra. "It's money! Wait just a minute! Wait till I get it all and I'll sing a lot." The delighted audience applauded as the stage manager hurried out with a handkerchief to help the boy collect his prizes. Charlie thought the man was going to keep what he picked up and objected strenuously. When he realized all the money was to be his—almost three easily won pounds—the boy turned to the audience and concluded his song smartly:

> "For to see the way he treats all his old pals
> Fills me with nothing but disgust.
> Each Sunday morning he reads the *Telegraph*,
> Once he was contented with the *Star*.
> Since Jack Jones has come into a little bit of cash,
> Well, 'e don't know where 'e are."

The applause was warming and Charlie sang next an Irish march song from his mother's repertoire, danced, and did several impersonations. These imitations were a vital part of his mother's act.

She mimicked popular actresses of the day, and in repeating these impersonations Charlie was not only demonstrating the wares of his first and best teacher in that art but also initiating a custom that would last the rest of his life. Shakespeare had his sugared sonnets among his private friends; Charlie Chaplin always entertained privately with an astonishing array of impersonations.

The Aldershot experience was a significant milestone for Charlie. "That night was my first appearance on the stage," he said, "and Mother's last." Hannah never regained effective use of her singing voice and her livelihood was seriously threatened. Legal action against her husband for financial aid failed and she was reduced to pawning her jewelry. Although she could no longer sing, her dancing was lively enough and when Charlie was five she joined the Katti Lanner ballet at the Empire Theatre. She took Charlie to the theatre with her every night. Ten-year-old Syd could and did fend for himself on these occasions. Charlie was quite the spoiled darling of the chorus ladies and Nellie Richards, a star turn, had clear memories of him forty years later.

He was mischievous, she recalled, and she had to spank him occasionally when he was in her care. "He was a regular little demon at times. He would stop there in the wings, singing my choruses half a line ahead of me, and so vigorously that I'm sure people in front must have heard him. The harder I frowned at him, the wider he grinned, and went right on with it. I was always threatening to spank him, so usually he ran like a hare when the last lines of my song were on his lips. I smacked him where he sat down—and more than once! . . . but he had a wonderful ear for music even then, and picked up almost everything I sang."

There was little for Charlie to sing about in life at home. This is why the dazzling upbeat life of the music halls was so appealing and would all his life remain a lovely memory. Into his life unceasingly, it seemed, came such inexplicable moments of sorrow as the time when his mother took him to Kennington Park to play. She sat on a bench as Charlie skipped away to play in a nearby children's gymnasium. A few minutes later he returned and, wanting to surprise her, moved up quietly behind the bench, where he heard her soft weeping. Shocked, he ran to her side and wept with her. Hannah spent an hour trying to comfort the distraught boy. For the rest of his life Chaplin detested public parks, and when it was necessary in his early film years to make movies in them he was always disquieted.

Hannah tried valiantly to make life easier for her boys. In the more desperate days of their poverty she provided them with peerless entertainment. The mimetic skills of Syd and Charlie Chaplin were developed under the superb tutelage of their mother. Not beautiful, but with a piquant charm radiating from strongly expressive dark blue eyes, her other attractive features were her long, silky brown hair and small, eloquent hands which her son inherited. A multilinguist, Hannah was a great actress (our source for this is a great actor, her son) who could one moment imitate a frippery music hall turn, then swing back into the golden-toned voice of Ellen Terry, England's best actress. Anecdotes were always vivified by her inimitably taking all the roles in conversation described, another habit her son took up from her and continued for the rest of his days.

"If it had not been for my mother," Chaplin said in 1918, "I doubt if I could have made a success of pantomime. She was one of the greatest pantomime artists I have ever seen. She would sit for hours at a window, looking down at the people on the street and illustrating with her hands, eyes, and facial expression just what was going on below. All the time, she would deliver a running fire of comment. And it was through watching and listening to her that I learned not only how to express my emotions with my hands and face, but also how to observe and to study people.

"She was almost uncanny in her observations. For instance, she would see Bill Smith coming down the street in the morning, and I would hear her say: 'There comes Bill Smith. He's dragging his feet and his shoes are polished. He looks mad, and I'll wager he's had a fight with his wife, and come off without his breakfast. Sure enough! There he goes into the bake shop for a bun and coffee!'

"And inevitably during the day, I would hear that Bill Smith had had a fight with his wife."

What is generally not remembered is that Charles Chaplin, Sr., was a mimic too. Although this was only an incidental part of his act, he occasionally incorporated imitations of prominent English personages into his routines and was widely praised for them in theatrical trade papers.

Of his mother's tremendous acting abilities Charlie Chaplin has

told one particularly memorable story. He was ill. Sydney had
gone to night school and Hannah began to tell her invalid of the
Christian heritage. As she read the New Testament to the sick boy
she annotated her readings with comments on Christ's personality, acting out the various roles in the Bible account with great
fervor. As she reached the climax of the drama at Golgotha with
the words, "My God, my God, why hast thou forsaken me?" she
wept and Charlie wept with her. "Don't you see," she said, "how
human He was; like all of us. He too suffered doubt."

Impulsively Charlie declared he wanted to die at once to meet
Jesus. "Jesus wants you to live first," Hannah said, "and fulfill
your destiny here." In this vivid way, her son said later, had his
mother "illuminated to me the kindliest light this world has ever
known, which has endowed literature and the theatre with their
greatest and richest themes: love, pity and humanity." The themes,
one must add, of Charlie Chaplin's best films.

Hannah Chaplin was his best mentor. He would learn from
others, eagerly borrow concepts and skills and inspirations from
them, but humanity and an abiding passion for it was given Charlie in deep measure by his mother. In the first bloom of his success he gave her the ultimate accolade. In an autobiography written for *Photoplay* magazine in 1915 he said:

> It seems to me that my mother was the most splendid woman I
> ever knew. I can remember how charming and well-mannered she
> was. She spoke four languages fluently and had a good education. I
> have met a lot of people knocking around the world since; but I
> have never met a more thoroughly refined woman than my mother.
> If I have amounted to anything, it will be due to her.

Hannah was ceaselessly vigilant in attending to Sydney and
Charlie even in what seemed at the time small ways. Believing
Bernard Shaw's dictum that it is impossible for an Englishman to
open his mouth without making some other Englishman despise
him, she made sure that the boys never spoke with the harsh
Cockney accent of their playmates. She taught her boys what
religious values she could but she was a late convert to a working
Christianity and never became a skilled catechist.

The urgencies of the little family's growing poverty finally
forced her to take any kind of job. The theatre seemingly closed

to her as occupation, she did occasional jobs as a practical nurse but found her best skills as a seamstress. Having made her own theatrical costumes for years, she turned to her sewing machine as a livelihood. There was one brief and glorious holiday from poverty when Sydney one day brought home a purse of gold coins he found on a bus while selling newspapers. Because no personal identification was with it, Hannah felt no scruples about taking the money and giving the boys an excursion at Southend-on-Sea, the nearest seaside resort to London. It was surcease of sorrow of fairy-tale dimension, and Chaplin was never to forget it. Sixty years later, following a life pattern of searching for the scenes of his childhood, he returned to Southend hoping to find something of what he had known that enchanting holiday. Southend had changed inevitably but the memory of it was still exhilarating after all those decades.

But Southend in 1896 was quite temporary solace for the misery that descended on the Chaplins. The sewing machine needed for Hannah's seamstress work was repossessed for lack of payment and the most vital source of their income was thereby stopped. There was no alternative but to apply to Lambeth Borough for the family's admission to the local workhouse. To use a crueler phrase better fitting the degrading situation, to enter the poorhouse.

Hannah's earlier desperate attempts to maintain her family's self-regard were now vitiated. Just seven, Charlie was unable at first to recognize either the ignominy of the situation or the loneliness of it. It was rather a lark until he found that his mother had been sent to the women's ward and Sydney to the older boys'. Hannah herself was so devastated by separation from her children that a few weeks later she applied for their discharge, knowing well that she would have to apply for readmission at the end of a single day together. Yet it was worth it, amply worth it despite the disgruntlement of the authorities. But this precious day's joy of reunion was to fade away in the succession of grindingly oppressive months that followed.

Syd and Charlie were moved to a school for orphans and destitute children at Hanwell, a few miles outside London. Initially separated from Sydney because he was in the infants' division, Charlie experienced a sense of deprivation that was to last a lifetime.

To be destitute, friendless, and alone at the age of seven when you knew your family was not far away suffering the same indignity was traumatic. Charlie Chaplin's overwhelming detestation of poverty and concomitantly his need and concern for money through his adult life began in his Hanwell days. He never had enough to eat there, his clothing was inadequate, and all the children were treated like offending Adams and duly flogged for the slightest infraction of the rules.

Of warmth, physical or spiritual, there was almost none. One treat was given the children annually. At Christmas the boys were each given an orange and a small box of candy. Many weeks ahead of the holiday, Charlie planned minutely what he would do with his gift. He would keep the bag under his jersey, held up by his belt, a constant reminder of its bountiful presence. He would make the contents last as long as possible. But first he proposed to eat the orange peel bit by bit, then the sections a half at a time, making it stretch over a two-week period. Then he would begin eating the candy slowly, one piece a day, sucking a bit on it in the morning, a bit more in the afternoon, finishing it at night. But— very importantly for his plan—never more than a single piece of candy a day. This attenuated pleasure would last more than a month, and Charlie looked forward to it with unbounded eagerness.

He received neither the orange nor the candy. The day before Christmas, in giddy anticipation of the holiday, he forgot to make his bed, a cardinal sin at Hanwell. In a situation virtually out of *Oliver Twist*, the ward supervisor decreed Charlie was not to receive his gift. The stinging, crushing disappointment of that was almost unendurable. Some of Charlie's fellow inmates laughed but two of the boys understood. They each gave him one of their pieces of candy, a prodigious gift from boys starved for sweets. Charlie made those two pieces of candy last half a month. The people—and they were many—who were to accuse Chaplin in later years of being tightfisted would have profited by hearing of this and similar incidents of deprivation which marred even more signally an already unhappy childhood.

A few days later Charlie was beaten for nervously pleading guilty to burning a few bits of paper in the lavatory, something he did not do. But he refused to cry out when three stripes were laid on his back. Another time he suffered the contempt of his fellows because he developed ringworm, which resulted in his hair being totally clipped, iodine smeared over his shaven head, and a large kerchief tied over it. Confined to a special ward, this torture lasted for weeks. Another genteel torture began when a teacher noticed Charlie writing, as he did naturally, with his left hand. For this impertinence he was soundly rapped over the knuckles. Inevitably he continued to use his left hand; just as persistently the teacher smacked him across the left knuckles until they became black and blue. Desperately, painfully, the boy tried to write with his right hand and succeeded. The only benefit of that episode was a dubious one: all his life Chaplin was ambidextrous.

Charlie's single relief from these continuing indignities was an occasional glimpse of Sydney who, as a kitchen worker, could smuggle out to Charlie a random bread roll and butter. Shortly after, Sydney left Hanwell, taking an option open to eleven-year-old poorhouse boys: joining the Royal Navy. Charlie's sense of desolation deepened.

One ecstatic day Hannah appeared. She had set about to repair their fortunes and, as Charlie embraced her, her fresh loveliness increased his sense of self-loathing. The infirmary nurse asked Hannah to excuse the boy's dirty face. Hannah laughed, hugged and kissed him, and her exact words Charlie remembered to his old age: "With all thy dirt, I love thee still." She was able to take Charlie back to London and Sydney was released from his navy duties to join them. There was a brief St. Martin's summer of prosperity before Hannah's financial condition worsened, and both boys were again sent to the workhouse, this time in Norwood. The neighborhood was a shade nicer than Hanwell but the school itself was as depressing.

It was on the school grounds while playing soccer one day that a nurse walked out to tell Sydney of Hannah's descent into the maelstrom. She had been certified insane. Sydney continued the game, trying to credit the news, then went away to weep by himself. Charlie could not, would not, believe the news, preferring to think that she had deliberately left the world's harshness, taking this form of escape. If so, she went to an unsympathetic refuge, the barren lunatic asylum at Cane Hill.

The court placed Sydney and Charlie in their father's custody, and for Charlie at least it promised to be high adventure. He had only the vaguest memories of his father and leaving the work-house to live with him and Sydney—and, as it happened, with Louise, his father's mistress, and their little son—was all rather overwhelming. The two-room lodging at 287 Kennington Road was barely adequate for Charles, Sr., Louise, and the four-year-old offspring. The incursion of Sydney and Charlie was an irritant to Louise, a blowzy but attractive alcoholic, and the boys quickly learned how to stay out of her way.

Charlie's relief came in the form of school, a "bleak divertis-sement" he called it, but much preferable to the ungracious at-mosphere of the Chaplin rooms. Sydney concentrated on football. Charlie particularly dreaded Saturday because it was a half holi-day when he was put to work at home scrubbing the floors and cleaning knives. Despite the great love which even nine-year-old Charlie saw between his father and Louise, the woman's resent-ment of the man's drinking triggered her own and caused her some evenings to throw Sydney and Charlie out of the house. The boys would wander through South London streets, dossing down where they could in alleyways and doorways.

It was during these dispirited days and nights on the streets, when it seemed that life could hardly descend lower, that Charlie had an experience destined to have the most profound artistic effect on him, an impact lasting and infinitely rewarding. As the active example of his mother made him indelibly a mime, a brief experience in a London street—almost a mystic experience—al-tered the boy by committing him forever to music.

One bitter midnight as he was walking past Kennington Cross, hungry, looking for a place to sleep, Charlie suddenly became aware of a clarinet and harmonica in a curiously engaging duet playing a popular song of the day:

> You are the honeysuckle; I am the bee.
> I'd like to sip the honey, dear, from those red lips, you see.
> I love you, dearie, dearie, and I want you to love me—
> You are my honey, honeysuckle; I am your bee.

At the time Charlie did not know these words. He was captivated by the music; it taught him immediately what melody was. He had heard, indeed knew, many sprightly songs from the music hall, but this was quite different. He understood for the first time that music could be beautiful as well as funny, that melody could create and hold forever the most poignant emotions, could crystallize charm. "The Honeysuckle and the Bee" symbolized for him thereafter the "sweet mystery" of music; it had a "rare beauty, a beauty that has gladdened and haunted me from that moment." Heard today, "The Honeysuckle and the Bee" indeed has a plaintive charm, a simplicity and direct emotional appeal typical of the music Chaplin was to write in middle age.

In their tatterdemalion days on the street Sydney and little Charlie never blamed their father for his shiftlessness. He was not a bad man, simply a genial alcoholic trying desperately when sober to do what he could for his family. He had an innate elegance and Charlie would watch him, enthralled, as he cut his meat in genteel fashion, holding the knife as he would a pen. Charlie imitated that for years after. When he was sober, Chaplin père would hold his four auditors enthralled with descriptions of the music hall performers he knew. But increasingly he failed to come home and sobriety vanished for good. Most days he would eat only six raw eggs in port wine just before leaving for the theatre. The early part of his day was spent sleeping off the aftershow drinks of the previous evening.

The deep residual instinct Hannah developed to protect her children surfaced again after a year in the asylum, and she came to Kennington Road to claim the boys. They were suitably entranced, and Louise, too embarrassed to meet Hannah, sent them off with great relief.

Syd, Charlie, and Hannah were by now united in the most durable of bonds, a seal of love and self-protection. They moved to a room at 3 Pownall Terrace in the Kennington Road, close to the acrid fragrance of a pickle factory, but they were together. Hannah's health seemed excellent. During this tenancy a little incident occurred which Chaplin was later to call the premise of his best films, an event combining the tragic and comic in just about equal measure. Sheep were driven daily past Pownall Terrace on their way to a nearby slaughterhouse, and when one of them escaped in the neighborhood there was much excited hilarity. The animal ran pell-mell among the hooting youngsters on the street as they fell over each other trying to grab it. Charlie laughed with all the others; it seemed grand fun. But after the sheep was caught and borne away to its death, Charlie realized that the capering was over with sad finality. Weeping, he ran to his mother crying, "They're going to kill it! They're going to kill it!" The memory of that encounter was lasting. Sorrow and laughter, he could now see, were sometimes inextricably combined and that mixture somehow made both elements more striking.

Hannah both directly and indirectly stimulated Charlie's theatrical talents. Her superb mimicry was a training stimulus for his recitations in school, and gradually from a mouselike status among his school chums he advanced to a kind of star billing with repeated renderings in all the classrooms of *Miss Priscilla's Cat*, a humorous monologue his mother taught him. The new acclaim even helped his studies. It was sterling preparation for Charlie's first professional engagement.

Both he and Sydney as a part of Cockney street life had learned the fundamentals of clog dancing. It was in effect one of the games to be learned and in some instances, with clever youngsters, to be mastered. Charlie's father knew a middle-aged ex-schoolmaster, John Willie Jackson, who managed The Eight Lancashire Lads, a troupe of youngsters specializing in clog dancing. Mr. Chaplin told Jackson that Charlie was an able performer, well qualified to fill a recent vacancy in the act. Because of this defection Jackson had been considering renaming the act The Seven Lancashire Lads, but on balance he could ill afford to waste the large number of posters bearing the old billing. Charlie was hired, given intensive rehearsal, and went out on the road. His professional career had begun to the upswing of a music hall band.

Jackson was a most amiable and understanding man. Charlie was given the quite decent wages for one of his total inexperience of a half crown a week (sent to Hannah) in addition to room and board. Four of the Lads were Jackson's own but all the performers were treated as family, Mrs. Jackson mothering them indiscriminately. She took them all except Charlie to a Catholic church every Sunday. As the only Protestant in the troupe, Charlie felt lonely and would join them occasionally, thus sparking the only time in his life when he was tempted to active church membership. He was attracted by the colorful ceremonials of the

Roman church and would have converted on the spot had it not
been for Hannah's demur. His Huguenot heritage was not to be
slighted.

Charlie's debut with the troupe was trying. He was much more
nervous than he anticipated being and it took him several weeks
before he was dancing as easily as the others. But once the routine
had become just that, he settled down into a consideration of his
deeper skills and ambitions. Before this time he had thought of
his future exclusively in terms of prestige and money. "When I
was a little boy," he said in 1915, "the last thing I dreamed of was
being a comedian. My idea was to be a Member of Parliament or
a great musician. I wasn't quite clear which. The only thing I really dreamed about was being rich. We were so poor that wealth
seemed to me the summit."

Charlie, of course, was never to lose that deep-seated need for
wealth but the ambition to be an M.P. vanished during the Lancashire Lads period. Like the other boys, he wanted to graduate
from their dancing line into a single act, to become a boy comedian. Interestingly—and this has some bearing on Chaplin's later
statement in life that his screen character bloomed almost unpre-
meditatedly in full fig on the Mack Sennett lot one day—young
Charlie during his Lancashire Lads tenure yearned to be a comedy
tramp. Indeed he envisioned a double act with one of the Lads
named Bristol. They dreamed of calling themselves Bristol and
Chaplin, the Millionaire Tramps, wearing beard stubble and
sporting flashy diamond rings. The act died aborning but it is
revealing that Chaplin's first impulse for comedy was a foreshad-
owing of his permanent comic persona.

During the Lancashire Lads tour Chaplin had the opportunity
to play on the bill with numerous (to use the British designation
for variety performers) "artistes," and it is indicative of his prime
artistic concern even then that he found the most engrossing ones
those with what he termed "unique personalities offstage." People became his life theme. Years later, novelist Jim Tully, a close
friend and adviser, would say of Chaplin, "His instincts are not in
art—not in work primarily—not in lands or ships at sea—but people." The spiritual kinship between Chaplin and Dickens has
been frequently cited through the years, once by no less a person
than Winston Churchill, who said they "both quarried in the

same rich mine of common life and found there treasure of laughter and drama for the delight of all mankind." Both deprived and insecure as children, both raised in a cruel London slum, temperamentally both Chaplin and Dickens were a curious mix of the recluse and the exhibitionist, and they found life essentially comic with deeply pathetic overtones. In confronting their mass audiences with concerns of class and social structure, they used extravagant, deeply alive caricature. Chaplin was profoundly influenced by Dickens. He first encountered Dickens' characters in the liveliest possible fashion—on the music hall stage in the single person of Bransby Williams (1870–1961). The Williams impersonations of Dickens' characters turned Chaplin to literature in general and Dickens in particular. Williams, when Charlie first saw him on the Lancashire Lads tour, presented in monodrama fashion a kaleidoscopic encounter with a number of Dickens' most memorable creations. Charlie was so enthralled with Williams' impersonations that he began to rehearse an impersonation of Williams impersonating. He also bought a copy of Oliver Twist although at the time he was barely able to read. Developing skills learned from Williams and his mother, it is not to be wondered at that Chaplin's astounding abilities began to flower at this time. Parenthetically, it is regrettable that some of the most compelling personalities Chaplin has created have never been seen by his public. This brilliantly wide range of people, real and fictional, we know of only vaguely from the testimony of Chaplin's many dinner guests over the decades. This testimony persistently attests to a skill which blended comedy and pathos in brilliant caricatures, to (using the precise adjective) a Dickensian skill. Bransby Williams was the catalyst of this skill.

After the Lancashire Lads toured the provinces they played the London Hippodrome, a vast pleasure palace, in its annual Christmas pantomime, Cinderella. The Lads that 1900 holiday season were cast as lively cats and dogs in the show, and Charlie in keeping with his darting grace was a cat. His feline headpiece had one of the eyes built to wink when Charlie pulled a string. During a children's matinee Charlie ventured some added comedy by going to a dog's rear end, sniffing energetically. The audience roared, Charlie turned to them and winked his large eye. They roared again; more sniffs, more winks, and Charlie completely ignored the frantic posturings of the stage manager in the wings exhorting him to stop the vulgarities. Carried along by the laughter, Charlie padded over to the proscenium arch, smelled it too, and then in quite uncatlike fashion lifted his leg to it. The audience exploded.[1]

After this engagement Charlie was reduced to taking various odd jobs. One of them he was glad not to be paid for—the hauling of blouses his mother was sewing at home to the factory which had commissioned the piecework. "I wanted to go back to the music halls," he said, "but [Mother] roused almost into a fury at the idea. All her most painful memories were of music hall life and she passionately made me promise never to act in one."

One day as he was taking a bundle of blouses to the factory he saw his father through the swinging doors of a pub, and his father saw him.

Mr. Chaplin called the boy in and proudly insisted he perform for the barroom cronies. The boy obliged, dancing and impersonating odd characters. His dad enjoyed it very much and gave Charlie a sovereign, a considerable piece of money. Charlie continued his journey to the factory, proudly giving the money on return to his mother. His dad had given him something else: a kiss and an embrace—the first and only time he did so. This was the last time Charlie saw his father.

A few days later Hannah was told that her husband had been taken to St. Thomas's Hospital. She visited him daily for a time, giving reports to Charlie. According to one Chaplin autobiographical account, his father on his deathbed alternated between despair and the euphoric conviction that he would become better and ultimately take his family to live in the country. Hannah, who knew her man, realized that talk of reunion was for him simply a pleasant thing to say. In later years Chaplin came to the belief that his mother never really loved his father deeply but always had a great compassion for him. That compassion was called up with some bitterness one day at Chaplin's deathbed when an

---

[1] In his 1933 reminiscences Chaplin recalls that he was a dog in this production. He may have been for certain performances but there is no doubt that he played a cat most of the time.

evangelist gravely told the sinner that his sins had indeed brought
him to where he was.

Shortly after, the *Era*, a theatrical newspaper, carried the story:

> Our readers will hear with regret, but without surprise, of the death
> of poor Charles Chaplin, the well-known mimic and music hall co-
> median. Of late years poor Chaplin was not so fortunate, and good
> engagements, we are afraid, did not often come in his way. Mr.
> Chaplin was removed to St. Thomas's Hospital suffering from
> dropsy, from which malady he died on Tuesday evening.

That was the evening of May 7, 1901. And poor indeed he was, in
many senses. Only thirty-seven, his talent wasted, his family suffering, almost penniless, never to see his son grow and prosper.

When Hannah called for his effects she was given some bloody
clothing and a pair of plaid slippers with oranges stuck in the toes.
She took out the oranges and a single coin fell from the slippers.

This trauma was succeeded by another. Hannah's mind, ad-
versely affected by malnutrition and worry about the future, began
to waver again. Charlie had to bear this alone because Sydney had
recently gone to sea. Hannah's normal vivacity would flag and for
long hours she would stare uncomprehendingly out of the window. Unusually neat by disposition, she now would fail to clean
their little apartment for days. One time when Charlie was out
playing, she got up from the window, took several pieces of coal
from their grate, and knocked on neighbors' doors, handing in the
coal, saying they were birthday presents for the children. She became obsessed with the idea that Sydney was being forcibly kept
away from her. There was nothing to do but remand her once
again to Cane Hill Asylum.

Charlie was allowed to stay on at 3 Pownall Terrace by the
landlady, who warned however that he would have to give up the
lodgings if a new tenant appeared. Charlie knew that unless he
could find a job the Hanwell orphanage was his next residence.
He was not far from it and in a state of near vagabondage when
Sydney returned unexpectedly, shocked to see Charlie almost in
rags and literally one of the great unwashed. Horrified, Sydney
bought his brother a new suit and sternly supervised a prolonged
bath.

Charlie was now in such high spirits that he became almost

cocky. He had at times in the past almost lorded it over Sydney because of his success as a performer. "I even assumed," he said, "a lot of my old patronizing attitude toward Sydney who had never been considered the clever one of the family, and promised him large returns for all he had done for me as soon as I should become a famous actor. This matter of cleverness I believe now to be greatly overrated. The clever person is too apt to let his cleverness excuse the absence of most of the solid qualities of character. . . . All my life I have been going up like a rocket, all sparks and a loud noise, and coming down like one again, but Sydney has always been the standby of the family, ready to pick me out of the mud and start me up again. He is the better man of the two." And such was always to be Chaplin's opinion of his brother.

Sydney was influenced by his brother in one vital area—his vocation. He resolved to quit the sea and become an actor too. The Chaplin boys began a daily circuit of the theatrical agencies, interrupting it only once to visit Hannah at Cane Hill, twelve miles out of London, a difficult journey for them then. She was somewhat better but still far from well. She told Charlie, for instance, that if he had only given her a cup of tea the afternoon the authorities came for her she would have been all right. He realized the irrationality of the remark but it was to stay with him for a long period, another of the many wound stripes of his depressing youth.

When the boys returned to London Charlie had something of a reputation to fall back on. An agent who had seen him in *Cinderella* found a role for him in a drama quite seriously entitled *From Rags to Riches* and Charlie was to be Reginald, the boy hero. "I wandered in rags," he said, "through three acts, which contained a couple of murders, a dozen hair-breadth escapes, and comic relief by the comedian, and I came triumphantly into my own in the fourth act, where the villain died a horrible death. [I was] an earl's son, defrauded of my rights by the villain after my mother had pitifully died in the streets of London with property snow sifted on her from the flies."

It was Charlie's first appearance as an actor and he made much of it. Fortunately much of the play was ad-libbed by the actors and he was never put to the task of memorizing his lengthy role. Offstage Charlie affected a cane and ostentatiously carried a copy of *Floats*, a British equivalent of *Variety*, under one arm. At twelve he was a leading man and he wasn't letting anyone forget it. The excitement was intense. "I liked it all," he said, "I liked the thrill of having to pause in a scene while the audience applauded, as they did pretty often after I became used to the stage."

After several months on tour Charlie returned to London and a fallow period of more odd jobs. For a time he was a printer's devil and he dignified his new job by wearing some aristocratic holdovers from his *Rags to Riches* wardrobe—a slightly used morning coat and a dashing black bow tie. As he walked into the workroom of the printing press his first morning there, the printers, working class all, stopped the presses and shouted at him with mock deference, "Morning, my lord!" and "He's a regular toff, and no mistyke!" Charlie easily surmounted his sharp embarrassment by a comic riposte, assuming at once the mien of a self-infatuated aristocrat. The workmen enjoyed the performance.

After that job ended, Charlie was for a time a page boy, a rare instance of life casting him for a role he was shortly to play on the stage, a role that would give him his first fame in the British theatre. Before that heady moment however he met and acted with the man to whom, in Chaplin's words, "I owe more . . . than to anybody in the world." This was his debt for the gift of professionalism. H. A. Saintsbury (1869–1939), a director and playwright, was a minor actor-manager at the time he began his tutelage of Charlie Chaplin. Although never a star of the first rank, Saintsbury had a large following in Britain over a very long career. Little remembered now except by very old members of the Savage, the Garrick, and the Green Room clubs, Saintsbury made a quiet reputation among his peers as a perfectionist, as the ultimate professional. It was his unending attitude to detail that was to impress itself most strongly on Charlie's creative processes. Charlie was by now an excellent actor and a skilled mimic but he had little control or focus of these gifts.

Saintsbury had just written a play of London life, *Jim: A Romance of Cockayne*, and Charlie was ideal for the part of Sam, a Cockney urchin.[2] Because Charlie was barely literate at the time,

---

[2] In several of his memoirs Chaplin variously and mistakenly calls the play *Jim: the Romance of a Cockney* and *Jim: the Romance of Cocaine*, the latter probably a ghostwriter's error of transcription. Chaplin, of course,

Sydney read his part aloud to him and Charlie ingested it easily. The rehearsals at the Drury Lane Theatre were a constant revelation to the boy. Saintsbury with exquisite precision told Charlie how to wait on stage for a laugh to die away, how to turn on a pinpoint cue, how to listen, literally listen, to his fellow actors, how to walk and sit with quiet control, and how to master all the intricacies of that mysterious and most difficult function of the actor's craft—timing. Charlie needed to be told in each instance but once and Saintsbury realized in rehearsals that the boy knew these things naturally, needing only the shaping of a skilled hand for initial guidance. Charlie's only fault was a tendency to mug, a tendency Saintsbury took well in hand and obliterated.

When the play opened at the Royal Court Theatre, Kingston-upon-Thames, on Monday, July 6, 1903, it was scored by the critics. The *Era*'s reviewer during the play's second week said:

> Master Charlie Chaplin is a broth of a boy as Sam, the newspaper boy, giving a most realistic picture of the cheeky, honest, loyal, self-reliant, philosophic street Arab who haunts the regime of Cockayne.

The play closed the night that review appeared.

But Saintsbury had another play, a sure-fire play, in hand. William Gillette's *Sherlock Holmes* was available to him and Saintsbury looked more like Holmes than even the aristocratic-featured author of the play who had crafted it for his own talents. Charlie was cast as Billy, Holmes's page boy, the aggressive street lad instrumental in aiding Holmes at a vital point in the play and who shares with his master the tag line of the second act just after the villainous Professor Moriarity has been repulsed:

HOLMES: Billy! You're a good boy!
BILLY: Yes, sir! Thank you, sir!

And good indeed Charlie was. The *Era*, by now taking quite a shine to the youngster, praised him for making ". . . the smart pageboy a prime favourite with the audience."

played a Cockney in the production. "Cockayne" or "Cockaigne" is a traditional cognomen for London, as witness Sir Edward Elgar's delightful Cockaigne Overture.

The Saintsbury production of *Sherlock Holmes* toured the provinces for almost a year before returning to London and engagements in suburban theatres there. Now it was Charlie's turn to help Sydney. Charlie asked Saintsbury to give his brother a small role then available, and this was done for the second tour of the play commencing July 1905. Sydney, barely twenty, played the role of a middle-aged nobleman with great assurance and complete credibility. It was during this tour that the boys were cheered immeasurably by the news from Hannah. She had quite recovered, recovered indeed to the point that she could join them on tour. This she did at Reading and during the few weeks remaining of the tour she supervised their meals and living arrangements.

And yet a curious reserve was now apparent between the boys and Hannah. She almost seemed a guest of theirs rather than their mother, Charlie thought. The closeness of childhood days was gone forever because Sydney was adult in every way and Charlie had grown well beyond his years. His precocity as a child, following a familiar pattern among child performers, had robbed him of any real childhood. But there was no real unhappiness in the reunion with Hannah. Charlie came to realize that she knew even before the boys did on this occasion that they were no longer children. This endeared her to them even more.

The second tour ended, Hannah returned to London and a newly furnished flat which marked forever the end of her poverty. From that time forward her boys were always affluent enough to keep her in comfort. Charlie and Sydney stayed with her briefly before returning to yet another tour of *Sherlock Holmes*, this time in what could be called a pickup company under the management of a cut-rate entrepreneur, Harry Yorke. The previous Saintsbury tours had been under the enlightened management of Charles Frohman, but Yorke paid bottom wages and played tank theatres only. It was at one of these, in Warrington, that Charlie received exhilarating news.

It was a telegram from William Postance,[3] manager of the great

---

[3] Chaplin was very fond of Postance but his memory falters on the name. He refers to him as Postant not only in *My Autobiography* but in *Limelight,*

William Gillette, asking if Charlie was available to play Billy again but this time with Gillette, the master himself, in London. Moreover, this was to be in a new play—a one-act curtain raiser, *The Painful Predicament of Sherlock Holmes*, a ten-minute dramatic joke in which Holmes utters not a word. The piece consisted of a madwoman forcing her way into Holmes's flat despite Billy's earnest efforts to prevent her. In extended, staccato monologue, she exhorts Holmes to solve a mysterious case, and Holmes beckons Billy over to give him a note. Billy dashes out and, shortly after, two burly men come to remove the lady. Billy comes forward and gives the last line of the play: "You were right, sir. It was the right asylum." Holmes nods gravely, then smiles at Billy.

The Painful Predicament of Sherlock Holmes was intended as a jolly divertissement before the chef d'oeuvre of the evening, Gillette's new play, *Clarice*,[4] which featured the author and an exquisite actress, Marie Doro. But the curtain raiser was the hit of the evening, the critics finding little to like in *Clarice* save the contour of Miss Doro's nose. Both plays were taken off a few days later, and in the same theatre, the Duke of York's, a few nights later, Gillette's old reliable, *Sherlock Holmes*, was substituted. Once more Charlie walked the stage as Billy, but this time with the author of the play, the man Booth Tarkington apotheosized a few years later by writing, "Mr. Gillette, your return to the stage is a noble and delightful event and speaking for myself, I would rather see you play Sherlock Holmes than be a child again on Christmas morning."

This kind of affection for Gillette was felt by all the London critics that October night in 1905. Gillette had played *Sherlock Holmes* to London acclaim four years before and that acclaim was repeated enthusiastically. Charlie was thrilled to be playing not only with Gillette but with the enchanting Miss Doro, and he quite lost his heart to her. As a very reserved sixteen-year-old he had little recourse but to love her principally from afar. They had

---

where he is memorialized as a kindly impresario (played by Nigel Bruce). To further complicate, in Chaplin's 1916 autobiography Postance becomes Postham.

4 In *My Autobiography*, Chaplin erroneously calls the play *Clarissa*.

no scene together in the play but nightly on the backstage stair
Charlie would time his passage up as she walked down, whereupon he would stammer out a "Good evening" to her gracious presence. Ten years later they would meet as peers in Holllywood but
by then his heart would be elsewhere.

Sherlock Holmes played all the fall of 1905 and went on tour
for a few months in early 1906. Then Gillette and Miss Doro returned to the States and Charlie was again at liberty. He was
confident however that London was his oyster, and when the
haughty Mrs. Madge Kendal, one of England's most prestigious
actresses, offered him a chance to audition for a provincial tour,
Charlie refused. He could not, he said, accept anything out of
town. "And with that I raised my hat, walked out of the foyer,
hailed a passing cab—and was out of work for ten months."

Chaplin's memory is faulty. It was just for eleven weeks. On
May 21, 1906, Charlie opened as the star of a vaudeville turn, The
Casey Circus,[5] in a Liverpool theatre. Sydney, early anticipating
his usefulness to his brother as a business manager, signed the first
contract ever written for Charlie committing him to a run-of-the-
tour engagement. The Casey Circus was much like its very popular predecessor, Casey's Court, an act featuring boys in burlesques
of currently famous people. Charlie appeared very briefly in Casey's Court to get the hang of it before he opened in The Casey
Circus. In the latter he came into his own as the featured player.
He was given the task of parodying the person of a "Doctor"
Walford Bodie, a very popular quack of the day who professed to
cure cripples during his performances by the showmanlike applica-
tion of electricity.

The producer of The Casey Circus, Harry Cardle, directed
Charlie in his Bodie impersonation, emphasizing the most obvious
points of claptrap caricature. Charlie pretended to accept the direction. Secretly, under the Bransby Williams influence and having had the advantage of seeing Bodie close at hand as they sat
near each other at Sir Henry Irving's funeral, Charlie decided to
play Bodie from life. It was to be an acting performance, not an
overstated burlesque as Cardle would have it. Charlie was certain

[5] So, and not Casey's Circus as Chaplin has it in his autobiography.

that the audience would accept the great acting and that this triumph would bring him back to a West End theatre.

On opening night Charlie made up alone, copying as realistically as he could the familiar spiked moustachios of Bodie. Then he made his entrance before the stunned Cardle could see him. "Once in the glare of the footlights," said Chaplin, "I dropped into the part, determined to play it, play it well, and hold the audience. . . . I advanced slowly, impressively feeling the gaze of the crowd, and, with a carefully studied gesture, hung my cane—I held it by the wrong end! Instead of hanging on my arm as I expected, it clattered on the stage. Startled, I stooped to pick it up, and my high silk hat fell from my head. I grasped it, put it on quickly, and paper wadding falling out, I found my whole head buried in its black depths. A great burst of laughter came from the audience."

Desperately Charlie rearranged his topper to some semblance of normality and tried to catch his audience up in the gravity of his interpretation. But the graver he became the louder the audience laughed. "I came off at last, pursued by howls of laughter and wild applause, which called me back again. I had made the hit of the evening."

He had made something else—the key discovery of his comedy style. "I had stumbled on the secret of being funny—unexpectedly. An idea going in one direction meets an opposite idea *suddenly*. 'Ha! Ha!' you shriek. It works every time. I walk on the stage, serious, dignified, solemn, pause before an easy chair, spread my coat-tails with an elegant gesture—and sit on the cat. Nothing funny about it really, especially if you consider the feelings of the cat. But you laugh. You laugh because it is unexpected. Those little nervous shocks make you laugh; you can't help it. . . . In the two years I was with *The Casey Circus* I gradually gave up my idea of playing great parts on the dramatic stage. I grew to like the comedy work."

The Casey Circus played its last performance at Sadler's Wells Theatre, London, on July 20, 1907, and Charlie lived for a bit on his earnings but finally had to borrow from Sydney. Sydney had done rather well for himself. From unimportant supporting character roles in the West End he had graduated to the status of a leading comedian in the Fred Karno Speechless Comedians, the leading comedy troupes in the United Kingdom.

Through Sydney, Charlie was to meet the most intriguing of his mentors, the man who would bring him unerringly into the highest rank of comedy—Fred Karno.

2
SUPPLE KARNO

"Fred Karno didn't teach Charlie and me all we know about comedy," said Stan Laurel. "He just taught us most of it. If I had to pick an adjective to fit Karno, it would be supple. That's what Karno was mentally and physically, even when he was an old man. He was flexible in just about everything, and above all he taught us to be supple. Just as importantly he taught us to be precise. Out of all that endless rehearsal and performance came Charlie, the most supple and precise comedian of our time."

Fred Karno (1866–1941), born Fred Westcott, was a jovial Jekyll and Hyde, an astute showman who brought pantomime slapstick to the region of high art. He took the conventional English pantomime with its somewhat arcane British orientation and made it universal. In his early years a music hall acrobat, Karno began with the principle of run-tumble-and-fall and invested it with a *plastique* or unbroken line of movement almost balletic in its function. Karno created wordless plays, usually burlesquing current fads or fashions of the day, and sharpened the satire with well-coached emphasis on swift and unerring movement. He influenced Chaplin profoundly in this way, and Chaplin has always admitted that his Karno work gave him the solid basis for his film comedy.

Karno, for instance, helped influence Chaplin to commingle laughter and pathos. In the midst of rehearsals for the most uproarious slapstick, Karno (as Stan Laurel remembers) frequently shouted out, "Keep it wistful, gentlemen, keep it *wistful* as well.

That's hard to do but we want sympathy with the laughter. Wistful!" Charlie Chaplin, one might say, was born wistful. In this and other ways he ranked first among the Karno comedians.

Wistful [Stan Laurel said]. I don't think I even knew what in the hell wistful *meant* at the time. But I gradually got at least part of the idea when Karno used to say it to some of the old-timers in the troupe. I don't remember if he was the one who originated the idea of putting a bit of sentiment right in the midst of a funny music hall turn, but I know he did it all the time. I recall one or two instances of that. I forget the Karno sketch but there was one in which a chap got all beat up—deservedly. He was the villain, a terrible person, and the audience was happy to see him get his. Then Karno added this little bit after the man was knocked down. He had the hero—who, mind you, had *rightfully* beaten up this bad man—walk over to the villain and make him feel easier. Put a pig's bladder under his head or what the hell have you. It got a laugh, and at the same time it was a bit touching. Karno encouraged that sort of thing. "Wistful" for him I think meant putting in that serious touch once in a while. Another thing I seem to recall: you would have to look sorry, really sorry, for a few seconds after hitting someone on the head. Karno would say, "Wistful, please, wistful!" It was only a bit of a look, but somehow it made the whole thing funnier. The audience didn't expect that serious look. Karno really knew how to sharpen comedy in that way.

Karno was also the first music hall showman to synchronize pantomime with music, Chaplin claims, and this rhythmic influence was to leave its effect on Chaplin's pantomime. Chaplin said:

At the time [I joined Karno] he had between eighteen and twenty companies touring all over England and in many parts of the world, America, South America and Africa. No language was necessary because the acting of the troupe was vivid and expressive enough to bring laughter from any race. All of the pieces we did, as I remember them, were cruel and boisterous, filled with acrobatic humor and low, knockabout comedy. Each man working for Karno had to have perfect timing and had to know the peculiarities of everyone else in the cast so that we could, collectively, achieve a cast tempo.

It took about a year for an actor to get the repertoire of a dozen shows down pat. Karno required us to know a number of parts so that the players could be interchanged. When one left the company it was like taking a screw or a pin out of a very delicate piece of machinery.

In his personal life Karno was a tyrant, a sadistic wife-beater, who boasted to her and anyone who would listen of his efficient use of the casting couch. As a director, like Saintsbury, he was the ultimate professional, aware precisely of effects needed, and if he was unrelenting and sometimes harsh in his work methods he was considerate and kindly to his performers. His two most distinguished protégés, Charlie Chaplin and Stan Laurel, retained grateful memories of him all their days.

Karno had seen Sydney Chaplin act for the first time in Repairs, a slapstick sketch by Wal Pink, in which Syd as a loutish agitator tried to get a gang of inefficient paperhangers and plumbers to go on strike. Syd got Charlie a job in the sketch as a plumber's helper with a good scene in which he knocked a nail through the wall into a water pipe. Karno saw both Chaplins in the act but he was impressed only with the older brother. It was some months before he would agree to Syd's importunities to interview Charlie. Charlie went to Karno's office, terrified.

In later years Karno described the scene: a young—extraordinarily young—boy, standing in the doorway. "He looked undernourished and frightened," Karno said, "as though he expected me to raise my hand to hit him. I thought he looked much too shy to do any good in the theatre, particularly in the knockabout comedies that were my specialty." But the actor in Chaplin assumed control and he faced the rotund little Karno with a great show of confidence. He spoke of his long experience in the music halls and the West End but Karno thought him too young. He told the lad that he did not even look the seventeen years he admitted to. "That's a question of make-up," Chaplin said, and shrugged casually. Beguiled by the shrug, Karno gave the boy a small part in the sketch G.P.O., featuring the leading Karno comedian, Fred Kitchen. In the Karno company, Charlie came to man's estate. Now he was "Chaplin," preparing to hold his own

with some very aggressive comedians. The first of those was Fred
Kitchen.

Kitchen, a large man not unlike Eric Campbell, Chaplin's
comic foil in later years, was instrumental in influencing one aspect of Chaplin's screen self. He had, says Fred Karno's biographer, J. P. Gallagher, "a curious shambling walk, a cross between
a shuffle and a hop. Karno, as usual improving on nature, fitted
him out with a pair of enormous boots—the direct ancestors of
the Charlie Chaplin boots." ("Boots" in the British sense: ankle-
high laced shoes.) Kitchen proved to be something of a Chaplin
rival, at least initially.

But Chaplin's real rival in the company was another Karno featured player, Harry Weldon. Weldon was the star of *The Football Match*, one of the five sketches Karno had on tour when
Chaplin joined the company. Each Karno company was virtually
a separate unit in that extensive rehearsals emphasizing ensemble
playing had welded the group into a strongly cohesive unit. Weldon, like Syd Chaplin, Kitchen, and every other featured Karno
player, was instinctively jealous of any potential usurper of his em-
inence. Chaplin, after being transferred to the *Football Match*
company, looked like just such an intruder.

But Weldon failed to note this in the two rehearsals held to accommodate the newcomer (who was replacing a somewhat color-
less player). Chaplin was cautious in rehearsal, being slow of
study. Weldon, irritated at having his daily golf game twice interrupted by the need to acclimatize Chaplin, was not kindly disposed to the newcomer. He was even less disposed on the London opening night of *The Football Match*, following a provincial
tour. That evening, February 3, 1908, at the Coliseum Theatre,
was in effect Chaplin's debut to comedy greatness.

Tense to the point of nausea, Chaplin made his entrance with
great trepidation. He played the villain, come to bribe Weldon,
the star goalkeeper, into throwing the game. Attired in slouch hat,
oversize Inverness cape, and small black mustache, Chaplin also
reddened his nose vividly to make the effect more piquant. He entered threateningly, his back to the audience to establish a tension, then turned with great unction, his nose dominating the proceedings. The great gust of laughter told him he had scored his
first point and he made several more in quick succession: tripping

over a dumbbell, then entangling his cane with a upright punching bag. The bag punched him in the face, Chaplin punched back, contriving to make his cane smack him on the ear. The world was to see more of that cane. The laughter grew. Stimulated, he pretended to lose a button and resorted to one of burlesque's hoariest laugh-getters, dropping his pants. In looking for the button he picked up something, threw it away distastefully, and ad-libbed, "Those confounded rabbits!" A roar from the audience.

Weldon, who was just about to make his entrance, listened incredulously. There had never been laughter at that spot in the show before. In Weldon's view, the villain's function in *The Football Match* was to contribute feed lines to the principal comedian, Harry Weldon. Weldon entered hurriedly to re-establish his dominance but Chaplin actually turned him into a stooge. Clutching his pants, Chaplin grabbed Weldon by the wrist and ad-libbed again, "Quick! I'm undone! A pin!" The sketch continued with similar contrivances and by evening's end a great many more laughs, all Chaplin-contributed, had been added to the show. Weldon grudgingly admitted their value but he resented them. He was further infuriated by the welcoming round of applause that Chaplin began to receive nightly on his entrance.

Karno realized Chaplin's value and signed him to a year's contract at four pounds a week, a very good salary for a mere supporting player who also had the audacity to be just eighteen years old. Weldon resented those things but he was not stung into reprisal until the provincial tour that followed. In Belfast, further irritated by reviews that seemed to praise Chaplin at his expense, Weldon in a knockabout jostling sequence hit Chaplin full force, causing a nosebleed. Backstage, Chaplin threatened redress on stage with one of the dumbbells, accusing Weldon of jealousy. Weldon, outraged, said, "Why, I have more talent in my arse than you have in your whole body!"

"That's where your talent lies!" Chaplin said. The feud continued until the end of the tour a few weeks later. The other members of the company were initially prone to favor Weldon because, outside of his blind spot where Chaplin was concerned, he was amiable enough and his name in certain towns was an undeniable drawing card. But the cast soon began to realize that Chaplin was no one-shot success. His careful crafting of gags and effects had built up the number of laughs to the point where it was virtually the funniest show Karno had ever produced.

But that designation was to be given shortly to a new production of a standard Karno production, *Mumming Birds*. This sketch was four years old and it had been done very well but its full humor did not come to life until Karno picked Chaplin to play a key role in a 1909 revival at the Folies-Bergères. The sketch derives its comic strength from the concept of eight excruciatingly bad vaudeville acts playing to a scornful audience of three, a fat boy, his uncle, and a man in evening dress identified in the program as "Inebriated Swell." This was Charlie Chaplin in the days when the act reached extraordinary heights, meriting its description in *Billboard* as "perhaps the funniest act ever to hit vaudeville." It was in *Mumming Birds*, three years after the Folies-Bergères engagement, that Chaplin would be seen by Mack Sennett, thus changing the face of cinematic history.

Mumming Birds (later known in the United States as *A Night in an English Music Hall*) reproduces the stage of a small variety theatre. The audience sees a false proscenium flanked by four empty theatre boxes, two on each side of the stage; between the boxes upstage is a tab curtain drawn to reveal the acts-within-the-act. As a tinkly overture begins, the fat boy in an Eton suit and his staid old uncle enter the box downstage right. The boy carries a hamper full of Bath buns which he uses for both sustenance and ammunition. Seconds later an usherette brings the drunken swell into the box downstage left. He smiles tipsily, bows, takes his right glove off, swaying delicately. He tips the girl, then peels the glove again from his bare right hand. The girl corrects him and leaves as he takes a cigarette from his case and attempts to light it from an electric light just outside his box. Infuriated because it fails to light, he is about to smash the bulb when he notices that the fat boy on the other side of the stage has lighted a match and is holding it out to him. The drunk smiles, bows gracefully and, in leaning forward to get his light, falls out of the box and sprawls on the stage.

The variety acts commence and they are so uniformly dreadful, causing such indignant reaction from the fat boy and the drunk, that the actual audience has a double measure of humor: the hammy acts and the splenetic reactions of the two in the boxes. As originally staged by Karno, the drunk's reactions were pointed and humorous but genteel almost to a fault. Chaplin made the drunk's reactions robust and highly physical, yet keeping almost all his activity within the confines of the box.

The acts come in quick order: a pair of scraggly cancan girls, a comic singer so awful that the drunk chases him offstage, a lady vocalist who destroys a song, "Come, Birdie, Come and Live With Me," a rancid ham actor who recites "The Trail of the Yukon" to agonized groans from the fat boy and the drunk, a quartet of male rustics singing interminable verses of "Hail, Smiling Morn That Tops the Hills With Gold" until they are pelted off the stage with buns, a soubrette dancing and rending a song called "You Naughty, Naughty Man," causing the drunk to imagine he is the object of her attention, and finally Marconi Ali, "The Terrible Turk, the Greatest Wrestler Ever to Appear Before the British Public."

The Turk appears, sporting a ferocious mustache, and apparently the victim of malnutrition. Notwithstanding, he proudly flexes his rubber-band muscles. The fat boy throws a bun before Marconi, who leaps forward and devours it summarily to the embarrassment of the "Number Man" who announces all the acts with great flourish. "Back, Ali, back, back!" he says. The Number Man now announces that one hundred pounds will be given to anyone in the theatre able to throw the redoubtable Ali within fifteen seconds. A plant from one of the top boxes challenges Ali and when he asks how he can get down to the stage the fat boy shouts, "Jump!" The challenger enters by orthodox means, rips off his coat, throwing it over the drunk's arm extended over the box railing.

The drunk throws it at the challenger, who throws it back to him, but before that brouhaha can extend itself the challenger is cajoled into fighting Ali. Ali defeats the challenger, and the drunk, in preparing to fight Ali, begins to take off his clothes. He is hustled offstage and returns shortly in long underwear tastefully decorated in red ribbons. The fight begins and the drunk gets Ali pinned to the mat by the simple device of tickling him into surrender.

The drunk receives the prize money, congratulations, and a

plaintive request. Is there anything else he would like? "Yes!" he
shouts. "First bring on the girls!" The entire company, for no better reason than that the sketch must end, rushes on for a finale of
simultaneous ructions: hooting, scrapping, food-throwing, and rip-
ping of clothes. This was Mack Sennett comedy years before it
existed.

During the Folies-Bergères engagement of *Mumming Birds*
Chaplin realized how fully his creativity could take him as a solo
performer. He had been given the Paris engagement as replacement for Billy Reeves, the originator of the drunk's role five years
before. Chaplin knew to a nicety just how Reeves played the
drunk; indeed he had seen Reeves play it long before working for
Karno seemed a possibility. Reeves played the role with a superb
inebriated doggedness and was deliciously funny. Chaplin was also
riotously funny but added a belligerent intensity to the role, almost audacious in its frenzy, yet totally under control. "He even
made those of us in the cast break up time after time," said Stan
Laurel. Stan adds:

> What has to be remembered about Charlie is that though he was
> essentially a pantomimist—and none better—still, with Charlie,
> things really began with his face. That may seem strange but it's
> true. He had those eyes that absolutely forced you to look at them.
> He had the damnedest way of looking at an audience. He had the
> damnedest way of looking at *you*, on stage. I don't think anyone
> has ever written about those eyes of his. They're very dark, the
> deepest kind of blue, and intense, just like him. And they can domi-
> nate anyone they look at. That's a part of the secret of his great
> success—eyes that make you believe him in whatever he does.

During these early days with Karno the first love of his life
came to Chaplin. Or, more accurately, overwhelmed him. On a
Mumming Birds engagement in London he was playing the drunk
at a suburban theatre, the Streatham Empire, where a dancing
troupe, Bert Coutts' Yankee Doodle Girls, preceded him on the
bill. One of the girls was a petite brunette with enormous brown
eyes. He had never seen such beauty.

Hetty Kelly was instantly aware of his feelings; when they first
met, she smiled, then grew embarrassed. Her shyness was equal to
his and his was ample. Deeply attracted to each other, they ar-

ranged to meet the following Sunday afternoon. Chaplin took three pounds from his savings to buy an expensive dinner at the Trocadero, a restaurant he considered adequate to grace her elegant beauty. But she had already eaten; it seems he had forgotten to specify dinner. He was not to be deterred from the rococo charm of the Trocadero, however, and she nibbled politely at a sandwich as he tried to impress her by ordering himself an expensive meal. She was not impressed. They met again for morning walks in dismal Camberwell where she lived, and he was excited when she allowed him to hold her hand. The fourth time they met he assumed that a special closeness had begun to grow but Hetty discouraged him. She was, she said, just fifteen. "After all," Chaplin said later, "the episode was but a childish infatuation to her, but to me it was the beginning of a spiritual development, a reaching out for beauty. . . . I went through the youthful misery of unrequited love." Hetty Kelly's memory was to persist with unusual tenacity for much of Chaplin's life. He met her casually a year later and much of the hurt had gone. But a part of him would be in agony for years to come.

Chaplin's success in *Mumming Birds* made Karno offer him the leading role in *The Football Match* opening in London's most prestigious music hall, the Oxford. To be featured player in such an important sketch at Chaplin's age was unprecedented. For an eighteen-year-old, slight, diffident in appearance, to appear in a role made famous by a seasoned trouper like Harry Weldon aroused much talk in the theatrical pubs. If Chaplin could succeed in the demanding role of Stiffy the Goalkeeper, he would be a made man, a star. Laryngitis, which had disturbed him in rehearsals, all but defeated him on opening night. The second night his voice was worse, and the following evening his understudy went on.

The Mr. Hyde half of Karno now emerged. Karno put Chaplin back into *Mumming Birds* with a demeaning implication that leading roles were not his métier. Yet Karno could not doubt the evidence of his own eyes or the report of the young man's success in *Mumming Birds* and other sketches on tour. Karno changed his mind and offered Chaplin the leading role in a new sketch, *Jimmy the Fearless, or The Boy 'Ero*. Chaplin, by now coolly determined to do only the things he liked, read the script and did not like it.

Karno promptly offered it to another youngster he had under contract, Stan Jefferson, not long down from the north of England where his father was a prominent impresario. Young Jefferson, six years away from his name change to Laurel, accepted the role with eagerness.

I never quite understood why Charlie didn't take the part in *Jimmy the Fearless* [said Stan]. It was really an awfully good show. Jimmy is a young lad from a working class family who comes home late after sparking with a "bit o' skirt." His mother scolds him, leaves him his supper, and after Jimmy eats, he sits down to read what in those days we called a "penny blood." What in the States was called a dime novel, full of melodrama and adventure. As Jimmy reads by candlelight, he gradually falls asleep, the stage darkens. And then after what we called in those days a transformation effect, the lights come up on Jimmy's dream world where he climbs high mountains, rescues a beautiful girl from some very naughty villains, fights all kinds of bad guys in the Wild West, has a great duel, finds fantastic treasures and at last wins the hand of a beautiful princess.

Then just as he is about to save his poor old parents from being evicted, the lights dim down and we're back in Jimmy's folks' humble cottage—where his dad pulls him out of his chair and starts to beat hell out of Jimmy with his belt!

I thought it was a wonderful sketch so I jumped at the chance to play Jimmy. Never had so much fun in me life, as the old saying goes. Charlie was out front the opening night and right after the show he told Karno he had made a mistake. He wanted to play Jimmy. And he did. No, I didn't feel bitter about it. For me, Charlie was, is, and will be always the greatest comedian in the world. I thought he should have played it to begin with. But after that I used to kid him—always very proudly—that for once in my life Charlie Chaplin was *my* replacement. Charlie loved to play Jimmy, and the memory of that role and of that production stayed with him all his life, I think. You can see *Jimmy the Fearless* all over some of his pictures—dream sequences, for instance. He was fond of them, especially in his early pictures. And when it comes right down to it, I've always thought that poor, brave, dreamy Jimmy one day grew up to be Charlie the Tramp.

Chaplin appeared with great success as Jimmy at the Stratford Empire Theatre a few days after his twenty-first birthday. By now

he was in full command of his artistic resources and he knew it.
Just as importantly, Karno knew it. He gave Chaplin a raise and
featured him in other Karno sketches. A few weeks after the crit-
ically acclaimed opening of *Jimmy the Fearless*, Alf Reeves, who
was managing the tour of various Karno companies in America,
returned to London because his principal comedian, Albert Wes-
ton, was no longer interested in touring the States and longed for
home. Chaplin, much intrigued by all he had read of the States
through the years, heard of this and campaigned for featured roles
in the American company. Providentially, one of the cancan
dancers in *Mumming Birds*, Amy Minister, who had entered
Karno's employ when Chaplin did, married Alf Reeves at this
time. She liked Chaplin personally and admired his prodigious
talent. She spoke earnestly to Reeves, who needed little more urging after going to Birmingham to see the new Karno star in a
sketch called *Skating*. Reeves asked Karno for Chaplin's services
in an American production of *Jimmy*.

Karno was well disposed to let Chaplin go to America but he
felt that *Jimmy the Fearless* was perhaps a bit farfetched for (as
he considered them) prosaic American tastes. He proposed that
the company take over a new sketch, *The Wow-Wows* by Her-
bert Sydney. Both Chaplin and Reeves argued strongly against it
but Karno was adamant. Stan Laurel was assigned a role in the
new peice.

Karno was dead wrong [said Stan]. *The Wow-Wows* was God-aw-
ful. Everybody in the company said so all during those dreary days of
rehearsal, but we weren't too despondent. In fact we were all
thrilled and excited. After all, we were going to the States, and we
all had heard enough about show business there to know that anything and everything could happen. And it sure as hell did.

3
AMERICA

Chaplin shared the exhilaration of the new Karno company. The United States had been in his mind for months, and the more he read and heard the more fitting a destination it seemed. As a comedian in England there was little beyond Karno's troupes he could aspire to; as an individual, stung by the cruel experiences of his childhood, he knew that the English caste system had in large measure already foreclosed on his future. America was clearly an open, unstructured society and he felt it would be sympathetic to his hopes.

Like his fellow actors, he considered *The Wow-Wows* totally inappropriate for American audiences. Chaplin played the leading character, the Honorable Archibald Binks, the role Sydney had created when the sketch made its debut a few months before. Chaplin kept the broad outlines of Sydney's interpretation but added a touch of casual athleticism here and there. As a hearty slap at the English upper classes, he made up his face as a cadaver.

The company rehearsed for two weeks in London, then in late September 1910 embarked on the S.S. *Cairnrona*, a cattle boat. Stan Laurel had vivid memories of the crossing:

> The *Cairnrona* was a cattle boat but it didn't carry any cattle unless you could call *us* cattle, and sometimes that's just how we felt. For that matter, the food did mostly taste like fodder; and the weather was pretty rough. But we had fun because we were all in a great business, we were young and we were delighted to be going where

we were going. One morning we heard there was land in the distance. I'll never forget the details of what happened next. We were all on deck, sitting, watching the land in the mist. Suddenly Charlie ran to the railing, took off his hat, waved it and shouted, "America, I am coming to conquer you! Every man, woman and child shall have my name on their lips—Charles Spencer Chaplin!" We all booed him affectionately, and he bowed to us very formally and sat down again. Years later whenever I met any of the old troupe, that was the one thing about those years that we remembered the best, and we used to marvel on how right Charlie had been.

The company found America living up to its expectations. The tempo of life was much quicker than in London and they were pleased to see how important vaudeville was in the fabric of American show business. Not only theatrical trade papers but many of the regular newspapers reviewed variety acts, and the public seemed to read these assessments. If *The Wow-Wows* was a success, the troupe had a very good chance of extending their only booking in the States, a six-week slot on the Percy Williams circuit. The company rehearsed diligently but there were ominous signs of inadequacy. A few of the company were not up to the mark, and a leading player, "Whimsical" Walker, a personal favorite of Karno's and a clown who had made his fame at the Drury Lane Theatre for many years, was a mumbler. Age had reduced his intelligibility. Since most of the plot exposition depended on his dialogue, Chaplin was apprehensive, and with reason. Opening night at the Colonial Theatre, New York, October 3, 1910, Walker was heard only half the time. The audience, accustomed to the typical Karno wordless play, was also puzzled by this twenty-nine-minute fast-talking farce.

Dash., the *Variety* "mugg" who reviewed *The Wow-Wows*, put it:

> A Karno company that talks seemed to hit the Colonial audience as a bit queer. Having seen *The Music Hall*, *Slums* and *Dandy Thieves*, it is but natural that American audiences should expect only pantomime from a Karno group. Anyone familiar with London music halls at all will not be surprised for most of the Karno productions over there depend to some extent upon dialogue. *The Wow-Wows* is the real English type of Karno act with the red nose comic in the fore, and the proceedings built around him.

Laid in three scenes, the act consists merely of a burlesque on a secret society initiation. To "get even" on the "tightwad" of a summer camp, the rest of the bunch frame up a phoney secret society into which they initiate M. Neverloosen.

Charles Chaplin is the "mark" and chief comedian. Chaplin is typically English, the sort of comedian that American audiences seem to like, although unaccustomed to. His manner is quiet and easy and he goes about his work in a devil-may-care manner, in direct contrast to the twenty-minutes-from-a-cemetery makeup he employs.

The makeup and the manner in themselves are funny. That is what will have to carry *The Wow-Wows* over, if it goes that way. Chaplin will do all right for America, but it is too bad that he didn't first appear in New York with something more in it than this piece.

The company amounts to little, because there is little for them to do. Dialogue in the opening doesn't amount to anything and at intervals during the piece there are talky places which drag the time when Champlin [sic] does not occupy the center of the stage. . . . The Colonial audience laughed at the show Monday night, but not enough. An act of this sort, erected solely for comedy, should register a bigger percentage of laughs.

Both Chaplin and Alf Reeves had warned Karno of just such a reception but he was obdurate, convinced that America was full of Masons, Elks, and similar secret societies who would take *The Wow-Wows* to their bosom. Reeves sent the *Variety* review to Karno but it was no use. Karno was convinced *The Wow-Wows* would have its day. The term "flop sweat" originated in American vaudeville, and the Karno troupe came to know the meaning of it during their six weeks in Williams' theatres in and around New York City. Alf Reeves added another sketch which they played occasionally, the old *Mumming Birds*, altered slightly and appearing under a new title, *A Night in an English Music Hall*. It was, by contrast with *The Wow-Wows*, rapturously received. But Karno insisted that the latter constitute the burden of the company's repertoire.

And *The Wow-Wows* did have a moment of glory one evening at the Fifth Avenue Theatre when the British colony in New York City (mostly English butlers, valets, and nannies constituting the St. George Society of Brooklyn) came in a body to see the show. They roared with delight at the British topicalities scattered heavily through the text. Fortunately an agent for the prestigious Sullivan and Considine vaudeville circuit saw *The Wow-Wows* that evening and, impressed by the audience reaction, booked the company for a tour through the Midwest, Canada, and California.

Stan Laurel was Chaplin's roommate on the tour.[1]

It was a whole new world [said Stan]. We were thrilled at the excitement of New York but seeing the whole country, mile after mile, was really the way to see America. I was Charlie's roommate on that tour and he was fascinating to watch. People through the years have talked about how eccentric he became. He was a very eccentric person *then*. He was very moody and often very shabby in appearance. Then suddenly he would astonish us all by getting dressed to kill. It seemed that every once in a while he would get an urge to look very smart. At these times he would wear a derby hat (an expensive one), gloves, smart suit, fancy vest, two-tone side button shoes, and carry a cane. I have a lot of quick little memories of him like that. For instance, I remember that he drank only once in a while, and then it was always port.

He read books incessantly. One time he was trying to study Greek, but he gave it up after a few days and started in to study yoga. A part of this yoga business was what was called the "water cure"—so for a few days after that he ate nothing, just drank water for his meals. He carried his violin wherever he could. Had the strings reversed so he could play left-handed, and he would practice for hours. He bought a cello once and used to carry it around with him. At these times he would always dress like a musician, a long fawn-colored overcoat with green velvet cuffs and collar and a slouch hat. And he'd let his hair grow long in back. We never knew what he was going to do next. He was unpredictable.

The one predictability about Chaplin on that long, tiring tour (playing three shows a day instead of the usual two in London and New York) was his tremendous success with audiences. Even when playing the tiresome *Wow-Wows*, Chaplin always transcended his material, but he also had the great pleasure of playing

---

[1] In his autobiography Chaplin speaks of living alone during his American tours. He may well have had a private room in New York but he certainly had Stan Laurel as roommate on tour. I have seen hotel receipts confirming this.

A *Night in an English Music Hall* together with a third sketch, A
Night in an English Club. The latter's subtitle, *or The Amateur
Entertainers,* states its essence. It was actually a hybrid of *Mumming Birds* and *The Wow-Wows:* various members of a London
club are called upon to entertain fellow members. The critic of
Show World during the Chicago engagement savored something
of the wistfulness that Karno always encouraged in his comedies:

> The offering somehow suggests Dickens. Seeing it one is re-
> minded of the gathering of the Pickwick Club. The caricatures of
> the individual members of the club are done with a graveness which
> makes the comedy stand out. The comedy is rough but the charac-
> ters are well drawn. . . . Various members of the club are called
> upon to entertain. There is a woman singer who gets her key
> repeatedly but cannot strike it when she begins to sing . . . an am-
> bitious tragedian who, after reminding the master of ceremonies
> several times, is at length permitted to start a scene of a play, only
> to be interrupted by the "drunk" (played by Charles Chaplin)
> which has come to be recognized as the leading comedy character
> of the Karno offerings.

An astute showman who recognized Chaplin's tremendous abilities, Sid Grauman, proprietor of the Empress Theatre in San
Francisco, marveled at the way Chaplin rose above the obscurities
of *The Wow-Wows.* He told Chaplin that if he ever left Karno
there would be ample backing at the Empress for any kind of
shows Chaplin would like to create. Chaplin was not yet tempted
to strike out on his own although, unaccountably, a few months
before he had discussed the possibility of buying a pig farm with a
fellow vaudevillian.

After San Francisco the Karno company went on to Salt Lake
City where the tour ended. Returning to New York with the intention of sailing to England, the company was booked unexpectedly for another tour. Alf Reeves was approached by William
Morris who owned a vaudeville roof garden, the American Music
Hall, at Forty-second Street and Eighth Avenue. The company
opened there with its sure-fire piece, *A Night in an English Music
Hall,* and won tremendous success. They played at the American
for six weeks and during this run Mack Sennett, then working as
an actor for D. W. Griffith at the Biograph Studios in New York,
saw Chaplin for the first time.

I was impressed [said Sennett], more than impressed. Stunned might be a good word. I think I was so struck by him because he was everything I wasn't: a little fellow who could move like a ballet dancer. The next week I couldn't remember his name but I sure as hell never forgot that wonderful easy grace of movement. I had seen nothing like it. I've seen nothing like it since, except in Chaplin films. And to think it was luck, pure chance that I saw Chaplin the first time! I had an appointment with a friend that night on Eighth Avenue. I waited, he didn't show up so I thought I'd kill time by wandering into the nearby music hall. Bless my friend for missing our engagement.

After the Morris engagement the Sullivan-Considine circuit began to receive requests from managers of their various theatres across the country for (as one manager put it) "those crazy Limeys." The company was booked for another twenty weeks cross-country to California.

During the San Francisco engagement Chaplin casually dropped into a fortuneteller's parlor on Market Street. He was a trifle embarrassed at this giving way to what some might call superstition but perhaps his Gypsy blood was in the ascendancy that day. In any case he quickly became intrigued by the brisk middle-aged lady who asked him to cut the cards three times toward her, then hold out his hands. After examining the cards and without looking up at Chaplin, she told him unhesitatingly that he was on the verge of a long journey out of the United States, that he would return again shortly after to enter a new business. At this point she faltered and allowed that the new business would be in the same general area he was presently following, but that the monetary rewards for it would be tremendous and his career extraordinary. She could not see what that career was. She then looked at him for the first time, examined his hands, and told him he would be married three times (two of the marriages failing), he would have three children, and would die of bronchial pneumonia at the age of eighty-two. After giving the dollar she asked, Chaplin left. The lady was not far out in her predictions but she did not foresee a father of ten children zealously avoiding drafts all of 1971.

The second Karno tour across the States was triumphant, and at its conclusion, when the company sailed for London, Chaplin was euphoric. He knew he had done well, and he was certain he had found his home. He would return to America, he knew, not only because of the theatrical opportunities but because there was a freshness, particularly in the West, that he found stimulating. Unlike England, this was a classless society where talent could soar to the top on nothing but its own credentials. He told this to Sydney when he returned to London, and Sydney was interested but distracted. He had married during Charlie's absence and this together with his own growing career kept the brothers from their old intimacy for a time.

They went to the mental institution where Hannah had now been confined for a few months. She had been violent of late, the doctors said, and was confined to a padded room. Charlie could not bear to see her under these circumstances so Sydney went in. Under a regimen of ice-cold showers for shock treatment, her face had taken on a bluish cast. Sydney was tormented at the sight. He returned to Charlie with the suggestion that now surely they could afford to put her in a private hospital.

When this was done and Chaplin returned that evening to a cheerless room he had rented in Brixton Road he was totally disconsolate and more than ever determined to return to the United States. He toured for several months with a Karno company in London music halls. The company was also booked for a week in Jersey, one of the Channel Islands south of England, and it was to be in Jersey that Charlie Chaplin conceived his first plot for motion pictures.

He had talked of the possibility earlier. During his first days in New York he and Alf Reeves often went to the movies and one day, according to writer Jim Tully (citing a letter Reeves wrote to a film trade journal in 1916), Chaplin got the idea of using the Karno company to make "picture comedies" in their spare time with theatre scenery for backgrounds. Chaplin explained his idea to the cast with enthusiasm, pointing out quite inaccurately that all they needed for their purposes was a movie camera. Reeves and Chaplin were certain that their venture would work, and they took on the task of financing it with an informal partnership, each agreeing to put up $1000 to buy the camera. At the time, Reeves said, they had no idea of their incredible naïveté. The project died aborning because all spare time was taken up with new sketch rehearsals. But it is intriguing that Chaplin had the idea of making movies as early as 1910.

When the Karno company played the island of Jersey early in 1912, the making of films was once more brought to Chaplin's attention. Alf Reeves (in his letter to the unidentified film trade magazine quoted by Jim Tully) said that the film idea discussed in New York persisted in Chaplin's memory. He talked about it frequently. During the Jersey tour a street pageant, part of an annual carnival of flowers, was held, and a newsreel cameraman was filming it.

Charlie [said Reeves] was more interested in this cameraman than in the carnival. The cameraman was here, there and everywhere, but wherever he went, a very pompous gentleman, who was apparently *chargé d'affaires*, would always be found in the foreground of the camera lens. He would shake hands with different dignitaries, but would always turn away from the person he was greeting and face the camera, bowing and registering his greetings to the camera, while his guests were in the background off to one side. Charlie was fascinated by this incident and told me that this bit of real comedy he would put in pictures should he ever be in a position to do so.

Chaplin was in that position almost two years later, the Jersey incident becoming the heart of Chaplin's second film, *Kid Auto Races at Venice*. But fascinated as Chaplin was with films in 1912, they were not much on his mind when, to his great pleasure, Karno summoned him to head a second tour of the United States. Once again the detested *Wow-Wows* was trotted out but this time Chaplin insisted on adding some solid slapstick to it which almost transformed the sketch. During this tour in 1912–13, *The Wow-Wows*, although never getting the laughs given its alternate piece, *A Night in an English Music Hall*, developed into what one member of the troupe called "a ruddy good show which Charlie really built up out of nothing."

But outside of audience response, the second tour provided something of a letdown, perhaps inevitably. The company was doing three shows a day, sometimes four, every day of the week. Travel pressures were constant and sightseeing was either impossible or marred by *déjà vu*. The tour was no longer an adventure.

Chaplin tried to read more. He was now a fervid admirer of

Ralph Waldo Emerson and became marked forever with the Emersonian theories of the primacy of the individual. Toward the end of the national tour the company had a single respite, a week off in Philadelphia. Chaplin resolved to relax in depth. He threw aside his natural frugality, bought a luxurious dressing gown and an expensive overnight bag, and took the train to New York where he checked into the Hotel Astor.

He was barely able to conceal fears of his social inadequacies as he registered and took possession of a beautiful room. (His sense of delight in this experience was so marked that fifty years later he was able to say fervently that the worst thing to befall a man would be getting used to luxury.) That evening, despite an aversion to grand opera (of which he knew very little), he went to the Metropolitan Opera to see *Tannhäuser*. Not knowing the story, unable to understand German, he was passive until the dead queen was brought in during the Pilgrims' Chorus.

Chaplin was then swept up into an emotional experience as poignant and memorable to him as his childhood encounter listening to "The Honeysuckle and the Bee." But that earlier moment was ecstatic: he had entered forever into the world of music and he knew it. This moment at the opera was trauma. He wept in agony. It seemed to him at this instant that he was crying in one spasmodic agony for all the intense deprivations of his earlier years—for all the injuries done his spiritual and emotional self. This was a moment when the façade he had created for himself since childhood was well and truly rent, and more than anything else it made him realize just how intensely alone he was. It was dramatically fitting that this, the nadir of his life to that moment, should immediately precede one of his life peaks.

He returned to Philadelphia next day. Alf Reeves had just received a telegram:

ALF REEVES MANAGER   MAY 12 1913
KARNO LONDON COMEDIANS
NIXON THEATRE, PHILADELPHIA, PA.

IS THERE A MAN NAMED CHAFFIN IN YOUR COMPANY OR SOMETHING LIKE THAT STOP IF SO WILL HE COMMUNICATE WITH KESSEL AND BAUMAN 24 LONGACRE BUILDING BROADWAY NEW YORK

Since Chaplin was the only person with a name remotely like
Chaffin, he left for New York titillated by the news given him
that the Longacre Building was home base for many lawyers. The
prospect of a legacy from an obscure relative came to mind. It
proved to be rather more interesting than that.

Adam Kessel, Jr., and Charles O. Bauman were the owners of
the New York Motion Picture Company, the parent of four sub-
sidiaries: Kay-Bee Films (named for the owners), Bronco Pictures
(they made Westerns), Domino Films (the heavy drama), and
Keystone Comedies. The latter was the sole province of Mack
Sennett, who in his unsigned telegram to Philadelphia had almost
remembered the name of the English comic he had seen in 1911
at the American Music Hall. Sennett was losing his star comedian, Ford Sterling, and in thinking of adequate replacement the
memory of the graceful little Limey came to mind.

Sennett was willing to give Chaplin a hundred and fifty dollars a week, exactly double the Karno salary, but Chaplin bar-
gained until he got a year's contract for $150 the first three
months and $175 for the remaining nine. He first had to finish the
Karno tour and then report to Keystone Studios in six months'
time. Chaplin played his last performance for Karno at the Empress Theatre, Kansas City, on November 28, 1913.

I missed him, I must say [said Stan Laurel]. To some of the company I know he appeared standoffish and superior. He wasn't, he
wasn't at all. And this is something a lot of people through the years
don't know or refuse to believe about Charlie: he is a very, very shy
man. You could even say he is a desperately shy man. He was never
able to mix easily unless people came to him and volunteered
friendship or unless he was among people who didn't know him.
Then he wasn't so shy.

Arthur Dandoe, a chap in the Karno company with whom I
teamed one time in a vaudeville act, didn't like Charlie. Arthur
didn't like him because he considered him haughty and cold. So in
Kansas City on our last night with Charlie, Arthur announced to everybody that he was going to present a special good-by present. He
told me what it was—about five pieces of old brown Leichner grease
paint, looking just like turds, all of this wrapped up in a very fancy
box. "Some shit for a shit" is the way Arthur put it. This was
Arthur's idea of a joke. I tried to argue him out of it but all Arthur
said was, "It'll serve the superior bastard right."

The so-called presentation never took place however and later Arthur told me why. First of all, Charlie stood the entire company drinks after the show. That fazed Arthur a bit but the thing that really shamed him into not going through with the so-called gag was this: just after his final curtain with us, Charlie hurried off to a deserted spot backstage. Curious, Arthur followed, and he saw haughty, cold, unsentimental Charlie crying.

4
KEYSTONE

With great apprehension Chaplin arrived in Los Angeles and burrowed into a rickety hotel on Bunker Hill. He was too nervous to call Sennett and for anodyne visited the Empress Theatre, the same vaudeville house the Karno troupe had played just weeks before. By a coincidence, the same night Chaplin visited the Empress, Mack Sennett and Mabel Normand went to the theatre, sitting just two rows behind him. An usher who knew Chaplin took him back to meet his new boss. Chaplin was very nervous and showed it; Sennett was very shocked and did not show it. He was under the impression that he had hired a man in his late thirties. Without make-up this sprig of a youth looked like a prop man's assistant, not the replacement for a reigning comedy star. After the show Sennett took the party to a rathskeller and frankly admitted his concern. "I can make up as old as you like," Chaplin said. He was asked to go out to the Sennett studios in Edendale next morning.

Chaplin took a streetcar out to the studios and felt like taking it right back again. The Mack Sennett studio looked like a combined secondhand lumberyard and aborted construction site. Chaplin was horrified. Across the street he walked up and down for half an hour, then took the streetcar back to the hotel. He did this two more days, absolutely unable to summon up the courage to walk into a building he had no doubt was as ramshackle within as without. The third day Sennett phoned and asked why he had not shown up.

Chaplin went down, toured the studio, and after talking with Sennett began to understand why this curious mélange looked as it did. Sets were continually being built or torn down (there was room for five good-sized sets on the lot), and the roof and sides of the building were translucent, diffusing the strong California sun needed for natural lighting. On cloudy days the roof could be rolled back and/or the sides of the building raised for additional light. There were three films then in production, and it was all, in Chaplin's words, "a roar of confused sound—screams, laughs, an explosion, shouted commands, pounding, whistling, the bark of a dog. The air was thick with the smell of new lumber in the sun, flash-light powder, cigarette smoke." But Chaplin soon realized the adequate order in this disorder. Although much of the comedy was improvised during shooting, a general story line and key gags had been worked out by knowledgeable directors with the help of players who were masters of pantomime.

The Sennett company by and large was a group of hedonistic clowns given to rough humor both on and off camera. Chaplin was not of their element although he manifested a cheerful row-diness equal to their own when the cameras rolled. Off camera he tended to go his own way—when, that is, his co-workers permitted it. In his early days at Keystone he became something of a butt of jokes. Charlie Chaplin, Jr., tells of one practical joke the Keystone gang planned for Chaplin. The gag had first been conceived for Jess Dandy, the stock Sennett fat man, who spent much time in the washroom reading the newspapers. The jokers wired the toilet seat and, when Dandy went into the booth and sat, the juice was turned on. Dandy emerged howling, claiming great injury. A bit later Chaplin, who was not in on the gag, entered the compartment and again the juice was turned on. The conspirators waited gleefully, but there was silence—followed by a loud thud.

More silence. And more silence. The gagsters grew frightened and one of them suggested that the electric charge might have been too strong. They pushed open the door to the compartment apprehensively, finding Chaplin face down on the floor, deathly quiet. As they stared in fascinated horror, he glanced up, smirked triumphantly, and vigorously thumbed his nose.

Chaplin resorted to nose-thumbing increasingly at Keystone both in self-defense against the practical jokes (which he mainly managed to circumvent) and as a comic device in his early films. Only he referred to this gesture of insult by its hearty British name, "cocking a snook." Chaplin cocked many snooks literally and figuratively in the years ahead.

At the studio he had occasional need to cock his snook vehemently. Chaplin was regarded not only as an odd fish but as something less than an artist in his first Sennett days. Mabel Normand told Samuel Goldwyn:

"They didn't really appreciate Charlie in those early days. I remember numerous times when people in the studio came up and asked me confidentially, 'Say, do you think he's so funny? In my mind he can't touch Ford Sterling.' They were just so used to slapstick that imaginative comedy couldn't penetrate."

Too, Ford Sterling was popular among his co-workers and the idea of a newcomer, especially a reserved and slightly overdressed Englishman, replacing him was not a welcome thought. There were no separate male dressing rooms at Sennett's; there was only a large mirrored locker room where all the men dressed, and passed the time of day. Chaplin spent very little time there. When rain stopped the working day he much preferred to sit in Mabel's little dressing room and discuss current life and letters. She preferred that too because although her well-known affection for Mack Sennett precluded any possibility of romance with Chaplin she liked him very much and found his conversation engrossing.

The opposite situation obtained with Chaplin's first boss on the Keystone lot, Henry "Pathé" Lehrman, an abrasive ex-streetcar conductor. The nickname derived from his fraudulent claim to his first boss, D. W. Griffith, that he was the American representative of Pathé Frères, the great French film company. Lehrman's obtrusive vanity irked Chaplin but he tried to follow the director's chaotic instructions. The first Chaplin film, *Making a Living*, went into production the last week of 1913.

Chaplin was cast as a glib swindler who finds a job as a newspaper reporter. Trying to scoop another's scoop by stealing his rival's news camera, Chaplin has the purloined news picture published. Chased by his vengeful rival, he runs about town to insure that issues of his paper are distributed. *Making a Living* in its fifteen-minute span lacks everything but a sense of urgency. It is a typical Keystone gallop. Chaplin volunteered a number of gags which the jealous Lehrman removed in editing, and the film looks it. Yet a distinctive Chaplin hallmark is established in his very first film—his serene belligerence in times of self-need. Chaplin is at the newspaper office trying to browbeat an editor. He keeps slapping the man on the knee, and when the man moves his knee away, Chaplin simply pulls it back automatically in order to continue the intimidation, not even looking at the knee. Chaplin, Walter Kerr points out, has "established what would become a permanent, immensely productive pattern: he is adjusting the rest of the universe to his merely reflexive needs." Charlie making the world his.

In *Making a Living*, the Chaplin costume and make-up are as barren and bizarre as the plot: Fu Manchu mustache, monocle, high hat, frock coat but shirtless, with tie, dickey, and attached collar and cuffs. The costume was basically the one worn by Chaplin as the Honorable Archibald Binks in several of the Karno sketches.

Mack Sennett was fond of using events of the day as background for his comedies when they were congruent with his plots. Although the story is apocryphal that Sennett comics joined public parades to cavort along as cameramen filmed these improvisations, Sennett certainly took advantage of news events for lively background. Early in 1914 he dispatched Lehrman and Chaplin to Venice, California, to see what larks they could film against a background of the annual children's auto race there. The result is *Kid Auto Races at Venice*, a plotless episode of Chaplin mugging, posturing, gesticulating as he stands in the way of a cameraman (Lehrman) attempting to film the event. All of this is very trivial, yet two vital things happen in the film: Charlie the tramp is born even if only embryonically, and Chaplin, by confronting the camera, joins not the characters in the film but *us*. He joins us, his audience, forever. "He wished," says Walter Kerr, "to communicate with his audience in the first person, and to belong to its world— not to the world of the characters. Essentially, Chaplin established himself as one of us, not one of them, whoever they might be."

In *Kid Auto Races at Venice*, Charlie makes his first fuss. This childlike figure does not emerge as a character (it is only a five-

minute film) but Charlie's basic costume is there for the first
time. For this film Sennett had simply asked him to put on a comedy make-up: "Anything will do." Chaplin had an idea that his
costume should exist in terms of contradiction: baggy pants, tight
jacket, large shoes and small hat. He added a small mustache to
age his youthful features and carried a cane for comic panache.
All of this, Chaplin says, occurred almost casually and in a matter
of minutes. It undoubtedly happened quickly but evidence exists
that most of these accouterments had been dormant in Chaplin's
mind for some time.

But as for the creation of Charlie the tramp, that, Chaplin
emphatically assures us, happened quickly:

> I had no idea of the character. But the moment I was dressed,
> the clothes and the makeup made me feel the person he was. I
> began to know him, and by the time I walked onto the stage he was
> fully born. When I confronted Sennett I assumed the character and
> strutted about, swinging my cane and parading before him. Gags
> and comedy ideas went racing through my mind.[1]

That the tramp came precipitately and full-blown into the
world cannot be doubted. But Charlie's costume has antecedents,
indeed may have originated *in toto* in previous theatrical incarna-
tions. There is the basic account amplifying Chaplin's that out of
odds and ends—Fatty Arbuckle's pants, Charlie Avery's coat, Ford
Sterling's size 14 shoes put on the wrong way, a small derby
belonging to Minta Durfee's father, Mack Swain's mustache cut
down—instantly and a little miraculously emerged the tramp's
costume. Charlie Chaplin, Jr., disputes this story. He is emphatic
in saying that Chaplin told him the costume really originated
years before he joined Sennett. One evening when Chaplin was
working temporarily as a janitor at a London music hall the featured performer became ill and the manager, knowing Chaplin
had worked as an entertainer, asked him to fill in. Chaplin agreed
and hurriedly put on the star turn's costume. It was far too big:

[1] Chaplin then proceeds to describe his third film, *Mabel's Strange Predicament*, as the one in which his tramp costume was first employed. His
memory fails him here. Minta Durfee and Chester Conklin both recall the
tramp's genesis in *Kid Auto Races* and the film's date also verifies this.

the pants ballooned out, the shoes were huge, but the derby was ridiculously small. Chaplin had a larger than average head size. It · was a ludicrous ensemble.

"I just put them on and there was my tramp outfit," Chaplin told his son. Almost swimming in his clothes, Chaplin went out before the audience and got the first laugh of the evening on appearance alone. He ad-libbed a zany routine, climaxing it by falling into a big tub of water. The pants billowed out and he floasted around cheekily for a few moments to great audience acclaim.

This story, which Charlie Chaplin, Jr., wrote knowing his father would read it, indicates that there were past influences on Chaplin as he stood in the Keystone costume room selecting the elements of his costume. He would also doubtless remember the laughs Fred Kitchen, the old Karno comic, got from his oversized shoes. Moreover, Chaplin still had a very active memory of "Rummy" Binks.

In *McClure's* magazine, July 1916, Chaplin recalled the origin of his splay-footed shuffle. At the age of twelve he watched an old "rum-soak" called Rummy Binks hold the horses for coachmen as they descended for a quick drink at the Queen's Head, a celebrated pub on Lambeth Walk. Rummy had large misshapen feet which shuffled as he walked horses to the trough. The old man tried to hurry but his tired old body restrained him. The coach drivers coming out of the pub for their horses rewarded Rummy with a coin, and from this he made his livelihood. Chaplin knew it must have disturbed the old man's spirit to live on such trivial bounty. Endlessly fascinated by Rummy, the boy watched him until it was obvious the old man was annoyed at the scrutiny. Chaplin would describe Rummy to his mother and imitate his walk. "Oh, you wicked boy!" Hannah said in horror.

"Well, that was the origin of my walk," said Chaplin. "I never had the idea then of using it. Even later, when I was in vaudeville, the only use I put it to was amusing the company behind the scenes. The walk was saved for the movies." Edward Smith, the *McClure's* reporter quoting Chaplin, goes on to say that the "pathos of the old beer-sot living on halfpenny tips and teaching a walk worth millions . . ." was not lost on Chaplin.

Another, and very authoritative, opinion on the origin of Chaplin's tramp costume comes from R. J. Minney, the only Chaplin biographer who knew Charlie and Sydney Chaplin as a family friend. Minney says that Chaplin based his costume "roughly on the clothes he wore when he played the rag-and-bone man in a Karno sketch called *London Suburbia.*" There is evidence that this is basically the same costume Chaplin described to his son.

There is no essential disharmony in these accounts. More than likely, Chaplin, faced with the quick need to throw a comedy costume together, called on his conscious and unconscious memory to help define his new character. Years later Chaplin came to realize that the costume was taking on almost mythic significance and this may have prompted him to authorize Rob Wagner's definition of the costume in 1918. Wagner ("a sun-kissed Aristotle," Gene Fowler called him) was a teacher of Greek and art in the Hollywood school system. He became Chaplin's publicity man during World War I and frequently issued Chaplin opinions on a wide range of things.

As to the costume, Wagner spoke of the symbolism which Chaplin "carefully" structured into it: "Each part of his ensemble is a symbol, and if you misplace symbols, they then become ridiculous. All [Chaplin's] stuff had to be shabby. He personified shabby gentility and to top it off, he used a walking stick because it is the keynote of much of Dickens' work." And thus allusively and justifiably having brought Chaplin into proximity with the nineteenth century's greatest popular artist, Wagner set forth a proposition with which most film critics and scholars concur. Deliberately selected to create a particular impression or not, the Chaplin ensemble does evoke a specific feeling, one well stated by Theodore Huff who, following Wagner, says:

> Chaplin's costume personifies shabby gentility—the fallen aristocrat at grips with poverty. The cane is a symbol of attempted dignity, the pert moustache a sign of vanity. Although Chaplin used the same costume (with a few exceptions) for almost his entire career, or for about twenty-five years, it is interesting to note a slight evolution: the trousers became less baggy, the coat a little neater, and the moustache a little trimmer through the years.

Most critics find in the tramp's costume the key element of drama itself—conflict: the warring of rich and poor, posh and plain, high and low estate. This may have been Chaplin's carefully planned structuring. And there is the likelier possibility that he created the tramp and his costume simply because they looked funny. If Charlie and what he wore attained a mythic dimension as the years went by, that is a pleasant accident of history.[2]

Chaplin's co-workers found the tramp character as odd as its interpreter but they came to realize the gag-making skill of the "Little Limey," as they mostly called him behind his back. The Sennett comedians, for all their roughhouse approach to life and their profession, were an amiable lot. Ford Sterling (1880–1939), the comedian Chaplin was replacing, always made up as a Dutch comic. As the "chief" of the Keystone Kops, he was a very vigorous comedian not notably subtle in his "takes" and "double takes" of reaction. Roscoe "Fatty" Arbuckle (1887–1933), who despised his aptly bestowed nickname, was a man whose superb pantomimic skills Chaplin much admired. Like the other famous fat man of film comedy, Oliver Hardy, Arbuckle moved and reacted with superlative ease. Arbuckle's wife, Minta Durfee (1897–1975), a petite comedienne with a tartly sweet personality, was Chaplin's leading woman for several films. Massive Mack Swain (1876–1935) was the first of the elephantine foils Chaplin was to employ as representatives of the Disloyal Opposition—be they minions of society, the law, or the underworld.

Also on the Keystone lot were the two prime scene stealers before Chaplin arrived—gentle Chester Conklin (1888–1971), who wore his walrus mustache as a badge of genial stupidity, and athletic Hank Mann (1887–1971), whose hangdog look invariably broke up the most laugh-hardened of his peers. There were also veteran character actress Alice Davenport (1853–c. 1931) and the formidable Phyllis Allen (1861–1938), archetypal battle-ax, ample of height and heft. The supporting players included Sennett himself (who played a rube with such distinction because he was one), Edgar Kennedy before his "slow burn" days, eye-popping Charlie Murray, Al St. John, the very youthful Charlie Chase, and

<hr>

[2] Too, Chaplin may have been creating a blowsy version of Max Linder's costume. Linder (1883–1925), France's greatest screen comedian, dressed as a boulevardier, got into scrapes boulevardiers specialized in. Chaplin has acknowledged a debt to him.

gangling Slim Summerville. And leading all these was the ineffable Mabel.

Mabel Normand (1894-1930) was Sennett's distaff Chaplin. Working for D. W. Griffith at Biograph in New York, she met Sennett, who became the love of her life and vice versa. Not only a versatile performer and enchanting to look at, she had a first-rate comedy mind. It was she who threw the first pie in film comedy,[3] and the Keystone Kops were also her idea. It was inevitable that when Chaplin became the star of the Keystone aggregate Mabel would be teamed with him. In his third film, *Mabel's Strange Predicament*, Chaplin was an afterthought. Sennett had asked him merely to enter a hotel foyer as a drunk and do what comic business inspired him as he confronted Mabel in elegant attire. What came to him was to trip over her dog's leash and get his foot caught in a cuspidor. This and a later chase sequence in and out of hotel rooms were so expertly executed by Chaplin that the veteran Sennett crew—and Mabel—were fascinated.

He failed to enthrall his director, Pathé Lehrman, who, against the evidence and probably stimulated by jealousy, insisted that Chaplin act in the frenzied Ford Sterling run-chase-and-tumble style. There was little Chaplin could do about that in his fourth film, *Between Showers*, because Sterling played the leading role. But Sennett saw the fundamental disagreement between the director and their new star, and in the next film, *A Film Johnnie*, Sennett supervised. *A Film Johnnie* (the high point of which is Charlie, after a forceful fire hose drenches him, twisting his ear and spouting water from his mouth) and the next, *Tango Tangles*, were location films—the former at the Keystone lot itself, the latter at an actual dance hall. The films almost directed themselves, with Chaplin and others improvising at need. But the next, *His Favorite Pastime*, with Charlie as a rather obnoxious drunk chasing a lady, was directed by George Nichols, a Keystone vet-

[3] At Slim Summerville, as a gag during lunch hour, a moment incorporated into her next film (according to Stan Laurel). It was not the first pie thrown in comedy history. Puddings had been thrown in English pantomimes in the eighteenth century and Fred Karno had thrown actual custard pies as early as 1897. For the record, the first custard pies ever thrown in the American theatre were in *The Corn Curers*, which opened March 17, 1898, at the Weber and Fields Music Hall, New York.

eran who also regarded the Ford Sterling pace as the only conceivable one for comedy. When Chaplin tried to interpolate his own more restrained gags, Nichols complained to Sennett, who again took over, supervising the next two Chaplin films, *Cruel, Cruel Love* and *The Star Boarder*.

Up to this point—his ninth film—no specific Charlie persona had really emerged. Although in most of these one-reel films the tramp costume is present and the free-wheeling, audacious, confidential charm dominates, this is not yet The Tramp. By the tenth film, *Mabel at the Wheel*, Chaplin's first two-reeler, Sennett may have contemplated forcing Chaplin into the mold of the now departed Ford Sterling because the tramp costume is gone and Chaplin actually wears Sterling's old frock coat. Sennett also unwisely forced a new director on Chaplin—Mabel Normand—and the easy comradeship between the two master performers vanished. Mabel brusquely disagreed with a Chaplin-suggested gag and there were angry words. Inevitably Sennett was on Mabel's side but, when it looked as if Chaplin would quit, Sennett took over and finished the picture.

This was the perfect time for Chaplin to suggest the obvious. Chaplin pictures should be done by Chaplin. Sennett's worry about an untried director taking over was mostly relieved by Chaplin promising to make up any loss if the picture failed. Chaplin apologized to Mabel for losing his temper and a relieved Sennett took them both out to dinner.

Mabel and Chaplin congenially shared the direction of his twelfth film, *Caught in a Cabaret*, before he took over his own films for good. The first Chaplin-directed film was *Caught in the Rain*, in which Charlie chases a married lady who in turn sleepwalks right into his room to the jealous consternation of her husband. As in most Keystone comedies, it was not the fast tempo but the gags which were funny. But Chaplin began to see that the Keystone rush-rush had a certain inherent virtue: swiftness allowed poor gags to be quickly left behind and, more importantly, the more gags in a film the better. Chaplin's films were soon the premier money-makers at Keystone. Occasionally Chaplin would wander over into other production areas of the studio to do a cameo appearance as in Fatty Arbuckle's *The Knockout* in which Charlie appears as an ebullient fight referee. It is, expectedly, the highlight of the film with the referee receiving a large percentage of the blows, one a knockout clout prompting him to count the stars he sees circling his head.

Chaplin learned film making quickly. One stimulus was a twenty-five-dollar bonus from Sennett for every film completed, and another was Chaplin's discovery that films were more adventurous than the stage. By camera placement and careful editing he found one could create one's own world, even in the pell-mell atmosphere at Keystone.

One clear professional difference between Chaplin and his fellows in what justifiably came to be called the "laugh factory" was the earnestness of Chaplin's screen character. Chaplin mugged in traditional fashion; his grimaces were as wide and elastic as Ford Sterling's and Mack Swain's. Technically the Keystone comics were alike in many ways. Where Chaplin dominated them, however, was in Charlie's overwhelming earnestness, a suggestion of deeper dimensions in a one-dimensional character. This pervasive sincerity soon caught the attention of the public. Also in contrast to some of the Keystone comedians, there was nothing self-congratulatory in Chaplin's comic acting. He is dedicatedly unself-conscious as he lopes through his world of hotel lobbies, restaurants, and public parks, getting into prodigious kinds of trouble, trouble from which he extricates himself with wonder-provoking ease and rapt sincerity.

Sincerity is certainly the hallmark of his appearances (and they are many) as a drunk. In *Mabel's Married Life*, Charlie comes home from a bender to face a stand-up punching bag which Mabel has purchased for his exercise. The boxing dummy, wearing a cap and sweater much like Charlie's rival, Mack Swain, has a rounded base allowing it to pop forward and back with driving strength. In his complete inebriation, Charlie confronts the dummy as an intruder and attempts to convince "him" of the folly of remaining in the house. In ordinary hands this scene would be mildly amusing; with Chaplin, it is hilarious because Charlie's certainty that the dummy is real is so profound that we almost share it. The authenticity of Charlie's drunkenness is an acting lesson. Unlike other comics who cleverly simulate drunkenness, Chaplin —like a real drunk—summons up his thoughts in an attempt to be *sober*. He is trying desperately to be sober. Chaplin looks at the drunk he is portraying from the *drunk's* point of view, not from the view of a skilled comedian trying to be drunk. It is the difference between great acting and clever impersonation. Reality.

Reality is also in another new note Chaplin introduced to his work, a tentative form of sympathy for Charlie. In the title role of *The New Janitor*, Charlie is unjustly dismissed and in consequence becomes something of a martyr. This is purely a side note and a good distance from the pathos yet to come in Chaplin films. He is still an integral part of the savage slapstick that is Keystone.

Certainly Chaplin used every device of slapstick including the stick itself. This double-lath of antique humor which, when smacked on head or backside caused a maximum of noise and a minimum of pain, necessarily lacked one of its prime elements in silent films. But Chaplin knew that a similar effect could be simulated by facile use of his cane—or a broom, mop, board, and ladder—inflicting a smart blow and an openmouthed reaction from the victim. This is funniest when Charlie inflicts the pain unknowingly—as he bends over or looks the other way or is distracted. Almost any object Charlie was capable of carrying becomes an extension of his own body. It is not extraneous to him; that cane or broom extends his whole bodily instrument and he uses it as a third arm.

A cheerful cruelty characterized many of Sennett's films in 1914–15 when Chaplin reigned there, and Chaplin became master of the process. Raymond Borde, speaking of *The Property Man*, describes Charlie lifting a heavy trunk and then asking a battered old man to carry it for him. Charlie loads the trunk on to the back of the human wreck. The man staggers forward, leaning on his cane. Charlie beats him like a mule, and the other collapses altogether, to lie, crushed under his burden, on the ground. To get him going again, Charlie leaps up on the trunk, thus adding to the burden of the old man, who now resembles nothing so much as a pathetic beetle pinned to the ground by some sick wit. And *The Property Man* is no exception. In his short films, Charlie's sadism is incessant.

Raymond Durgnat agrees with this, citing Chaplin as "easily the cruelest of Sennett's comedians." One need not challenge this to point out also that the millions who loved these films in 1914 and later were not necessarily laughing at cruelty. One does not laugh at a cartoon—which is what *The Property Man* is—because it is real, but precisely because it is unreal, a caricature of life's troubles. We, all of us, soon or late get someone on our backs.

Cruel or simply uncomfortable, a persistent ingredient of Keystone comedies was what Chaplin called the arse-kick. This device he developed in his Keystone days and carried it well into the years of his artistic majority. During a bond-selling tour in 1918 a judge Chaplin met in the South said he admired Chaplin's knowledge of fundamentals: "You know that the most undignified part of a man's anatomy is his arse, and your comedies prove it."

Perhaps his comedies tend to overprove it. That at least was Robert Benchley's privately stated opinion. He abominated Chaplin's films because he considered them too full of what he called "Charlie's ass-kicking humor." Too full surely, but no one, be it said, ever ass-kicked like Chaplin, and if the thing is to be done at all, it is a pleasure to see it done with such emphatic grace.

Charlie arse-kicked in every conceivable variation known to humankind, attacking his goal either from behind, to one side, or spinning past on the bias. In *The Property Man* the locus of the kick changes at one point from backside to the teeth, and a kicking duel begins. In *Mabel's Married Life* Charlie kicks the firm-set Mack Swain over and over until his foot is injured. In *Dough and Dynamite* after some preliminary kicking early in the film Charlie is attacked by the usually genial Chester Conklin, who arse-kicks him five times in pile-driver fashion. And on and on. As a Chaplin gag, this is not a sometime thing.

A frequent companion device to the arse-kick at Sennett's was the somersault, and it too had variations. Quite frequently as a result of a kick, Charlie or a chum (ladies never somersaulted for obvious reasons) would make a complete revolution, heels over head. Chaplin became the master of this on the Keystone lot. He was in any case the master pantomimist there and Sennett appreciated the fact: "We seldom used chase sequences with Chaplin. He was not the man to take part in those. . . . His style is intimate, not panoramic—the one shot instead of the crowd scene. We understood that early in the game."

Chaplin perfected the somersault until he became the master of its cleverest variation, the "108" or backward somersault. His only

rival with the 108 was Ben Turpin, who joined Keystone after he
left. Turpin loved the 108 and did it on demand from perfect
strangers until Sennett, fearing injury to his valuable property,
posted signs declaring a hundred-dollar fine for anyone who
"bribes, asks or demands a 108 from Ben Turpin." Chaplin used
108s as exclamation marks following a rough-and-tumble gag.

Sennett had the inspired idea of teaming his leading comedian
with America's best-known comedienne, the Broadway-based
Marie Dressler (1869–1934). The happy result was *Tillie's Punctured Romance*, the first full-length film comedy. Miss Dressler
was signed at the not insignificant sum of $2500 a week, $2300
more a week than her leading man was getting. But Chaplin did
not object; he sensed, correctly, that exposure to the wide public
this film would reach could do him nothing but good. *Tillie's
Punctured Romance* (for a while Sennett thought of calling it
She Was More Sinned Against Than Necessary) was based on
Marie Dressler's 1910 Broadway success, *Tillie's Nightmare*, which
gave to the world that singular ballad, "Heaven Will Protect the
Working Girl." The film took fourteen weeks to shoot and could
easily have been done in ten. Miss Dressler, personally amiable,
was professionally stern. She insisted on following stage rather
than screen procedures in rehearsal until Sennett asserted himself.
After that all went well.

Tillie's Punctured Romance is still a lively and interesting comedy. Miss Dressler, whose overriding mugging makes Ford Sterling
at his worst look like Henry Daniell in rigor mortis, must be
seen to be believed. The film begins with Miss Dressler as the
bovine Tillie, out in the spring of all the world, playing with her
dog. She accidentally heaves a brick at a stranger, sleek Charlie, a
charming con man. Considerably battered, he is taken to her
farmhouse. Tillie's father befriends Charlie, who repays him by
stealing the old man's wallet. Tillie cavorts coquettishly as Charlie
projects his dubious passion for her. He convinces her to steal
more of her father's money and run off to the city with him.

For city garments Tillie has brought her best finery. As she
strolls about in the *haute* of her *couture* she resembles nothing
quite so much as an ambulating Persian pagoda. She walks fear-
fully through the tearing traffic on her loved one's arm. The couple is spotted by Mabel who, upon realizing that Charlie, her con-

federate and paramour, has been ostentatiously untrue, knocks
him down with deep sincerity. The police arrive and Tillie drags
her man away by the hair. Mabel flirts with a cop who incredibly
—like a dry fly refusing the succulent trout—walks away.

Charlie takes Tillie to a café where, slightly unhinged by strong
waters, she does a dance in which she undulates like a crumbling
silo in the storm. It is an extravagant event. Charlie sneaks off to
an alcove with Mabel where she urges him to take Tillie's purse.
Tillie, reaching the climax of her seizures, collapses happily on the
dance floor—and five men cannot lift her. Charlie and Mabel flee
with her purse, and Tillie's violent reactions to this force the
police to take her in. At the station, beatifically sozzled, she kisses
the sergeant on the brow, which stuns him. She is released when
it is found that she is the niece of Mr. Banks, the local millionaire.

Meanwhile Mabel and Charlie have bought new clothing with
their spoils. Tillie's uncle refuses to have anything to do with her
on unstated grounds. Perhaps he just doesn't like big women. He
goes off mountain climbing to forget the entire thing. Tillie gets a
job in a café to which inevitably come Mabel and Charlie to
spend some of Tillie's money. When Tillie sees them, it is in the
best *Punch* tradition of collapse of stout party, and Charlie being
pulled to the ground with her. He runs away and Tillie runs
amok until restrained by the café staff. In the interim, her uncle
has plunged from a mountain crag and lies still on the slope
below.

In a park with Mabel, Charlie reads a newspaper account of
millionaire Banks's demise and Tillie's accession to his money.
Charlie sneaks away from Mabel, runs to the café before news of
her good fortune can be brought to Tillie and, kneeling in the
spill of her slop pail, protests his undying love. They marry at
once and when they return to the café Tillie is told of her uncle's
death and her inheritance. Rolling her eyes like oscillating bal-
loons, she says (via title), "I wondered why he married me so?"
Charlie feigns passionate hurt at this lack of confidence in him,
and she succumbs, taking him to her uncle's mansion where Charlie as lord of the manor now has a grand opportunity to insult all
the servants. He does—by hearty arse-kicking and flicking cigarette
ashes in one flunky's face. He trips over a tiger rug which he

spanks. Mabel gets a job as maid in the house to be near her cad of a lover.

A posh ball is given and a desiccated slice of café society attends. Tillie changes her dress during the ball from a disastrous one to a dance costume, a cross between a belly dancer's harness and a haystack cover. She descends to the company from her room above, determined to outshine a professional dance team that has just done a decathlon version of the Turkey Trot. Tillie dances elaborately with her husband as Mabel tries to pull him away for a rendezvous. Ultimately Mabel and Charlie sneak off for some chaste cooing and Tillie dances on in an extraordinary *pas de seul* that shakes the dance floor. She looks for hubby, discovers him with Mabel, and hurls cream pies at them vengefully. This failing to win him, she finds a revolver and blasts away. Charlie flees upstairs and hides in a lady's boudoir as she is *en déshabillé*. Tillie, shooting like a peck of popcorn at climax, follows. Charlie hides in a large vase, pushing Mabel rudely away when she wants to share it. Mabel creeps under the rug, making quite a bulge. Tillie comes in the room flailing a cane, breaks the vase, and proceeds to choke her husband.

At this moment Tillie's uncle appears. The fall from the mountain was a bit less than fatal. He is outraged at the scum profaning his noble halls and chases them all out. Mabel spirits Charlie away and a servant telephones the police. These prove to be the Keystone Kops and at the station they line up before the sergeant in traditional bowling pin crash-down.

The scene shifts to Venice Pier where Tillie follows Mabel and Charlie, still shooting wildly. (Her six-shooter has the capacity of a Gatling gun.) Tillie falls in the water and when the Kops arrive to rescue her they succeed in typical fashion by hauling her up and down out of the drink on the rescue rope like a yo-yo. When she is finally brought in gasping, the ladies both give Charlie short shrift. Their rejection makes him swoon and the Kops grab him for past malfeasances. Tillie and Mabel commiserate with each other and embrace tearfully and happily.

Tillie's Punctured Romance is still vital comedy, perhaps too vital. It is funny although much of its basic appeal may be to folks who enjoy cockfights and mud-wrestling. It is arse-kicking brought to apotheosis, and Marie Dressler's stock in trade seems to be falling down, which she does unceasingly and with little provocation throughout. She is barely up before she is down again, flailing wildly about. One gets the idea she *enjoys* falling down.

Described in print, this may all seem like farcical overkill, but in the viewing, *Tillie's Punctured Romance* does hold up, for two reasons. First, Miss Dressler's abounding energy and volcanic mugging take one along with them. She is too energetic and changeable to get tired of: she will not let you ignore her. Then there is as always Chaplin's urbane dexterity, amusing and baffling in equal measure. One wonders how any human can so smoothly and so quickly become someone so smooth and quick.

The rude charm of *Tillie's Punctured Romance* can serve as an extended epigraph for Chaplin's work for Keystone. The film's strenuous and cheery physicality *was* Sennett. At Keystone, Chaplin was manifestly much better than his material, yet he never stepped beyond its framework, fittingly. He proved to himself that he could hold his own with any comedian or comic situation and that he could play *en ensemble*.

The release of the film brought other job offers but Sennett was determined to keep his prize. He offered Chaplin $750 a week and Chaplin refused. Sennett offered him one half of his interest in Keystone. Chaplin asked for $1000 a week, stunning Sennett, who pointed out that even *he* didn't make that kind of money. Sennett countered by offering a long-term contract: $500 weekly the first year, $700 the second year, and $1500 the third year, averaging out to $1000 a week for the contract. Chaplin replied that he would take the contract if the terms were reversed: $1500 the first year, $700 the second, and $500 the third. Sennett thought this was a bad joke but the joke was that Chaplin was not joking. That joke cost Sennett over a million dollars.

Chaplin made two more short comedies for Sennett before completing his contract. Sydney Chaplin, who had recently begun work at Sennett's at a salary higher than his brother's, was asked by Chaplin to form their own company. The conservative Sydney did not want to give up a contract that still had a year to run at a salary he had never before commanded. He elected to stay with Keystone. Charlie told Sydney he was serenely optimistic despite the prospect of immediate unemployment. He was certain someone would offer him what he was worth, and someone quickly did. The Essanay Film Manufacturing Company signed him, triumphantly. Essanay was to allow him greater freedom than he had at Keystone although Keystone was hardly a restrictive place to work. But two things hampered Chaplin at Keystone—the need to turn out films quickly, and the pervasive influence of the heavily physical gag. For all that, it was marvelous training and experience, and Chaplin learned a few things about comedy pace. He had appeared in thirty-five films at Edendale, playing a wide variety of roles.

As to his great comedy creation, Charlie the tramp, the Keystone Charlie was frenetic of personality, at times charming but often downright nasty, and rarely in repose. Since strife in one form or another is farce's framework, Charlie's basic situation in these films is the getting in and out of trouble. Much trouble. The gentleman tramp, Charlie's permanent screen character—the suave, compassionate, wry savager of pretentiousness—was not yet born. But he had been conceived.

5
ESSANAY

The first cowboy star of the movies, G. M. "Broncho Billy" Anderson, was a warmhearted young man from Little Rock who, after some years as an unsuccessful performer in vaudeville, learned that the way to success was to give the public what it didn't realize it really wanted. Anderson invented the Western just before there was a need for it and, great salesman that he was, convinced the motion picture industry that the best place to make Westerns was the West, something not easy for Eastern financiers to credit. Anderson took as partner George K. Spoor and from a compound of their initials formed the Essanay company.

One of the Essanay executives, Jess Robbins, was both an innovative technician (the first man to use reflective lighting in films) and a competent director. Robbins urged Anderson to sign Chaplin and to be quick about it before Universal or other interested studios did.

Gossip had pushed Chaplin's asking price from $1000 to $1250 a week plus $10,000 bonus. When Robbins met Chaplin over dinner to discuss terms, the Essanay man assumed that these were Chaplin's terms, and Chaplin did nothing to change the impression. He had, in fact, no terms in mind at all. Robbins was sure Essanay would meet the salary but the bonus was another thing. Anderson came to Los Angeles and seemingly obviated the difficulty by saying his partner Spoor would give the bonus when Chaplin began work at the Chicago Essanay studios. Chaplin signed with Essanay and finished his last Sennett film, *His Prehistoric Past,* with barely concealed impatience.

His good-by to Sennett and the Keystone gang was never made. He had never learned how to say good-by well. He simply left Keystone one Saturday night and began his new job the following Monday. But everyone at Keystone knew he was going and there was regret. Still, a sense that he was never one of them prevailed. "As for Charles Spencer Chaplin," Mack Sennett said, "I am not at all sure that we know him."

Chaplin went to Chicago and hated it. The mid-January weather was appalling but he had been assured that the Chicago studio was better than the indifferently equipped one at Niles, California. He had visited Niles briefly and agreed that it was not much. But Chicago was worse in a different way. It irritated Chaplin considerably that Mr. Spoor, the supposed source of his $10,000 bonus, was nowhere in evidence. Also, the studio at 1333 Argyle Street was depressing—a former warehouse with unimpressive equipment. The shooting lights, incredibly, were turned off promptly at 6 P.M., everyone going home even if a scene was in progress. This for Chaplin was a baffling approach to making films. The final turn of the screw was word that he could pick up the script for his first film from the chief scenarist, a young widow who rather fancied herself as a writer, Mrs. Louella Parsons. Chaplin declined with tart thanks, explaining that he wrote his own scripts.

The only bright spot in Chicago was a comedian he had been given to use as he would. Ben Turpin (1874–1940) had gone from burlesque to a janitor's job at Essanay, from there to *playing* janitors at Essanay. Turpin's cross-eyes were considered his comic good fortune, as proved to be so when he made considerable money with Sennett in 1917 after Essanay. But Chaplin, true to his instinct that a good comedian was the sum of his parts and not just a freak part of his sum, wisely withheld close-ups of Turpin in *His New Job*, the first Chaplin Essanay film. He wanted Turpin, in his role of a carpenter's assistant, to succeed *in toto*. The film satirizes life in a movie studio and has Charlie rising from extra to stagehand to star understudy in a matter of minutes. Chaplin is kidding here his Sennett days, but lovingly, and everyone gets into trouble uncomplicatedly, like the leading lady who, sweeping up a stair, loses her skirt as Charlie kneels on it.

There were some casting difficulties before the proper actress (Charlotte Mineau) could be found. Chaplin had auditioned several girls, among them a sharp-eyed little unknown, Gloria Swanson. She was finally given the bit part of a secretary (and can be seen fleetingly in existing prints) but the leading role was not for her. She explains:

"One gag called for Chaplin to kick me in the rear. Perfectionist that he is, he called for take after take, and I started to ache. I really wanted to be a dramatic actress. I loathe comedy, and the reason I *was* so funny was that I was so serious when I did comedy scenes. I finally protested about being kicked in the rear so much and I was fired."

Miss Swanson was not the only one fed up. Chaplin gave an ultimatum: he must see Spoor. Spoor was nowhere about and no one in the front office could speak for his presence *or* absence. Spoor, it later came out, was actually hiding from Chaplin. Appalled at his partner Anderson giving Chaplin a contract only top stars were receiving, Spoor was trying to tread water until Chaplin proved himself at the box office. On the contingency that he would not, Spoor planned to renege on the bonus by claiming he had not (as indeed he had not) been consulted.

When Spoor got strong evidence from the film exchange in Chicago that exhibitors were crying for Chaplin films, he made himself aggressively available and affected to be hurt by Chaplin's lack of trust in him. Spoor had assumed that Chaplin was simply a clever comedian from the Sennett lot who had mastered the tricks there and would bring some of them to Essanay. Spoor, like some critics of the day, just couldn't make Chaplin out.

Chaplin's press in early 1915 was typified by the film critic of the Fort Wayne *Journal* who, in reviewing *Tillie's Punctured Romance*, was hard put to label the rising new comedian:

> Chaplin's ability to make people laugh is a difficult thing to analyze. He has the funniest facial expression imaginable but other screen artists can twist their features through laughable contortions. He has a funny walk but other comedians can do that too. There's something else and it is purely Chaplinesque, as this odd specimen can bang a man over the head with a mallet, or merely walk across the screen and a laugh that comes from the heart greets him. He's simply Charlie Chaplin without a successful imitator, and to miss

him in *Tillie's Punctured Romance* is to miss the laugh of a lifetime.

Spoor did not think Chaplin very funny but it was amply clear that filmgoers did not agree. The critic in the February 20, 1915, issue of *Motion Picture World* was also puzzled by Chaplin's curiously effective antics in his first Essanay release. The reviewer marveled that such a plotless effort, depending principally on fights, smacks on the bottom, and concentrated mayhem, could summon up such hearty laughter. It was, said the critic, "a hard proposition to analyze. . . . Ben Turpin proves a good foil for Chaplin. For him the comedy star has no respect whatsoever. He pushes his face in, kicks him, slams the swing doors in his face, and finally walks on the unfortunate's stomach. In fact he abuses with sturdy vigor most people who happen to cross his orbit." *Motion Picture World* couldn't understand it but ". . . if the audience thinks it's funny, it must be so."

These were Spoor's sentiments exactly, and he overwhelmed Chaplin, after the bonus was paid, with queries as to how his working situation might be made more comfortable. Chaplin preferred California.

The Essanay studios at Niles, California, were a few miles outside San Francisco in ranch country. The amenities were not impressive but in contrast to Spoor's lair it was a gain. Broncho Billy made his films here, and there was at least an air of professionalism. Not the least professional aspect was Roland H. Totheroh, a cameraman working for Broncho Billy. Rollie Totheroh (1891–1967) was to be Charlie Chaplin's cameraman for thirty-seven eventful years in which they created some of the greatest moments in film comedy.

The cinematography of Chaplin's films has been criticized various times for its extreme simplicity. Simplicity. One wonders why this is so damning a word. "Unimaginative," "straightforward," "plain," "unadorned," "not fancy" are other words used pejoratively to characterize Rollie Totheroh's camera work. What is perhaps not remembered about that camera work is that it was not being called on to recreate the murky atmosphere of Edouard Tisse's Odessa or the grandiose detail of Billy Bitzer's Babylon. Totheroh had to keep in sharp focus the frantic gyrations of a single man, a man prone to much movement—the greatest pantomimist of this century—who, whatever the setting, was by far the most interesting thing in it. Rollie Totheroh never became a great cameraman as such because he never had the chance to become one, perhaps a salutary gain for the film as art. "I never cared for tricky shots," said Chaplin. Totheroh did precisely what Chaplin wanted, and that was not easy. Trying to get all the action Chaplin planned as well as accommodating to his frequent improvisations of movement required a nimble mind and two very strong arms.

The cameras then [said Totheroh in an interview with Timothy J. Lyons] were so different from today. First breaking in, my trouble was in cranking the camera. As a rule for comedy it was fourteen frames a second, for instance if somebody's running away from the camera and you wanted to speed it up. The cameraman regulated everything! We didn't have a change of focus apparatus on the camera; we'd have to reach over while still cranking and turn this apparatus we had on the mount that held the lens. Say we're on a twelve-foot focus and it comes to a six-foot focus: we'd have to reach over while still cranking and turn to six feet. So both hands were really operating things at one time. You get used to it. It comes to you naturally. After a while, you can get it pretty well on the nose. Charlie used to say, "Rollie, let's see: we'll make this a happy twelve." He left it up to me. I would then find what I thought was a happy twelve, or a good fourteen.

Sixteen frames per second was the standard silent camera speed. Chaplin at times emphatically wanted his pace faster than normal.

As to what was filmed, Chaplin gave Totheroh very clear instructions: Chaplin was to be the center of all his scenes. All lighting, setting, and placement were calibrated to Charlie's doings. This required not subtlety in camera work so much as concentration and nimbleness.

Chaplin's first film at Niles was A Night Out,[1] with Ben Turpin and Charlie as a pair of roisterers out on the town, with overtones of chaste bedroom farce. The film is now notable for two things. The first is a glorious moment when a reeling Ben hauls Charlie along a sidewalk by the scruff of his coat. "His toes trail," says

[1] Not His Night Out as Chaplin has it in his autobiography.

James Agee, "he is supine as a sled. Turpin himself is so drunk he can hardly drag him. Chaplin comes quietly to realize how well he is being served by his struggling pal, and with a royally delicate gesture plucks and savors a flower."

A *Night Out* is also memorable for the debut of Edna Purviance (1894–1958), who was to appear in thirty-five Chaplin films and remain on his payroll all her life. Her beauty was intensely feminine, almost ethereal in its blonde radiance, but she was at the same time *zaftig*, luxuriously lush and rounded. Nevada-born, she had gone to San Francisco and attended a business college there. When she met Chaplin in San Francisco (through a mutual friend at Essanay), she had just ended an unsatisfactory love affair and Chaplin was touched by her gentle air of melancholy. But feeling that she would at least be very decorative, he signed her and by the time of their fourth film, A *Jitney Elopement*, he knew she could do comedy.

In addition to Edna Purviance and Ben Turpin, the Essanay company included Manchester-born Leo White (1887–1949), a former musical comedy actor. Sharp-nosed and lean, White excelled in playing excited French counts in the Chaplin comedics, usually looking like a demented ibis. There were also Billy Armstrong (1869–1943), an old Chaplin comrade from the Karno tours; John Rand (1872–1940), who as a former circus acrobat was able to bounce himself and others around efficiently; William "Bud" Jamison (1894–1944), round of face and figure, later to be typecast as a comic cop and frequent nemesis of the Three Stooges; and Wesley Ruggles (1890–1972), in time to be a prominent director.

Edna Purviance actually came into her own with *The Tramp*. Indeed Chaplin came into his own in this, his first masterpiece, the film in which the quintessential gentleman tramp—the character Chaplin frequently called The Little Fellow—emerged. Interestingly, until this film, his forty-first, Chaplin had played an actual tramp only once, in Mack Sennett's *The Face on the Barroom Floor*. In all his other films his character had a variety of gainful occupations or was at least solvent. It should be noted that in Chaplin's native land a tramp is not so disdainfully regarded as in the United States, which may be a factor in the sympathy quotient Chaplin extends to his character. In the United

States the word "tramp" connotes a seedy vagrant, unwashed, eternally on the beg. Not so much in England where the name derives from the English phrase, "on the tramp." A tramp the Oxford English Dictionary identifies as "one who travels from place to place on foot, in search of employment, or as a vagrant; also, one who follows an itinerant business."

In *The Tramp*, Charlie saves Edna from a gang of crooks, shooing them into a lake, and is rewarded with a job on her father's farm. As a hired hand, he is a resounding failure, accidentally dropping a sack of flour on the farmer, puncturing another worker with a pitchfork, and trying to milk a cow by pumping her tail. The crooks assault the farmhouse, mounting a ladder to a window where appear Charlie with a club and the farmer with a shotgun. Charlie pursues them, is wounded in the leg, and is celebrated as a local hero. Edna admires him but when her fiancé appears it is clear Charlie can do only one thing—walk away gallantly, and—because he is the new Charlie—with at least a show of gaiety tingeing the melancholy. So comes into existence the archetypal Chaplin exit.

His few possessions are in a bandanna, his shoulders droop in despair—when suddenly he whips his cane elegantly, gives a joyous little hop as he walks down the street to what he—and we—feel must be a better tomorrow. That syrupy statement becomes so only perhaps in retrospect. It is precisely the emotion Chaplin wants us to feel, and in 1915 that emotion prevailed. It still does for most of us.

Chaplin worked diligently on *The Tramp*, and it shows. He had talked Broncho Billy into allowing him to leave Niles and work in Los Angeles at the well-equipped if rather old Majestic studios on Fairview Avenue. *The Tramp* was shot on a nearby farm and great attention was paid to detail, some of the endless rehearsals irritating cast members. Here began the legend of Chaplin the Overmeticulous.

> Leo White, a friend of mine, worked on *The Tramp* [said Stan Laurel]. He said they repeated some gags until the actors felt that if they did it one more time they'd blow their corks. He said the business of the crooks going up the ladder was done so many times and in so many variations that they just couldn't tell what the hell

all the fuss was about. But they were wrong. That's just what made Charlie a great creator of comedy. He knew that sometimes you *have* to do a thing fifty times in slightly different ways until you get the very best. The difference between Charlie and all the rest of us who made comedy—with only one exception, Buster Keaton—was that he just absolutely refused to do anything but the best. To get the best he worked harder than anyone I know.

Chaplin's story sources were widely varied: an anecdote told by a friend, a newspaper report, a comedy routine seen years before in vaudeville or simply an ad-libbed confrontation of his character with trouble, in as wide a range of gag incidents as possible. Occasionally he publicly divulged the source as he did—or seems to have—in an article, "How I Made My Success," in *Theatre* magazine, September 1915, ostensibly written by him but bearing the syntactical mark of Rob Wagner. This would not alter Chaplin's function as source, and some interesting things are said, prime among them Chaplin's conviction that comedy is the most serious study in the world and that a comedian should have "intense sympathy" with his character's troubles. Thus far so good, but the article veers into a suspect account of Chaplin's source for *The Tramp*.

Here it is said Chaplin accidentally met a tramp on the street, took him to a saloon for lunch and liquor, and drew from him his life story, thus inspiring *The Tramp*. This is all a little too pat, a bit too press agency, and is marred by a premise hard to credit: Chaplin, a fastidiously shy and private man, meets a strange drunk on the street, strikes up an acquaintance, and takes him to a barroom to get his story (a story, incidentally, hardly likely to be the farcical doings in *The Tramp*). It may be true but the present writer does not believe a syllable of it. What further mars the authenticity of the *Theatre* magazine story are three completely false statements "Chaplin" makes: he went to Hern Boys' College near London for two years, he was "in Charles Frohman's company in London for three years," and his first film was *Tillie's Punctured Romance*. (It was his thirty-third.)

Chaplin's next film of consequence, *Work*, featuring Charlie as a paperhanger, is directly derivative from *Repairs*, a Fred Karno sketch of 1906. The film, like its Karno source, has for its best moments Charlie and his boss trying to paper the house and each other with thick white paste. This is all highly predictable and immensely funny in spite of it. The things making the predictable funny are two—Charlie's attitude and his overwhelming mimetic virtuosity. These two elements were cardinal to his work. This double compound as exemplified in *Work* creates outsize laughter of a kind not heard in film theatres before or since.

In *Work,* one of Charlie's foils is the head of the house who, in the face of burgeoning incompetence around him and his wife's supposed infidelity, grows increasingly splenetic. Charlie on the other hand remains imperturbable. This is a favorite Chaplin device: creating the tensions of anger about him while he stays placid in the eye of the storm. It is instructive to compare the two players. Billy Armstrong as the husband overflows with indignation throughout and it suits the provocation given. But the extravagances of his anger are unreal. Charlie's attitudes in the film are equally extravagant but they are real. Billy and Charlie are both comedy grotesques but one is straw, the other flesh and bone. Billy is a cartoon character inhabiting his strip, Charlie appears in the strip doing the same sort of footling thing as Billy but Charlie believes himself to be real, and he so convinces us. Like any great actor, Chaplin actually listens to his fellow actors when they speak; he does not merely wait for his cue as so many comedy actors do. He believes in the reality of Charlie; he plays Charlie on Charlie's terms.

In addition to attitude, Charlie's infinite ease in doing everything, simply everything, is literally marvelous. When he disposes of a cigarette butt he throws it over his shoulder, pivots his body, and without looking kicks the butt away in a graceful arc. In *Work,* Charlie spills a giant gob of paste on his feet and, in trying to get away, runs frantically in place, moving not an inch. A skilled dancer can do this but it strains credulity that a great actor can, and superlatively. It is rather like John Gielgud as a febrile Caliban doing an easy back flip on the high wire. When Charlie does these things they are not done as a stunt. Charlie does not "pull" the gag or "do" the gag; he *is* the gag. And the gags are mostly very old stuff. As Roger Manvell says of Chaplin, we are more caught up by his "skill and perfect action in the timing of the action than by the originality or invention in the gags themselves."

This stunning ability to perform authentically on all levels with complete ease was, Walter Kerr suggests, an artistic danger:

The secret of Chaplin, as a character, is that he can be anyone. That is his problem. The secret is a devastating one. For the man who can with the flick of a finger or the blink of an eyelash, instantly transform himself into absolutely anyone is a man who must, in his heart, remain no one. . . . Just as Don Juan, loving everyone, can love no one, so Chaplin, impersonating everyone, can have no person. . . . Infinitely adaptable . . . Chaplin now has no one identity to embrace. . . . The tramp is the residue of all the bricklayers and householders and bon vivants and women and fiddlers and drunks and ministers Chaplin had played so well, too well. The tramp was all that was left. Sometimes the dark pain filling Chaplin's eyes is in excess of the situation at hand. It comes from the hopeless limitation of having no limitation.[2]

By the time Chaplin was well along with Essanay, he ventured into pathos again. As a humble janitor in *The Bank* he has good fun with his mop, using it principally as a shoulder-borne slapstick. But here Charlie is also affecting, showing a deep devotion to Edna, the beautiful bank stenographer, the object of his hopeless affections. He sends her expensive flowers, and love seems at least not far distant. A robbery occurs, Charlie foils it, saves Edna. As they kiss, the scene dissolves. It has been a dream and Charlie finds himself in passionate embrace of his mop. He next sees Edna in blissful tête-à-tête with her boy friend. Kicking away the discarded bouquet of flowers he had given her—kicking it with beautiful dexterity on the back of his heel like a cigarette butt—Charlie returns to his lusterless job. The situation is poignant and it is funny; it is, to use a word which now means both of those things together, Chaplinesque.

Gradually Chaplin's stories began to take on at least some flavoring of satire. His *Carmen* not only burlesqued the opera but the two unwittingly funny Hollywood versions of it made in 1915, one by Cecil B. De Mille featuring Geraldine Farrar, and another by William Fox with Theda Bara. As Darn Hosiery, the

[2] This and previous Walter Kerr quotations are from his *The Silent Clowns*, a book that must be read to appreciate Chaplin's art fully.

Don José figure, Chaplin has wonderful opportunities for kidding derring-do, especially in the duels. In one, he is viciously skilled in cut, thrust, and parry. His opponent is equally ferocious and they slash away energetically. This grows rather boring for them after a bit and they concentrate on the graceful effects they can execute, going into a ritualized dance, wielding their swords, says Robert Payne, "like feathers or like billiard cues and gently cut one another down and as gently rise, and all the time their expressions are ferocious."

When Darn Hosiery must kill his vixenish Carmen, Chaplin does so with a disconcertingly real knife. He stabs her (Edna) with surprising viciousness, helps her softly to the ground, bends down and kisses her tenderly. We are utterly baffled to find ourselves moved by this: it is being played with utter sincerity. He stabs himself, falls over her as ever Romeo did his Juliet, and dies. What, pray, is this? Then as the toreador comes in upon them, we see gradually amidst this solemnity that a part of Charlie is not yet dead—his behind. It rises so that he can levitate his foot, which kicks the toreador out of camera range. Edna and Charlie rise beamishly, embrace, and Charlie shows us directly the death instrument, a dagger with collapsing blade. We have just been fooled—twice.[3]

Chaplin's last film for Essanay, *Police*, shows something of his increasing interest in depicting life's inequities. When Charlie is released from prison as the film begins, a title tells us that he returns to find "once again the cruel, cruel world." Which is verified by his meeting a bogus reformer who tries to bring him to righteousness, then steals his watch. Charlie resumes a life of crime until Edna reforms him and he is secure in his new convictions until an unfortunate encounter with the police again puts him on the run.

This is to be Charlie's essential status with the law or at least with its professional guardians through many of his films. From *Police* forward, more serious matters begin to occupy Chaplin's thoughts than heretofore. During the last months of his Essanay

---

[3] After leaving Essanay Chaplin was angered to find the company releasing *Carmen* with added extraneous footage featuring Ben Turpin. He could not stop this legally but it was salutary, he said in later years, because in future all his contracts specified that his work was never to be altered by anyone.

contract he started filming a feature-length film he planned to call *Life*, meaning *My Life*. *Life* was to be an account of the London he knew as a street boy in the savage days when his mother was in the asylum and Sydney was at sea. Chaplin wanted to show the tragicomic world of flophouses, grimy alleys, and living "on the beg."

There is only one long scene extant. In it Charlie is the inhabitant of a flophouse, encountering typical patrons. Among them we see a bawling old drunk, crooning and caterwauling endlessly until Charlie, unable to endure it, knocks him out firmly with a thick bottle. Then, forgivingly, Charlie kisses the old man on the head. This is one of the most delightful manifestations of the key Chaplin comic device—a sudden and surprising reversal. A physical onslaught followed by elaborate courtesy to the victim becomes one of his prize gags. Later, needing an ashtray for his growing cigar ash and seeing no proper place of deposit, Charlie drops it into the old man's gaping mouth. Before we have time to grasp the implication of any of this, Charlie drops to his knees quickly and says his beddy-bye prayers in the time it would take to light a match, then into bed.

These and a few other gags constitute all that was filmed of *Life*, and there is enough of it to realize that a masterpiece died aborning—something on the order of a richly comic version of Gorky's *The Lower Depths*. Unforgivably, two years after Chaplin left them, Essanay took the *Life* excerpt and jerry-built it into a two-reeler with snippets from other Chaplin films, *Police* and *Work*. The result was called *Triple Trouble*, a title as undistinguished as the film that emerged.

Life went unfinished because Chaplin was under constant box office pressure to turn out two-reel comedies quickly. His popularity was growing so phenomenally that Alan Dale, a New York drama critic, writing in July 1915, could say that the "two real triumphs of pictures are *The Birth of a Nation* and Mr. Charles Chaplin."

There was some resistance to Chaplin's films. The Chicago *Daily Tribune* editorialized about the increasingly "vulgar" content of some of them, instancing a July 1915 release, *A Woman*, in which Charlie disguises himself (and very convincingly) as a woman in order to enter Edna's house. In a scene with Edna's father, Charlie's skirt falls off, revealing his baggy long underwear. The *Tribune* and a goodly number of its readers found this hard to take. William E. Hamilton of Milwaukee wrote hotly to the editor that *A Woman* "certainly does outrage the sense of decent people."

But this censoriousness—and it was not to be the last—had little or no effect on the box office, Essanay found. Chaplin's fifteen films for them had been rapturously received. By the end of 1915 a Chaplin craze was in full swing across the United States. Children were wearing Charlie buttons and mimicking his walk at play. Popular songs—"The Chaplin Waddle," "The Chaplin Strut," "The Chaplin Wiggle"—were being churned out by Tin Pan Alley. The soldiers in France were singing (to the tune of "Red Wing"):

> The moon shines bright on Charlie Chaplin
> Whose boots are crackin'
> For the want of blackin'
> And his little baggy trousers
> They want mendin'
> Before we send 'im
> To the Dardanelles!

The *Ziegfeld Follies* featured the girls in Charlie make-up doing a number, "Those Charlie Chaplin Feet." Theatre owners instead of billing Chaplin's name on marquees placed a life-size photograph of Charlie in the lobby with the legend, "I'm here today." It seemed the public could not get enough of him. Certainly the public could not escape him.

Some people did not consider this an unmixed blessing. Occasional letters to the editor fulminated against what one man indignantly called "this deuced Chaplin craze." Berton Braley, a popular writer for family magazines of the time, had had enough. Writing in the November 1915 issue of *Green Book* magazine, he put it pointedly:

SATIETY

Charlie, old pal, we've no personal peeve at you—
None, anyhow, we at present recall;
Yet we are looking for something to heave at you—
Paving brick, building stone, hammer or maul.

Charlie, we're weary of every old trick of you—
Bored with your face and your moustache and cane.
Gosh, but we've seen you so much we are sick of you,
Charlie, we're breaking down under the strain.

You've been exhibited, touted and pageanted,
Billboarded, placarded, hither and yon.
Never was anyone half so press-agented;
Go where we will, we must happen upon
Busts of you, statuettes, photographs various,
Cartoons and comments and posters galore.
Honestly, Charlie, in ways multifarious
You're getting more of a spread than the war!

Vaudeville is crowded with acts imitating you;
Every old movie has you on the screen.
We who were strong for you soon will be hating you
Simply because you're so constantly seen.
Granted you're gifted with vim and agility;
Granted you're there with the pep and the zest:
Yct, ere you drive us to dull imbecility,
Charlie, we beg of you—give us a rest!

This minority opinion was clearly not denigration but the complaint of an overstuffed child on Christmas afternoon. There can be too much of a good thing. As it turned out, Chaplin won this round too. Berton Braley changed his mind, publicly—but not until seven years later.

6
MUTUAL

Essanay had been thriving on Chaplin films, thriving moreover
on a suggestion by Sydney Chaplin that it rent his brother's films
on a percentage based on theatre capacity. This now standard procedure was resisted by some owners but so eager were they to book
the films that any real resistance melted. Sydney, after his contract
with Sennett expired, took over all of his brother's business affairs,
the shrewdest move Chaplin ever made professionally.

Spoor of Essanay, realizing that Chaplin was aware of his popularity and box office value because of Sydney, hastened to offer a
contract of $350,000 for twelve two-reel pictures. At Sydney's urg-
ing, Chaplin said that any contract would have to include a
$150,000 bonus. Spoor bridled, insisting that no one in the film
business would give such a contract. Sydney left for New York to
prove or disprove just that. Before going, Sydney directed Edna
Purviance to make sure that his brother did not sign a contract
with Spoor or anyone else in his absence.

By 1916 Edna and Charlie had become lovers. Outside of casual
engagements with lovely ladies and an innocent fling with Peggy
Pierce, a Sennett ingenue, Chaplin's love life was not exactly extensive in his early Hollywood years. He was extraordinarily busy
building his career, and his social activities were mostly confined
to people in his profession. He and Edna were unlikely to escape a
relationship: both unmarried, attractive, professionally linked.
Their romance was not much in the public eye because Chaplin
was not given to ostentation, and Edna had a retiring disposition

too. She provided him with the loving stability he needed—a woman's comfort; he gave her deep affection and intellectual stimulus. At the time he was living in comfortable but modest quarters at the Los Angeles Athletic Club. He and Edna dined there quietly most evenings of the week.

When Sydney left for New York early in 1916 to negotiate a contract for his brother, Chaplin impulsively followed him a few days later. New York was to be his first real vacation since the Karno days. On the journey he was met with the first personal evidence of his incredible popularity. At Amarillo, Texas, at Kansas City, at Chicago, the huge enthusiastic crowds exhilarated and depressed him. The adulation was pleasing but it was unsettling for one of his inbred shyness. The New York Police Department insisted he get off at the 125th Street station instead of Grand Central Station because of the potentially unruly crowd gathering there. Sydney met him at 125th Street with a limousine and told him that the Mutual Film Corporation had agreed to a contract of $670,000, payable at $10,000 a week, together with a $150,000 bonus.

But Chaplin felt no elation, only self-pity. The great success coming so easily depressed him. He walked the New York streets alone and he felt alone. The people who cheered him were not his friends. He doubted if they had anything like a friendly interest in him.

He made only one public appearance. On a Sunday evening, February 20, 1916, he led John Philip Sousa's band in a benefit concert at the vast Hippodrome Theatre for the Actors Fund of America and a British theatrical charity. He conducted the orchestra with great pleasure, the only part of the evening he found supportable. Reporters noted that the huge audience was curiously restrained in its reaction to Chaplin. Seemingly they found it difficult to connect the wiry little rogue on the screen with this well-mannered handsome young man. Chaplin received polite applause, he bowed politely, took a polite curtain call, said a few polite words. It was all rather down. Then, realizing what the trouble was, Chaplin broke into the tramp's walk and sauntered about stage, twirling an invisible cane. The audience exploded. Now they saw *him*.

A week later he signed his new contract in a much-pho-

tographed ceremony with Mutual's president, John R. Freuler, at
the table with him, Sydney standing behind. The Chaplin boys
had come a very long way from Kennington Road and Chaplin
knew how much of that distance Sydney had brought him:

> At last I had an opportunity to repay Sydney the money part of
> the debt I have owed him since he came to my rescue so many
> times when we were boys. He could not refuse half of the bonus
> money which he had worked so hard to get for me, and that check
> for $75,000 gave me more pleasure than I can recall receiving from
> any other money I have ever handled.

There was one piece of unfinished business in New York before
the return to California. Chaplin knew Hetty Kelly was now living in New York with her sister, Mrs. Frank Gould, wife of the
prominent financier. Although Chaplin was in love with Edna,
the thought of at least seeing Hetty was irresistible. He walked
past the Gould home on Fifth Avenue, walked past it again, and
again and again. He did that for a half hour before he faced the
truth: he was afraid to see her.

Back in the city he was now unqualifiedly calling home, Chaplin moved into a new studio, fittingly designated the Lone Star
Studio, at 1025 Lillian Way, Hollywood. He had built around
him a small production unit: Rollie Totheroh as cameraman, and
performers Edna Purviance, Leo White, John Rand, James T.
Kelley, Frank J. Coleman, Charlotte Mineau, and Lloyd Bacon
(later to be one of Warner Brothers' legendary directors).
Among the newcomers to Chaplin's Mutual company were old
Karno comrades, the sparse and limber Albert Austin (1885–
1953), from Birmingham, England; and tiny Loyal Underwood, who was to play runt parts with distinction. The Mutual
company's counterpart of a giant Mack Swainish villain was Eric
Stuart Campbell (1878–1917), born in Dunoon, Scotland, who
after a few years with Fred Karno, partnering Sydney Chaplin,
went into musical comedy and was grandly typecast with the
D'Oyly Carte Company in the title role of *The Mikado*. He wore
variations of the Mikado's make-up in several Chaplin films. Finally there was roly-poly Henry Bergman (1870–1946), Chaplin
foil, confidant, and assistant director. Bergman had been a circus
and opera performer who entered films as an assistant to Chap-

lin's old bête noire, Pathé Lehrman. Bergman played a great variety of roles in the Chaplin comedies, among them some very robust ladies. Chaplin was his idol—a close friend and backer of Bergman's popular delicatessen-restaurant in Los Angeles. Bergman remained on the Chaplin payroll from 1916 to his death thirty years later.

Mutual had wide foreign distribution and as 1916 progressed Chaplin became the best-known man in the world. Even in the then prime temple of art, the theatre, Chaplin was not without honor. Minnie Maddern Fiske, a sweetly shrewd and intelligent Broadway star, rather shocked some of her peers and followers by writing an article, "The Art of Charles Chaplin," for *Harper's Weekly* in 1916. "The *art* forsooth!" was the reaction among some leading Broadway players. Mrs. Fiske was sincere and entirely persuasive.

Arguing that a growing number of people recognized Chaplin as a comic genius and that his work possessed a quality more vital than mere clowning, Mrs. Fiske insisted that thoughtful people were now seeking "to discover his secret for making irresistible entertainment out of more or less worthless material. . . . The critic knows his secret. It is the old fashioned secret of inexhaustible imagination, governed by the unfailing precision of a perfect technique." She recognized Chaplin's vulgarity, a quality she also found in Aristophanes, Swift, and Shakespeare among others. She allowed too that film was a brand-new medium and that Chaplin had been with it only two years. She foresaw great success for him in authentic burlesque, and how wonderful it was that this could be seen for just a few pennies! "It is said that he came from a life of sadness. And at twenty-six he has made the world laugh. Quite a beautiful thing to do!"

But Chaplin did not create that laughter alone. Creativity at Mutual was frequently improvisatory and collective. Chaplin did not depend on his own imagination exclusively by any means.

When Charlie was working on an idea [said Rollie Totheroh], often he would call me in. There was often a lot of his own people around. He'd hit on a certain situation where there was something he was building on and he'd want conversation more or less. If somebody came up with an idea that sounded as if he could dovetail it and it would build up his situation, it would sink back in his

head and he'd chew it over. And there'd always be someone there
to write things down . . . taking dictation. . . . Most of the time
Charlie pretty much had a basic idea when we started filming.

The basic idea for the first Mutual film, *The Floorwalker*, was
just an object, albeit a very interesting object—the escalator in a
department store. When Mack Sennett saw the film he was stung
with envy: "Why the hell didn't *we* ever think of that?" Chaplin
got the idea while in New York. He was ascending on an escalator
when the man in front of him made a misstep and nervously tried
to compensate for it.

On moving into his new studio, Chaplin had a solid department store set built complete with efficient moving stairs. The
resulting adventures with it are, in Stan Brakhage's words, "man
against Deus ex Machina"—Charlie going up or down in fruitless
desperation. It is about the only original gag in the film save one,
which Charlie carries off handsomely. Charlie and the store manager are look-alikes. The manager is absconding with the profits in
a bag; Charlie enters the office also carrying a bag. They confront
each other, the manager thinking, hoping, a mirror stands there.
Charlie mimics the man's movements flawlessly until at one moment the men's fingers meet. Shocked, the manager reaches out to
that visage that so resembles his, holds it, studies it.[1] Charlie, mistaking the movement for a homosexual advance, true to his pen-
chant for the completely unexpected, bends forward obligingly to
kiss the manager. With Charlie one can only expect the unexpected.

The next Mutual film, *The Fireman*, came directly from a walk
Chaplin took past a fire station not far from the studio. He
thought of himself as a fireman in bed at the mercy of the fire
bell, and with only this single situation in mind began to shoot
the film, trusting to his powers of improvisation. Perhaps for this
reason the film flows jerkily. It is principally false alarms versus
genuine alarms, authentic fire versus arson, to a kind of Keystone
Kops drill tempo, and with arse-kicking galore. *The Fireman* has a
few memorable gags (Charlie as the firehouse cook setting table
for the men by throwing out the plates like an expert poker

[1] The gag was used again in expanded form by the Marx Brothers in *Duck
Soup*, seventeen years later.

dealer, Charlie thoughtfully cleaning the horses with a feather duster) and a thrill ending in which he scales a two-story façade to rescue Edna. But *The Fireman* is simply rather good Mack Sennett. The critics enjoyed it and the public, as usual, came in very large numbers. Chaplin felt content, too content. He thought he now knew just what the public wanted. Then a letter from an admirer pulled him up short. It was, Chaplin admitted, a "jolt"—and one of the most important letters he was ever to receive. The admirer had seen *The Fireman* at a large Midwestern theatre and he was not impressed:

> I have noticed in your last picture a lack of spontaneity. Although the picture was unfailing as a laugh-getter, the laughter was not so round as at some of your earlier work. I am afraid you are becoming a slave to your public, whereas in most of your pictures the audiences were a slave to you. The public, Charlie, likes to be slaves.

It was a great lesson. Chaplin understood the logic of the situation at once and completely changed his work approach for the rest of his life. Henceforward, he would trust to what *he* hoped for and liked in his comedy, and never again would he try to project what he thought the public liked.

His next film, *The Vagabond*, like *The Tramp*, was a landmark film. It reinforced pathos as a Chaplin leitmotif, pathos made all the more memorable by wedding it to robust and sometimes vulgar farce. *The Vagabond* begins with Charlie's by now literally fabulous feet appearing beneath a saloon's swinging door. He is a violinist, of all natural things, come in to play for some coins, but his solo is interrupted by a German band that takes over. Charlie goes over to the free lunch and "helpfully" switches signs on the meat platter so that an old Jewish gentleman can take some ham. Then Charlie passes the hat, presumably for the band, which chases him out into the country.

There he encounters a charming girl (Edna) who has been slaving for a band of Gypsies. After rescuing her and fleeing in the Gypsy wagon, Charlie falls in love. He protects the girl, feeds her, plays his fiddle for her. (The audience could not hear it but the tune was his first great experience with music, "The Honeysuckle

and the Bee." Stan Laurel said of Charlie's abilities as a violinist,
"I wouldn't call him a good violinist but he sure as hell wasn't a
bad one.")

There are touches of cheery vulgarity in *The Vagabond* of the
sort Minnie Maddern Fiske speaks of: a gob of spit picked up in
mistake for a coin, Charlie offering Edna a rake to comb the fleas
out of her hair, and his kicking an old lady in the stomach (a
mean old harridan, well played by Leo White). But the exuberant
flavor of the Charlie-Edna scenes is tenderly warming, and when
a young artist (Lloyd Bacon) happens by their camp hoping to
paint the young beauty, Charlie's idyll ends. Edna and the artist
fall in love. His portrait of her winds up in a gallery where Edna's
wealthy mother recognizes her long-lost daughter via a striking
birthmark. With the artist she comes for the girl, gives Charlie a
cool handshake, offers him money which he proudly refuses, and
leaves with Edna in an enormous limousine. Charlie stands in the
road, looking wistfully after them.

And now, some critics insist, Chaplin should have ended the
film to preserve the honest pathos established by Chaplin. An
ending like *The Tramp*—Charlie walking down the road, sadly but
proudly—has been urged by some as the only valid ending.

Chaplin did not agree. He filmed two endings. In one he veers
sharply to farce: he tries to commit suicide by jumping in a lake.
A repulsive old crone rescues him and after one look at her face
he jumps back in the lake. The other ending, the one he used, has
Edna, during the limousine ride to her new life, considering how
much Charlie means to her, suddenly ordering the car to turn
back and pick him up. This done, all ends happily.

But does it? The ending is at least ambiguous. Edna is no fool,
her love for the painter seems real enough and, all in all, Charlie
is not for the likes of her. Mama at least will see to that. It may
well be that in entering that limousine Charlie is going to bigger
heartbreak than walking down that dusty road. Going into Edna's
world is the larger peril—the outcast forced into society's inner
circle that can never contain him.

Certainly the cleverest and conceivably the funniest film Chaplin made for Mutual is *One A.M.* Except for Albert Austin's fleeting appearance as a taxi driver, this is a stunning solo performance. The philosopher Henri Bergson in his essay, "Laughter,"

insists that the comic consists of the mechanical imposed on the living. *One A.M.* verifies that in reverse. This gloriously comic piece is the living imposed on the mechanical: the tipsy Charlie— on the interior of a repulsively stylish (1916) home. The entire film is a pun on drunkenness, says Stan Brakhage.

In full evening dress, the intoxicated Charlie is delivered to a friend's home where he is spending the night, or what is left of it.[2] Everything in the house seems dedicated to his literal downfall. The front door is recalcitrant and he must go through a window in order to open it. The rugs are treacherously alive when they skid, and Chaplin's artfulness lies in his making them seem to move Charlie rather than the opposite. Everything he approaches in the house takes on life through his delicate maneuvers—the full-bodied lion trophy that intimidates him, the stuffed open-mouthed bear whose silent growl is shattering, the revolving brandy table that refuses to stop for him, stair carpets like Venus' flytraps, and on the stair landing a giant clock pendulum that smites him down. (Charlie falls down dozens of times in the film, each time differently.)

Finally there is the impertinent Murphy bed, determined to wreak the ultimate chastisement on the drunk. Charlie presses a button to bring it out of the wall and it comes down halfway. He struggles with it and it captures him by whirling him up into the closet with it. He finally gets loose after several efforts, frees himself from it, pulls it down, and it crashes smartly on his head. Charlie settles in it, leans over to get a cigarette from the floor, and the bed snaps back up, hurling him onto the floor. The bed shakes like a bucking bronco when he grabs it; it kicks him to the wall, crashes down, turning over wrong side up. When the bed finally falls out correctly, Charlie jumps victoriously on it—and it falls to pieces. He spends the night in the bathtub.

Chaplin's surging popularity in 1916 brought forth professional imitators by the score. Billy West was the best known of the Chaplin imitators at the time; Stan Laurel the least. Stan, however, labeled his twelve-minute vaudeville sketch a direct imita-

---

[2] Extant prints offer no evidence of this being anything other than Charlie's home. But contemporary reviews refer to Charlie as staying at a friend's home. This would explain some of his seeming unfamiliarity with the interior. Perhaps an initial title has been cut in present prints.

tion. This was the Keystone Trio, in which he imitated Chaplin, and two fellow performers from the old Karno company played Mabel Normand and Chester Conklin. Later, using his own name for the act, Stan formed the Stan Jefferson Trio (with Alice and Baldwin Cooke) in which the Mack Sennett flavor was dropped although Stan continued his Chaplin imitation.[3]

What Stan did was flattering and totally inoffensive; what Billy West did was theft of a sort quite obvious yet very hard to prove legally. Various types of comedians had borrowed from each other over the years with little hope of determining original sources for their acts. Unlike Stan Laurel, then a smalltime vaudevillian, Billy West was in direct competition with Chaplin. West made one- and two-reel comedies, he engaged competent comedy support (Oliver Hardy, Leo White, etcetera), he copied Chaplin's make-up and costume—and he was rather good. West (1883–1975), a Russian-born comedian, imitated Chaplin in at least fifty films. In the movie business West was held in such contempt for his steal-ing from Chaplin that some trade journals would only print his name in lower case, presumably to make billy west feel small.

There was also Billy Ritchie (1879–1921), who went so far as to accuse Chaplin of imitating *him*. Ritchie was the original drunk for Karno in *Mumming Birds*, which may conceivably have given him the idea that he was entitled to use the Chaplin costume (which in any case he claimed he originated) for a series of L-KO films.

Chaplin resented West and Ritchie but he was infuriated with a Mexican actor, Charles Amador, who brazenly changed his name professionally to Charlie Aplin and copied outright prize Chaplin routines. Chaplin sued. Amazingly, Amador's lawyers made some detailed and verifiable points supporting their client's "right" to the Chaplin costume and walk. They proved through expert testimony that Chaplin's costume and make-up were not singular. The brush mustache had been worn by a Chicago actor named George Behan in 1890; Chris Lane wore a decrepit derby on stage in 1898; Harry Morris appeared in burlesque doing the

---

[3] Stan did his Chaplin imitation for me one glorious day. "Charlie is in my bones," he said, and verified it. For the first time I could see what Karno train ing had given both men: superb litheness, total mimetic grace, and an under-lying, ever so gentle, sadness.

splayfoot walk in 1892; Bud Meley and others used baggy pants
from 1895 on; at the turn of the century an act called the Nibble
Brothers did much stage business with a flexible cane; in early
vaudeville Sherman and Morrissey appeared with the large turned-
out shoes; in 1890 Byron of Byron and Langdon wore the tight-
fitting skirt coat; and Billy Ritchie undoubtedly wore a combination of all these a good five years before Chaplin ever entered
films.

Amador's lawyers were certain that these impressive and well-
documented statistics would prove that Chaplin had no claim to
the costume he insisted was so uniquely his. Chaplin's suit con-
ceded all the historical points established but made the sensible
rejoinder that, even if others had used elements of his costume,
the costume *en ensemble* together with the Chaplin name had become his exclusive property, and that under the law of unfair competition he was entitled to protection from imitators. The decision went against Amador. For years after, Chaplin enjoyed doing
a private parlor trick for fellow workers—an imitation of Amador,
West, and others of his mimics, giving their flaws eloquent pre-
sentment.

It is not known just who in 1916 suggested to Chaplin that an
autobiography would be appropriate. Chaplin has never mentioned the book, *Charlie Chaplin's Own Story*, published that
year by Bobbs-Merrill Company. It is a curious work, "being [the
title page says quite inaccurately] the faithful recital of a romantic
career, beginning with early recollections of boyhood in London
and closing with the signing of his latest motion picture contract."
(With Mutual.) Another sentence on the title page reads: "The
subject of this biography takes great pleasure in expressing his ob-
ligations and his thanks to Mrs. Rose Wilder Lane for invaluable
editorial assistance." Mrs. Lane was likely the ghostwriter of
Charlie Chaplin's Own Story, and if it is she who must be
thanked for the flagrantly Dickensian episodes of Chaplin's boyhood, it should be said that as a writer of fiction she is not without distinction. Written in the first person throughout, the book
has Chaplin claiming to be born in a little town in France. Charlie Chaplin, Sr., is described in a wealth of detail although in *My
Autobiography* Chaplin says he barely remembers his father. The
gentle and genteel Mr. Jackson from North Country England

who took Charlie into the Lancashire Lads is metamorphosed into a seedy Mr. Hawkins, a ferocious Cockney of dreadful temperament, a bush league Fagin. In this account, Charlie, while on tour with the Lancashire Lads, runs away from Mr. Hawkins, is pursued by dogs, and returns to London and his mother. And similar fancies. The book's galleys were obviously not read by Chaplin because he would have corrected two of the glaring errors: his brother Sydney is throughout referred to as "Sidney," and Fred Karno's surname becomes "Carno."

Yet at times the book is certainly accurate in spirit if not in detail. Chaplin's deep love for his talented mother and for Sydney is touchingly told, and the flavor of the Sennett days is well captured. The book was not a success. In the few places where it was sold the critics easily discerned the palpable fictionalizing. Chaplin quickly withdrew it, and it is now in the rare book category.

On the first day of shooting *The Pawnshop*, one of his best Mutuals, Chaplin told the cast that the set for the film reminded him of "the less than good old days—the seamy side of my life." But as always this was the life that he kept returning to literally and figuratively all his life. There was a pawnshop close to his birthplace.

In *The Pawnshop*, Charlie finds much pleasure in the very miscellany of the place and its customers. As an employee, Charlie is not ideal: he is quarrelsome with a co-worker, and in cleaning the shop he takes a duster to a whirring electric fan, filling the room with feathery detritus. Fired by his boss (Henry Bergman), Charlie pantomimes the height of his eleven dependent children from ground level to infinitude, and when the boss relents, Charlie embraces him in a running jump. Sent into the kitchen to help there, he does the dishes with Edna. He expertly wipes a plate, a cup, and then his hand, by passing them through a wringer. The cup isn't quite dry so it must go through twice. Ordered to the shop, he is entranced by an old Shakespearean actor who enters and sobs out his need to pawn his golden wedding ring. Finding only a ten-dollar bill in the till, Charlie gives it to him in deep sympathy; the old man takes it, pulls out a fat wad of banknotes, peels off the change, and gives it to Charlie. When the actor leaves, Charlie feelingly slaps himself with a hammer.

What follows is the most celebrated episode in the film and

one of the funniest pieces of business in film comedy. A seedy individual (Albert Austin) comes in with an alarm clock to pawn. Of course Charlie must examine it with stern objectivity, so he takes a stethoscope and listens intently to the works working. He taps it over crossed fingers. Something is not quite right, he suspects, so he takes an auger and bores into the clock. He applies a can opener with surgical care, cutting efficiently. The lid is now fully off and he evaluates the innards by sniffing. The odor is distinctly unwelcome. Confounded by this, the owner sniffs too. Charlie delicately applies dentist's forceps to the interior; he hits it with a hammer. Unscrewing the mouthpiece from a telephone, he uses it as a jeweler's loupe and peers intently inside the clock. He shakes out the contents and, in removing the mainspring, measures it out from his nose to the full length of the arm. The mainspring resists, coils up in insistent bounce, and Charlie oils it placatingly. He takes Albert's hat, sweeps the entire mess into it, and with polite disdain hands it back to Albert, indicating that it is manifestly worthless.

An old Karno sketch, *Skating*, was partial source for one of Chaplin's next Mutuals. In *The Rink*, as a waiter who spends lunchtime at a nearby roller rink, Chaplin has the best chance yet in his career to exhibit his incredible grace of movement. The film is not much more than an excuse for a love story and the display of Charlie's fandangos on the rink floor. There are clever incidental gags (Charlie, asked for the check by a sloppy eater, determines what the customer has consumed by carefully examining his lapel, tie, and ears) but basically the film is dance and bumps and falls and near misses so beautifully choreographed that even repeated viewing is unwearying. *The Rink* is a beautiful soundless waltz, and as in so many Chaplin films we identify consummately with Charlie. We become him totally; he is the hero of our living daydream. We inhabit Charlie particularly when, like some gravely cheerful bat, he swoops insouciantly about the floor, courting collision as carefully as he skirts it. Virtually a character in the film is Eric Campbell's giant belly, which is banged into periodically in little measured climaxes so that it becomes a mute ceremonial gong announcing the end of each episode. Even *The Rink*'s pratfalls are exquisite—forceful figures in a robust, gymnastic minuet.

The next film, the superb *Easy Street*, arguably his best two-reeler, derived from Chaplin's past. The basic set was a street scene from the Kennington of his boyhood which Chaplin built for $10,000, a then incredible expenditure for the set of a short film. It was money well spent. The street has the cold and grimy texture of a London slum, an effectively stark contrast to the humor it environs. In *Easy Street*, Chaplin appears in a role somewhat unusual for him at Mutual—a tramp. Charlie wanders into a mission as derelicts do, for what he can find there, and after being moved by the preacher's sermon and much more moved by the beauty of Edna, the minister's daughter, Charlie reforms on the spot—and returns the collection box he had hidden beneath his jacket. Nearby on Easy Street one sees why the street is so named: chaos and rapine reign unchecked. The police assigned to the area are hauled away to the hospital hourly. Unaware of this, the reformed Charlie sees a recruiting sign outside a police station. Instantly signed up, he is given a uniform several sizes too large and assigned to Easy Street. (Some critics wonder how the anti-establishment tramp could ever join the police. The answer is that Chaplin would join anything for an authentic laugh.)

Dominating the street is a giant tough (Eric Campbell), easily the dimensions of Popeye's old nemesis, Bluto, and twice as evil. But Charlie is no Popeye. When he meets Eric and sees the havoc wrought in the neighborhood, Charlie shakingly puts in a call at the police box and, to divert Eric's suspicions, first uses the phone receiver as a wind instrument, then peers through it as a spyglass. Eric picks up the receiver; Charlie eagerly pounds him on the head with his truncheon. Eric reacts as if someone has been scratching his head. To show the invincible thickness of his skull, he proudly inclines it toward Charlie so that he can give it some really good swipes. Charlie's stick rains blows on that formidable crew cut; it is a frankfurter swatting concrete. To show off the full range of his strength Eric casually bends a steel lamppost over as he would a cornstalk. In the process his back is turned and Charlie leaps on him, forcing Eric's head into the gas casing, and turns on the gas. Like an efficient anesthetist, Charlie feels Eric's pulse during the process and adjusts the dosage accordingly. Eric slumps and is taken to jail.

Charlie is now lionized by the residents of Easy Street and he

even helps out an old lady who has stolen a ham by gathering
"sample" vegetables from a fruiterer. His reward for this is a
flowerpot dropped from a window above. Edna takes him to visit
one of the poorest families on the street: ten little children, a sorrowful mother, and a scrawny father resembling a dissipated
jockey. Staring incredulously at the numerous children and at
their father, Charlie feels the man's muscle and pins his police
badge on him as a prize. To the children Charlie scatters food
from a box as if they were chickens.

Eric escapes from jail and is recaptured by Charlie pushing an
iron stove out of a window on him. Edna, in trying to help Charlie, is kidnaped, Charlie is thrown in with her and, after accidentally sitting on a dope fiend's needle, is euphorically regenerated
and conquers the entire mob surrounding him. Charlie conquers
their hearts as well and reform settles into the neighborhood, even
touching Eric. A title assures us

> Love backed by Force,
> Forgiveness sweet,
> Bring Hope and Peace
> To Easy Street.

The last scene shows Easy Street in decorous array, many of its in-
habitants walking to the new mission chapel at the end of the
street. Eric appears arm in arm with his once browbeaten but now
serene wife. Suddenly realizing that she is walking on the outside,
he gallantly reverses positions, tips his derby primly to Charlie and
Edna, and continues on his way to church. Charlie and Edna
follow.

Easy Street is a deliciously funny film yet its underlay of slum
life is authentic, a forerunner of the social concerns Chaplin was
to embed in his feature films. In later years he told Sergei Eisenstein that the scene in *Easy Street* where he throws food to the
children was indicative of his dislike of children. He also told the
English author Thomas Burke that he didn't like children. Eisenstein was not surprised at Chaplin's attitude. The only people
who do not like children are other children, he said. There is
something to be said for this but Chaplin was uncomfortable with
children by and large because they intimidated him. In one of
his autobiographical accounts he said that he loved children really

but he felt inferior to them. "Most of them have assurance, have not yet been cursed with self-consciousness. And one has to be very much on his best behavior with children because they detect our insincerity."

In creating his next for Mutual, *The Cure*, Chaplin reverted to one of the oldest of his stock characters, a drunk, but this is a drunk trying at least nominally to be cured. Charlie arrives at a spa, well fortified, and with a trunk, also well fortified with many varieties of booze. Formidable Eric Campbell is a visitor too, come to ease a gouty foot. Inevitably Charlie must tangle with that foot, and he does—in a revolving door. Later, in the lobby, Charlie, seated between Edna and Eric, not seeing her and facing him, is intrigued by Eric's heavy winking and hand waving intended for the girl. Charlie wiggles into a coy position, waving coquettishly in reply to the big man. Charlie is never afraid to give even homosexuals a little harmless fun. Eric is affronted.

The health regimen does not at all suit Charlie; he doesn't get into its swing. He throws the steam room into an uproar by not co-operating with the masseurs, among other things assuming that the massage given him is actually a wrestling match. In the interim one of Charlie's bellhops, after nipping at the contents of the trunk, is ordered by management to throw all the liquor out. The bellhop does, right out the window into the spa fountain whence flow the medicinal waters.

A very high-toned saturnalia follows drinking of the water with prim old ladies and dignified business types skipping about in desperate gaiety. Charlie must rescue Edna from several drunks. The film ends with Charlie, a block of hangover ice on head, walking with Edna to the fountain—where he falls in.

The Cure is perhaps the funniest of the Mutual films, and indeed all of them have an exhilaration never seen again in the Chaplin canon. Of all his employers over the years, the Mutual company was the most agreeable to him. They were not dismayed by either his lavish production spending or his growing tendency to introduce serious themes. His next film, *The Immigrant*, had some especially poignant ones.

"Of all his early work," says Isabel Quigly, "[*The Immigrant*] came closest to his darker and more directly satirical films of the late twenties and thirties." It is also indirectly autobiographical—

the outsider come to a new land that is hospitable and forbidding in about equal measure.

The opening shot of the film is, like so many good Chaplin gags, surprise lit by humor. We see Charlie's back as he leans over the ship's railing in what seem to be violent thrusts of nausea. Then he spins around—triumphantly, with a large fish he has just landed. He meets fellow immigrants Edna and her mother and befriends them. After various travails in a bucking sea, they reach New York, and the women lose touch with him. Later Charlie sees Edna in a restaurant, and as he delightedly holds her hands he finds she is holding a black-bordered handkerchief. At this moment the superb actor Chaplin is shows in a quiet, soul-poignant look as he gently lowers her hand. It is a look lovely in itself, Charlie's first deeply human look in all his films. Here he shows himself genuinely in love, genuinely moved by the girl's loss.

The rest of the film is mostly an attempt to evade the responsibility of paying the bill in the restaurant, high in comic flavor, but the ending of the film is, like Charlie's look, affecting and deeply serious. As Charlie and Edna leave the place, rain floods the streets and they scurry through it. Then, breathlessly happy, Charlie catches Edna up in his arms and carries her into the nearby marriage bureau. The rain is a statement by Chaplin that this romantic ending is real.

"The Immigrant," says Chaplin, "touched me more than any other film I made. I thought the end had quite a poetic feeling." He qualified that just a little by saying that as he carried Edna he realized she was growing heavier. They were, in any case, in love at the time and that flavor is apparent in the film. In his later Mutual films Chaplin was more carefully searching for mood than in his previous work, and this he frequently accomplished by having a small string orchestra on the studio floor playing mood music. For The Immigrant he used "Mrs. Grundy," an old tune Chaplin thought possessed a soft, pensive longing that defined two lonely souls on a rainy wedding day.

The Adventurer, Chaplin's last film for Mutual, is a very high-class Sennett film, if one can imagine such a thing. And Sennett turned inside out somewhat because it begins with a chase. Filmed in the wild and beautiful Los Flores Canyon in the Santa Monica hills, the chase is an exuberance of escaped convict Charlie outwitting some admittedly not very full-witted guards, swimming out to sea where he rescues two ladies from drowning, inevitably Edna and her mother. Under the impression he is wealthy (he is wearing a yachtsman's stolen swimming suit), they invite him to their posh home to recuperate.

Waking the next morning, Charlie finds himself in striped pajamas and for a horrified moment thinks he is back in prison. The brass bars of his bed seem to confirm this but the entrance of an obsequious servant recalls him to his pleasant new situation. That evening at an elaborate dinner Edna's truculent suitor—who could it be but Eric Campbell?—is much distressed at the favor Charlie is finding in Edna's eyes. In a stroke of luck Eric finds a newspaper containing Charlie's photograph in convict suit under the legend "WANTED." Eric tells Edna's father, and Charlie, seeing the newspaper meanwhile, deftly alters the photograph by penciling in Eric's heavily hirsute features.

Edna's father has called the prison guards, who chase Charlie in and through the house, up and down stairs, until the great moment—the finest moment in the film—when the guards quickly scuttle by Charlie after he has placed a lampshade on his head and stands rigidly as a piece of furniture impervious to their gaze. Eric is in the chase too until he gets his neck securely caught between sliding doors by Charlie. Charlie jumps over a balcony to escape but he cannot resist kissing Edna's hand and apologizing. A guard seizes him and Charlie quick-wittedly introduces the man formally to Edna. Who could resist shaking the hand of this lovely lady? As the guard does, he lets his grip on Charlie falter. Charlie leaps away and off, down toward his freedom road.

A few months after the filming of *The Adventurer*, Eric Campbell was killed in an automobile accident.

Eric was such a wonderful guy [Stan Laurel said]. People used to say he had a heart as big as himself—and Eric was a mountain of a man. I think he would have made a very big success in the movies when sound came in because he had a beautiful big voice, again just like himself. The odd thing, though, was that he was really a very shy man—like Charlie in that respect. Eric used to refer to himself as an elephant. I guess in a way he was right. Big, gentle, lovable.

Chaplin treasured his days at Mutual. He called it the happiest period of his career and, although the Mutual offer of contract renewal was excellent, Chaplin accepted a bid from the newly formed First National Circuit, a combination of theatre exhibitors formed to resist the monopolistic big studios. The contract called for First National to advance $125,000 for each two-reel film negative, this amount including Chaplin's salary. If it was longer than two reels, the company would give $115,000 for each extra reel. First National would also pay for all advertising and for all prints of the films. Distribution costs were estimated to be thirty per cent of total rentals, and after all costs had been met, First National and Chaplin would divide the profits equally.

It seemed ideal, and in some ways it was.

7
FIRST NATIONAL

By 1917, Charlie the Tramp's physical persona was very well defined.

Going to his local theatre, the 1917 filmgoer always expected to find in the skitteringly graceful Charlie an acrobatic emphasis on all his primary movements, even to the emphatic thoroughness of his arse-kicking. Charlie is also kicked, but mostly he instigates the action. He kicks backward a good deal, mostly as a gesture of defiance or retribution. His splayfooted, shuffling walk, punctuated by an occasional hop, can quickly accelerate into a quick run, a run usually highlighted by his perhaps most memorable physical movement—the corner skid, in which he makes a ninety-degree change in direction mid-run. Arms extended in balance, one holding the cane, he spins around on one heel, one leg in the air, and skids several times until reversal. A variation on this movement is a complete turn when he pivot-skips on his heel and returns swiftly whence he came.

His somersaults—half, three quarter, full, and reverse—are impeccably graceful. His cane, that artful extension of his body, is variously a slapstick, prod, club, support, tool, hook, and probe. He uses it to pull people into his orbit, to tickle, to lift up ladies' skirts, to initiate a teasing flirtation, to get attention, to redirect attention, as an ear swab, toothpick, or back scratcher, and to trip up nasty people. His derby, like the cane, is a sign of his gentility, and even when he is engaged in an act of consummate deviltry he never forgets to tip it—even to someone he has just reduced to insensibility.

Charlie's face is deceptively grave much of the time. He watches a very great deal. As he listens or ponders he can arch his eyebrows angelically as his mouth twitches, rabbitlike—this almost always an expression of anticipatory wickedness. His wide-ranging leers and smirks, for all their naughtiness, do not bear a burden of malice. He simply enjoys being a devil and we are with him all the way. Perhaps that is because to some extent he dominates us with his eyes: they are extraordinarily penetrating, and they mirror affection, severity, wonder, surprise, and serenity with astonishing rapidity. And when, as he so frequently does, he oversteps his bounds his face can instantly become winsome as, sitting, he coquettishly stretches his arms down over his extended legs and looks ingratiatingly at the one he has offended.

This 1917 Charlie is a Charlie not yet with a soul. He is a scamp, something of a rogue, not anywhere so nasty as his Sennett self, and much of the fun watching him comes from his cool and dashing bedevilment of the societal types his audience is frequently intimidated by: policemen, bosses, autocratic parents, love rivals, browbeating spouses, and those haughty types who confound us all—bored waiters.

Late in 1917, after completing his work at Mutual, Chaplin took a badly needed holiday in Honolulu with Edna. Along to preserve the proprieties were Rob Wagner, his press agent, and another employee, Tom Harrington, a bohemian ascetic, man of mystery and selflessly devoted to his new boss. The Honolulu trip was brief. Chaplin was anxious to return for a project that had been occupying his thoughts for months—his own studio. He was also beginning to find Edna's company a little wearing. He had been jealous of her close friendship with film star Thomas Meighan but he found that he was happier not getting so deeply involved and maintaining only a working relationship with Edna.

His real love at the time was the new studio being built at the corner of La Brea and Sunset Boulevard, then on the outskirts of Hollywood. It was, indeed it is, an efficiently structured studio block (today the home of A & M Records), the long side of which is designed to represent a row of English cottages. It took a year and a half to build, and its cornerstone still carries the imprint of Charlie's feet and the year of completion, 1918. Part of the grounds today are given over to a supermarket but for most of the years of Chaplin's tenancy there were extensive amenities: a large garden, a tennis court, trees, a residence, garage, stables, swimming pool, and a carriage drive in addition to a large sound stage, offices, dressing rooms, and a variety of workshops.

Most of Chaplin's First National acting troupe came over from the Mutual company: Edna, Henry Bergman, Albert Austin, John Rand, Loyal Underwood, Phyllis Allen and—vitally, to replace Eric Campbell—burly Mack Swain from Keystone. Sydney Chaplin acted, too, in addition to his business duties. Chaplin gained another valuable assistant, Charles F. "Chuck" Riesner, a former Sennett gagman and Broadway lyricist ("Goodbye Broadway, Hello France!"). Riesner was a jolly soul and an inventive gagman. He helped Chaplin direct the initial First National film, A Dog's Life, a three-reeler.

A Dog's Life is the life of both Charlie and his mutt, Scraps, described in a title as a "thoroughbred mongrel," which is also a pretty good description of Charlie, who plays a tramp, albeit one eager for employment. There was one irritating distraction during the making of the film when Chaplin received a number of letters from British fans, mostly ex-fans, who sent white feathers. Chaplin had in fact tried to enlist but was termed medically unfit. It was information that should have been more widely disseminated. Chaplin suffered from the slacker designation for many years.

A Dog's Life finds Charlie and Scraps on the very bottom rung of society, unable to find employment of any kind except that of scrounger, at which they are both pretty competent. Charlie finds a half-empty bottle of milk and, knowing Scraps cannot get her head into it, shows her a practical solution—dipping her tail in the milk and licking it off. The chums go to a food stand run by a sad-eyed vendor (Sydney Chaplin) who soon realizes he is at the mercy of two sharpers. Scraps grabs off a string of sausages as Charlie distracts Syd's attention, then Charlie, biding his time, watches Syd shuffling his pans. A plate of muffins stands on the counter and every time Syd turns to his duty Charlie pops a muffin into his mouth, assuming a bland look as Syd turns back suspiciously. The muffins diminish in this way, and Syd is frustrated. He knows those muffins are going down that gullet but he is determined to see at least one snatched before his very eyes even if he has to expend two dozen of them in the process. But no matter how he tries, a flash side look, quick twist, or double take, he always just misses. One cake left now, and Syd spins victoriously to see Charlie's hand hovering over the plate. Charlie pretends he is brushing nasty flies away from that splendid pastry. As Syd turns back to work Charlie gaily lifts the last muffin—to see a cop watching him, a cop who chased him earlier in the morning. Charlie replaces the cake and leaves hurriedly as Syd turns around vengefully to thwack the thief with a sausage. The cop gets it.

Charlie meets Edna in a café where she is a singer and typically befriends her to the point where they are talking of a little home in the country. But first there are two crooks who steal a wallet that they bury and Scraps digs up and gives to Charlie. The thieves steal the wallet again and Charlie takes revenge on them in a curtained booth of the café where they are roistering victoriously. He smacks one of the men with a mallet and, sticking his arms up behind the sagging crook, assumes his identity by becoming the crook's arms to the very life: admonishing quiet to his crony, straightening his tie, lifting a glass of beer for a sip, wiping his mouth, holding out his hand for a cut of the swag, shaking hands with his fellow thief, waving him closer, hitting him with a bottle when he leans forward.

As Charlie flees the café the crooks revive and chase him back to Sydney's stand where Charlie and Syd hide behind the counter as the crooks shoot. Scraps sensibly relieves Charlie of the wallet before the crooks do, saving the day, and the cops close in on the thieves. In the last episode Charlie and Edna are secure on their little farm, gazing down lovingly on a layette. Within are Scraps and a lovely litter of puppies.

A *Dog's Life* is at times almost disconcerting in its realism and we are certainly entitled to the pleasant compensatory ending, unreal as it may seem in context. With this film Charlie the Tramp leaves his sometimes mean, amoral little habits and for the most part becomes Charlie the gentleman tramp. He has been gallant before but gallantry has never been so deeply ingrained as here, as his embrace of a common mutt confirms. It was clear to Chaplin that Charlie now needed a deeper dimension. Roguish tricks as such could no longer sustain such a character. The problem was that as a slapstick comedian his farcical plots did not easily accommodate sentiment. This conflict Chaplin helped resolve by making Charlie increasingly more of a Pierrot, that wistful mischievous clown who so artfully combines tears and laughter. But Pierrot always had one trouble and Chaplin saw that as Charlie's too—getting women genuinely interested in him.

In his own life, Chaplin had the reverse of that trouble. Not very social in his early Hollywood days, he had only one real friend, Douglas Fairbanks. The two men were cast in the attracted-opposites relationship. Fairbanks was heartily gregarious and boundingly optimistic; Chaplin, already well wounded by life, tended to solitude and pessimistic caution. But they shared a passion for life's wide possibilities and a vigorous sense of humor.

In early 1918 Samuel Goldwyn asked Chaplin to a party at which there were a number of very pretty girls, and from among these butterflies Chaplin unerringly picked the prettiest and silliest. Mildred Harris, a very young film actress, was not sought out by Chaplin for the charm of her conversation or the scope of her worldly interests. She was overwhelmingly feminine, adoring, and completely pliable. She had exquisite hair and very beautiful eyes. When she told Chaplin a few weeks later that she thought a baby was on the way, he reacted without foresight. Vaguely considering the long-felt need of a wife, strongly attracted to her youth and engaging prettiness, he married Mildred on October 23, 1918, before a Los Angeles justice of the peace. He bought them a home at 2000 De Mille Drive, North Hollywood—the first home Chaplin ever owned. Their courtship, for want of a better word, was conducted during a particularly harried time for him, the making of *Shoulder Arms*, his contribution to World War I. It was a film that said many things to many people; it was by turns bravura slapstick, a realistic image of war's roiling discomforts, sentimental whimsy, and unashamed flag waving. Above all, it was funny.

Shoulder Arms begins with Charlie in boot camp as top man in the "awkward squad." His splayfeet continually getting in his way, he is ordered by the sergeant to turn his feet inward, something nature never intended for Charlie. They keep springing back. His awkwardly balanced rifle inevitably becomes a slapstick, a continuing assault on his buddies. Sent to France, he prepares for any need by affixing to his uniform several knapsacks, a blanket, tin bathtub, coffeepot, egg beater, cheese grater (perfect as a cootie scratcher), and a mousetrap. Yet he is not happy, lacking as he does the consolation of a letter from home. He must share one vicariously, looking over a buddy's shoulder and reading along with him. When Charlie does get a package from home it contains limburger so potent he must wear a gas mask to endure it.

Despite smashing his pocket mirror and an identity disc numbered thirteen, he goes over the top and captures just thirteen Germans. Asked how he did it, he says, "I surrounded them." A brave volunteer is needed for a new mission and Charlie steps forward. Warned of the gravity of the mission, Charlie steps backward, but he is sent out. Disguised as a tree trunk, branches for arms and eye-port through a knothole, he wanders through enemy territory and is surprised by a German fuel-cutting squad. He disposes of them with his twin advantages, a huge club and the ability to root where he will.

With the help of a lovely French girl (guess who) he befriends, he disguises himself as a German officer, bullies everyone in sight, and captures the Kaiser and Crown Prince, who happen to be in imperial headquarters nearby. On arrival behind the American lines with his presitigious prisoners, Charlie cannot— and who can blame him?—resist delivering a heartfelt kick on the Kaiser's arse. Charlie is hailed by his fellows—until two soldiers shake him out of the sleep that has brought him such a salubrious dream.

Chaplin had been advised by D. W. Griffith among others that a film like Shoulder Arms should not be made until after the war. Chaplin felt some apprehension until Douglas Fairbanks saw it and almost collapsed with laughter. Shoulder Arms, released in the last weeks of the war, was received rapturously, especially by the men he was trying hardest to please, the men in the trenches and the men who had been in the trenches. Chaplin had made a more overt propaganda film in the fall of 1918, following a Liberty Bond tour with Douglas Fairbanks and Mary Pickford. The Bond is an amusing half reel made for the Liberty Loan Committee and distributed without charge throughout the country. Charlie, Edna, Sydney, Henry Bergman, and Albert Austin show in brief vignettes how the bonds of friendship, love, and marriage are all inspiring but the most important bonds of the day are Liberty

Bonds, which constitute a blockbuster mallet capable of knocking out the Kaiser.

Chaplin's own bonds of marriage were unraveling. But he tried to concentrate on his work, and it was at this time that he said he began to think of comedy structurally, not as just an accretion of gags but as one scene begetting another. He had learned (he said) that a natural organic relationship between the individual scenes contributed more effectively to the whole.

Whereupon he made two rather bad films that have no organic growth at all. His next film, *Sunnyside*, like Stephen Leacock's fabled knight, seems to go in several directions simultaneously. Probably Chaplin was tired. It was not only his marriage that was disturbing him but First National. He asked them for more money to strengthen the quality of his films, thereby increasing the likelihood of their making more money, but First National did not see it that way. Sydney Chaplin had been hearing rumors that all the producing companies in the country were contemplating a secret merger. This would effectively place all film distribution in their hands by means of binding five-year contracts with every exhibitor in the country. Leading actors would have no recourse but to play the producing companies' game. The actors decided to play their own game and found United Artists, a company whose name expressed their operative function. Chaplin, Fairbanks, Mary Pickford, D. W. Griffith, and others planned to function together and distribute their own pictures.

But not yet for Chaplin. He had six more films to complete under his First National contract. He tried to buy his way out to no avail. He offered First National several kinds of financial advantage to let him go but they were adamant. If some of Chaplin's frustrations spilled over into *Sunnyside* in 1919 it is understandable.

In *Sunnyside*, Charlie is an overworked hired hand at a rural hotel-*cum*-farm. His daily twenty-four-hour grind forces him to get his meals on the run—milking a cow (kept in the kitchen) directly into his coffee, holding a hen above a sizzling skillet so eggs will emerge fried. Charlie loves neighbor Edna and tries to see her as much as his schedule allows; but her dour father dislikes him. Driving his master's cattle to pasture, Charlie dreamily allows them to wander off, and when he finds one of the strays, mounts it and is kicked off into a stream, insensible—and a dream dance with four nymphs in demi-Elysian fields begins. He is dancing, Robert Payne says, "because one dances in paradise, and there is no reason for it." Well, maybe. One suspects, however, that Charlie is dancing because Chaplin read reviews praising his balletic grace and now he is giving us balletic grace like crazy. Here we see the style and not the substance of Charlie. It is not enough.

When the dream ends and Charlie comes into the harsh world of love unrequited, there is ample suffering. A city slicker hurt in a car crash outside the hotel quite wins Edna's heart, and there is a touch of the gallant old Charlie as he tries pathetically to imitate city ways in rural fashion. He kisses Edna's hand but it is covered with glue, and the kiss extends itself ludicrously.

Edna rejects Charlie, who goes out suicidally into roaring traffic. He is about to be hit—and awakes; again this has been a dream, the *second* dream in this short film. This is overuse of a device, but a more serious disservice to the film is that the so-called highlights of the film occur during dream sequences. So much for film structure and organic relationships.

There was some critical revulsion. Harcourt Farmer in *Theatre* magazine, October 1919, put it in the title of his article, "Is the Chaplin Vogue Passing?" Mr. Farmer rather thought it had, which proves him a very bad prophet indeed, but with *Sunnyside* (which Farmer said filled "the analytical mind with grim foreboding") at hand, this critic may be forgiven something of his attitude:

> I contend [he said] that the extraordinary Chaplin vogue is based upon the simple law of repetition—that each film contains precisely the same elements—that the appeal of every Chaplin picture is to the lowest human instincts [that pain is diverting]—and that, in the natural course of events, the Chaplin vogue in five years will be a thing of remote antiquity.

One does not know if Mr. Farmer was around five years later when Chaplin made probably the greatest film comedy of all time, but if he was, it is to be hoped that no one was tactless enough to recall these words.

Chaplin suffered during the shooting of *Sunnyside*. Making the film he compared to the pulling of teeth. Like that harsh experience, usually the result of personal folly, he had brought it on himself: he had married in haste and was repenting in haste. With the shakiest sense of realities, Mildred was enjoying her new name but not much more. Marriage was largely beyond her, and Chaplin himself had no clear idea of marital responsibilities. She complained of Chaplin's moods and long silences but that was understandable. They had absolutely nothing to talk about. There was a brief reconciliation when, after announcing that she was not pregnant, she declared she was. Peace prevailed between them until just after the birth of a malformed son on July 7, 1919. The baby lived three days and was buried in a Los Angeles cemetery under a simple stone with the words, "The Little Mouse," the pet name she had given the baby. Years later Chaplin told a friend bitterly, "The undertaker put a little prop smile on its face. The kid never smiled." The baby's death affected Chaplin profoundly because he blamed himself for the child's affliction. Shortly after the death, he moved back to the Los Angeles Athletic Club and leased a new home for his wife on South Oxford Drive.

Ironically the split occurred at a time when Chaplin was starting to shoot a two-reel film on the jolly misadventures of a family man on a day's outing with his wife and children. A *Day's Pleasure* is a bland little domestic comedy. A daddy takes out his family in their rickety, frequently malfunctioning Model T Ford, gets into a traffic mix-up, and spends the day on an excursion boat. The best gag is when Charlie dashes off the boat to buy cigarettes just before it sails, then dashes back just as it pulls away from the dock. A hefty lady (Babe London) who has pushed a perambulator on board is caught by the boat's precipitate departure and hangs suspended, hands on the deck, feet on the dock—a natural bridge—and Charlie quickly takes advantage. He does help the lady in. Other than that, the gags are on the level of Charlie at one point trying to straighten out a folding chair. This is not adventurous comedy. But the film had a fairly pleasant critical reception. The Chicago *Herald's* critic marked its superiority over *Sunnyside* and continued that faint praise by saying A *Day's Pleasure* contained "fewer assaults upon posterior portions than Chaplin's other films."

When the youngest of A *Day's Pleasure*'s cast grew up, he saw the film and noted its shapelessness. Jackie Coogan, who played Charlie's youngest son in the film, said in a recent interview that his boss "kind of sloughed that picture off. You will notice if you see it, that it gets very jumpy. He lost interest in it." He lost interest, Coogan believes, because he was fermenting the story and production concepts for his next film, a quiet masterpiece, *The Kid*.

But before Chaplin could seriously get under way with that project there was Mildred. Animosity between the two was reported in the press, and Mildred's new manager, the redoubtable Louis B. Mayer, publicly scorned Chaplin's offer of a $25,000 settlement. Chaplin announced his contempt of Mayer and his intention to knock the hell out of him. They met accidentally in the dining room of the Hotel Alexandria, grappled and fell, Chaplin hitting his head on construction planking. Separated by house detectives, Mayer declared a victory because he had connected with a blow. Years later Chaplin told his son Charlie, "I trapped myself into something by talking too much."

In August 1920, Mildred filed for divorce, claiming mental cruelty and that she never knew where her husband was or what he was doing. In November 1920 in the divorce proceedings Chaplin settled $100,000 on Mildred together with some community property. Mildred did not spend the money well. After being declared a bankrupt a few years later she went back into films to display a pleasing if not unusual talent. She can still be seen on television wherever the 1936 Three Stooges short, *Movie Maniacs*, is shown. Playing a film star in that frantic two-reeler, she is not without charm. Mildred married twice after the Chaplin marriage and had a son. Marion Davies despite her avowed affection for Chaplin is quoted by Lita Grey Chaplin as saying, "Mildred Harris was no saint, but she wasn't really a bad kid, and Charlie, God bless him, loused her up good."

Marion Davies believed that Mildred saw Chaplin as her entry to stardom, and that this, aside from any affection she felt for her husband, was the impelling reason for the marriage. Once married, however, Mildred tried to be a good wife, Marion insisted, until Chaplin "kicked her out," treating her badly, thus triggering the alcoholism that was to plague her until her death.

For the record: Chaplin did not kick her out, and alcoholism is not a disease imposed on one by others.

Mildred Harris died July 20, 1944, in Los Angeles of pneumonia following surgery.

8
THE KID

After the making of *Sunnyside,* Chaplin spent agonizing days trying to think of an effective theme for a new film. Just a premise to get the film started was all he hoped for. To relax from this pressure he went to the Orpheum Theatre in Los Angeles one afternoon to see a vaudeville program. He particularly enjoyed an eccentric dancer, Jack Coogan, whose act ended with his four-year-old son Jackie rushing out on stage to do a sprightly little shimmy dance, smile, and wave. The boy was enchanting. A piquant personality, a warming smile. A week later Chaplin thought of the boy as a foil for Charlie, but he was sorry to hear that he had been signed by Fatty Arbuckle. The report was wrong; it was the father who had signed with Arbuckle, and shortly he was free to bring his son to the studio and go to work. Jack Coogan was signed to act and serve as production aide on the new film, the first full-length Chaplin film. The boy got some brief experience by working in *A Day's Pleasure.*

What was clear from the first day's shooting of *The Kid* was the scope of the youngster's astounding talent. The natural exuberance, the unfeigned sweetness, the outgoing charm of Jackie Coogan—if it could be caught—would give the film a distinction unique in movies to that time. Cute children had been a staple of films from the earliest days but only in brief dosage. This was to be a film devoted extensively to the tramp and a kid—two open-hearted children.

The genuine closeness between Chaplin and Jackie in the mak-

ing of the film was unforced. Jackie's quality in the film can be
summed up in a word perhaps inappropriate for one so young, a
word that can be used to designate the ageless Charlie as well: *gallant*.
A high-spirited bravery courses through the film as Charlie
and Jackie, who live so close to poverty's edge, face it with surging
cheerfulness. Jackie is a little tramp, Charlie *secundus*—bright,
pert, quick, and possessing one of Chaplin's great physical assets:
luminous, intensely alive eyes.

The Kid's opening title sets its tone: "A comedy with a smile—
and perhaps a tear." Perhaps, nothing. A woman (Edna) leaves a
charity hospital, infant in arms, and a title tells us delicately, "The
woman—whose sin was motherhood." Walking sadly by a church,
she sees an obviously unhappy young bride leaving on the arm of
her elderly bridegroom, and when a flower from the bride's bouquet falls, the old man steps on it unseeing. Our besmirched
flower, Edna, heart-riven, walks on, finding a parked limousine in
which she deposits the baby with a note asking that he be loved
and cared for. The car is stolen shortly by thieves who leave the
baby beside a slum garbage can.

Charlie appears on a pleasant morning walk, expertly ducking
garbage thrown casually from windows above. He stops for a
smoke, elegantly removing his fingerless gloves to extract a butt
from his sardine can cigarette case. A cry. He finds the baby, tries
to give it to various slum denizens, but is frustrated by a policeman who comes to believe the baby is Charlie's own. Charlie finds
Edna's note and ponders it. Edna meantime is about to commit
suicide when a tiny child rushing up to her on the bridge makes her
think of her infant. She rushes to the home where the limousine
was parked and is horrified to learn that the car has been stolen.

Charlie has settled in beautifully with the baby, who has been
placed in a little hammock close to a suspended coffeepot with a
nipple attached. Diapers have been reasonably cut and contrived
from old clothing. A splendid potty has been made by cutting a
hole in an old chair and placing it carefully over a cuspidor.

Five years pass. We now meet Jackie, sitting on a curb, mani-
curing his nails deftly prior to paternal inspection. When he presents himself to Charlie, there is a stern examination of not only
hands but ears, nose, and hair. The two partners must be in impeccable fettle as they set out for the day's work. Their job is an

instance of not only going where the work is but creating it on the spot. Jackie's task is to hurl a stone through a window and run. Charlie's is to stroll casually by wearing his glazier's harness, ostentatiously available to replace the glass. (Chaplin may well have gotten this idea from Fred Karno, who actually made his livelihood as a boy this way.) Jackie carries off his part handsomely until a stern policeman sees him wind up for a tremendous throw. Jackie smiles at the cop disarmingly, pretends the stone is a juggling ball, throws it down, and runs off. The cop's suspicions fix on Charlie, who pretends he doesn't know the boy, but with a sudden burst of speed the two elude their pursuer.

In the interim, Edna has made a great success as an opera singer but it is not enough. Yearning for her lost boy, she becomes a part-time charity worker helping slum youngsters and in the course of her duties unknowingly gives a toy to Jackie. He loses it to a tough youngster (Raymond Lee) and the boys fight. Raymond's burly brother (Chuck Riesner) happens by and sees the fight, telling Charlie, "If your kid beats mine, I'll beat *you*." Charlie hastily declares Raymond the winner even though Jackie is winning. Bending a lamppost to display his strength, Chuck is about to do the same to Charlie when Edna arrives to stop the fray. As Charlie lays Chuck low with a brick, Edna sees Jackie is ill and insists that a doctor be called. This vague old gent gives Charlie a thoroughly incompetent checkup. The doctor, asking how Charlie found Jackie, is shown Edna's original note, which Charlie has kept. Part of Jackie's recuperation is spent sitting quietly in bed reading the *Police Gazette* as Charlie prepares a mustard plaster. The doctor meanwhile has reported Jackie's situation to the County Orphan Asylum, which sends out a truck to take the boy. The asylum men are forced to call in the police to help them get Jackie, so spiritedly do he and Charlie resist. Jackie in bitter tears is hauled into the truck. (This episode comes from Chaplin's life. He was, like Jackie, literally torn from his mother's arms when he was taken to the workhouse.)

Charlie flees a pursuing cop over the rooftops, until in a hide-and-seek climax they both climb up the opposite sides of a steep gable to face each other, and Charlie pushes his opponent down. Taking a short cut across the roofs, Charlie leaps on the asylum truck, kicks out the attendants, and is reunited with Jackie. They kiss tearfully, and if there is a dry eye among viewers of *The Kid* at this moment it can only be due to defective tear ducts.

The dotty old doctor tells Edna of the note Charlie has shown him. Charlie, now on the run with his boy, goes to a flophouse and, having money for only a single admission, spirits the lad into his bed under the blanket, allowing him a fleeting moment to pop out for his prayers like a jack-in-the-box. Jackie, to frustrate the suspicious proprietor, assumes the posture of Charlie's raised knees. A pickpocket in the next bed goes through Charlie's pocket while he undresses and finds, incredibly, a forgotten dime. Charlie grabs the dime and, counting on the man's great skills, puts the thief's hand back in the pocket. The proprietor reads in the paper of a reward for Jackie and takes the boy to the police and Edna while Charlie sleeps.

Charlie searches forlornly and in vain for his foster son. Seated on the doorstep of his squalid home, he falls asleep and dreams a dream. The slum yard where he lives is transformed into an efflorescence of white flowers, and there is a food stand with a sign, "LUNCH. The price is love." All the ragged slum dwellers have turned into angels with quite efficient wings. The bully Chuck drifts by playing a spirited harp. Jackie comes in to wake Charlie, who is also consigned a pair of wings. "Sin creeps in," we are told, with devilish figures who slip past a dozing watchman. A devil tempts Chuck's wife to flirt with Charlie, and she reveals her ankle, almost felling him with desire. Chuck puffs into anger and angel feathers fly. Charlie tries to soar above the entire thing but a cop shoots him down.

At which point Charlie wakes and the dream ends, and a jolly good thing too. The dream is just too much for the film. (J. M. Barrie once asked Chaplin why in heaven's name he had interrupted his marvelous film with this curious irrelevancy. Chaplin replied that he got the idea from Cinderella's dream in Barrie's *A Kiss for Cinderella*.)

The cop who shakes Charlie out of the dream hustles him off to a limousine which takes him to a great mansion and a loving reunion with Edna and her long-lost son Jackie. The now affable policeman, symbol of the pursuing furies in Charlie's life to this very moment, shakes his hand and Charlie enters the house, presuma-

bly to a better and happier life. Presumably. But like the ending
of *The Tramp*, this may not be a happy ending we can accept
unreservedly. Charlie is clearly not of Edna's class and Jackie has
probably got Groton and Harvard in the distance. Charlie's like-
liest connection with the new family, if any, is to embody high
life below stairs, perhaps as an eccentric second footman. Charlie
wouldn't much like that.

The flirtatious angel in *The Kid*'s dream sequence was a beautiful young adolescent, Lillita Grey, the kind of young woman
Chaplin was always drawn to—the pert, immature, but intensely
feminine type, a type best defined in this generation's vivid
phrase, a living doll. Chaplin's previous doll was giving him a
great deal of trouble during editing of *The Kid*. First National
joined with her in plans for attaching the film. Because *The Kid*
was slightly over six reels in length, First National, scenting big
business in the wind, tried to cheat Chaplin by offering him only
$405,000, their contractual payment for three two-reel pictures.
The Kid, having cost over half a million dollars and with a potential return in the millions, was worth three two-reelers about as
much as a six-carat diamond ring is equal to six single-carat rings.
First National, said Chaplin, would freeze in hell before he con-
sented to such an arrangement. He had Rollie Totheroh and
others take the film out of state in the cutting stage, and when a
print was assembled, Chaplin showed it to First National executives in New York. They professed not to be impressed, and
Chaplin angrily gave them a week to make up their minds to accept the film on his terms. They took them—$1.5 million to
Chaplin, Chaplin to receive half the profits after First National
had regained the million and a half. The film remained for five
years on a rental basis, then reverted to Chaplin.

The Kid won everyone, particularly the critics. Hannen Swaffer,
in the London *Graphic*, sensing correctly that the film was actually a return to Chaplin's desperate Lambeth boyhood, said:

> He was born in a London slum. He was kicked around when
> he was a boy, and made ridiculous. All through his little silly boyish
> years he cried; and when you've seen *The Kid* . . . you know that
> Charlie Chaplin has put into that picture a thing that makes Glad-
> stone's speeches on Bulgarian atrocities merely ponderous nothings.

The whole social fabric is wrong, and Charlie Chaplin knows it. He is the only man in the motion picture business who does.

Swaffer goes to the heart of *The Kid*. Charlie himself is the kid; he and Jackie are identical, differing only in age, forlorn lambs in arid pasture. The artistic sympathy between them is too marked to think other than that Chaplin saw in Jackie Coogan the Lambeth boy of 1895. Chaplin was expressing nothing but himself.

"A man of Dickensian genius," the *New Statesman* called him, and England's best drama critic, James Agate, was not afraid to use the adjective "sublime," adding, "There is, at least for me, more emotion in a single tear of *The Kid* than in all the bucketfuls of 'Vesti la giubba.' . . . I do not laugh at Charlie til I cry. I laugh *lest* I cry, which is a very different matter."

Agate was puzzled, as some critics were, by the astounding talent of Jackie Coogan. The floods of tears Agate could not conceive of this six-year-old actually feeling; yet could he be professional enough to make them come at will? If the boy's emotion was real, said Agate, "then there are depths in this small soul which frighten me."

The answer is that the emotion was turned on in various ways. In 1976, Jackie Coogan, referring to his being taken away from Charlie and put in the orphan van, remembered:

Mr. Chaplin and my father told me what they wanted to do, what they wanted to see on the screen. Just as intelligently as you would tell someone to thread a needle or how to put a record on a record machine, they would tell me exactly what they wanted done, and I used to pay attention very closely. It was inherent in me, because the whole thing was like a wonderful game to me. . . . They told me . . . "Now you're being taken away from Charlie" —my daddy—"and you love this man and you don't want *this* man." You'll notice that when the fellow throws me in the truck, he really threw me in, so he identified himself as a bad man. A child reacts to size a great deal, and he was a big fellow. That's one thing they got in that shot, when they came in on a close up of me. That's where I'm turning them on, and I'm pretty hysterical. The musicians, of course, helped a lot. We had music on the set. And Chaplin used to talk, as every director did, while the shot was in process, being silent pictures. He'd say, "Now you really love this man, and he's gone, and they're going to take you. . . ." It works on you.

As to James Agate's question as to whether emotion or calculation dominated this superb performance, the answer is *both*—as all good actors unfailingly testify.

Chaplin cannot be better praised than to be called the mentor of Jackie Coogan's performance in *The Kid*. Robert Sherwood in 1923 said that the movies to date, whatever their merits or flaws, "can claim at least one great distinction: [they have] provided the only possible medium for the expression of Jackie Coogan's altogether inexplicable genius."

Jackie Coogan became the child star of the decade. His *Oliver Twist* (1921), recently found, reveals that his superb acting was not limited to one film. Jackie went on to make four million dollars, mostly under the guidance of his father (who died young), all of which was spent by his mother and stepfather before Jackie attained his majority. It did Jackie little good but this injustice— which left him surprisingly free of bitterness in later life—resulted in the Coogan Law of California which requires that child actors' earnings be held for them in strict accountability until maturity. Jackie Coogan became a character actor in later years, and a good one, with a solid flair for comedy. He never attained stardom as an adult, nor was there really much reason to. What need to scale Everest twice?

When Chaplin visited Los Angeles for his special Academy Award in 1972, he was reunited with Jackie after fifty years, Jackie now of portly build and balding head. "It was," said Chaplin, "touching."

9
THE GREGARIOUS LONER

To be both deeply shy and heartily outgoing is a rare form of temperament, and in possessing it Chaplin inevitably suffered at those moments when duty or circumstance forced him in one of the moods to display the other. As his own boss he could and did shut up shop whenever he liked but occasionally he could not. By mid-1916 his fame was so great that celebrities the world over sought him out, at times inconveniently, but the mutual publicity was not unwelcome to him. This was heady stuff for a former Lambeth street boy. Dame Nellie Melba, Ignace Paderewski, and Leopold Godowsky from the world of music were especially welcome because of Chaplin's deep love of the art. Great dancers like Nijinsky and Pavlova came and were suitably entertained. But writers and politicians and vaudevillians and film actors came too. Chaplin loved to show off his new model studio.

As a visitor to the studio came Max Linder, the only screen comedian Chaplin was ever indebted to. Chaplin to a certain extent imitated Linder's techniques of flirtation and comic drunkenness, but particularly, says Jack Spears, did Linder's "expressive, symbolic gesture become part of Chaplin's stock-in-trade. Linder and Chaplin were equally remarkable for the way they used facial expressions to provoke laughter—particularly the quick nervous movements of the mouth and eyes, and the gingerly testing smiles." Chaplin once sent Linder a photograph inscribed, "To Max, the Professor, from his disciple, Charlie Chaplin." In 1921, Linder bought a beautiful home next door to Chaplin's on Argyle

Street in Los Angeles. Chaplin was delighted with one Linder prank. Seeing that Chaplin had a black limousine with a Japanese chauffeur, Linder bought a yellow limousine and hired a black chauffeur. After small success in American films, he returned to France.

Following the divorce from Mildred Harris in 1920, Chaplin was understandably chary of involving himself with any woman in what looked like a long-term commitment. He played a wide field of attractive ladies and Edna had not altogether faded out of his life. Although not an alcoholic, she was given to nipping and weight was beginning to blur her lovely features. May Collins, a young New York actress, was a constant Chaplin companion for a while but when reporters asked if an engagement was possible denied it. Then admitted it. Then denied it again. "I like the young lady," Chaplin told a reporter. "*Like* her. That is all." Then, as one reporter described her, "stately, cool, beautiful Claire Windsor appeared on the scene." Chaplin supposedly described Miss Windsor as "restful," an adjective he withdrew when she bruited it about that they were engaged. To compound this injury there was the heavy drama of her disappearance. Miss Windsor went out riding one morning in the Hollywood Hills and the horse returned to the stables without her. She was missing for two days before being found by one of the many search parties in a brush arroyo that had been searched hours before. She claimed amnesia but Chaplin's astute press agent, Carl Robinson, noted her riding boots were shiny new. She admitted a hoax. For two days, from the attic of a house in the Hills, she had watched the weary search parties seeking her out. In the best American tradition Miss Windsor took the publicity she had courted and went on to be a movie star. Chaplin had no comment.

Anna Q. Nilsson, Thelma Morgan Converse, and Lila Lee interested Chaplin briefly but it was not until the arrival in Hollywood of the distinguished English sculptress, Clare Sheridan, that Chaplin found a woman with charm, beauty, and intellect in equal measure. A cousin of Winston Churchill, the widow of a direct descendant of Richard Brinsley Sheridan, she had also walked with common folk and in some ways rather fancied herself one. As a pro tem Bolshevik, she had been to Russia where she did busts of the leaders; she did the same for prominent Ameri-

cans. Her bust of Chaplin reminded him of a criminal's head. No
—of a genius, she said. There was scant difference between the
two types, Chaplin said. Mrs. Sheridan found only the most exalted aspirations in Chaplin's visage and spirit. After their brief
relationship ended, she called him "a great soul."

Shortly after *The Kid* opened in theatres across the country,
Chaplin sent Tom Harrington to England where the consummately tactful secretary arranged to bring Hannah Chaplin to the
United States, a potentially hazardous act because she was still in
uncertain mental health. Harrington was relieved that she remained lucid all during the ocean voyage and she seemed fine
until an immigration official in New York greeted her respectfully,
"So you're the mother of our famous Charlie!" Pleasantly, Mrs.
Chaplin said, "Yes, and you are Jesus Christ." Her escort employed diplomacy of high order to obtain an entry permit for her, a
permit renewable yearly on the condition that she not become a
financial burden on the state. The Chaplin publicity office issued
a story that she was going to California for recuperation from
shell shock induced by wartime Zeppelin raids.

When her two sons met her at Pasadena, nine years had
elapsed since their previous meeting and they were struck by how
she had altered physically. From the almost birdlike sharp-fea-
tured soubrette she had changed to a heavy-set, placid old lady.
Hannah knew her boys at once and settled down in a Santa
Monica bungalow with a trained nurse and a housekeeper to care
for her. She was perfectly at home and found special joy in shop-
ping at Los Angeles department stores. Once, Konrad Bercovici
reports, she went on a spending spree, running up a bill of several
thousand dollars, buying hundreds of yards of varicolored silk.
Knowing she would never use any of them, Chaplin ordered them
sent back, then suddenly reversed himself. "Let her have all that
and more," he told Bercovici, "and all that she wants of the frippery. The poor soul has been longing for such things all her
life."

Chaplin knew that Hannah had wanted them from the time
she went on the stage as a girl, and now the silks had come thirty
years too late. Let her have ten times what she had ordered, he
said, and wept.

With the completion of *The Kid*, Chaplin still had four pic-

tures to make for First National. Doug and Mary Fairbanks again
complained that they were the only members of United Artists
distributing their films through the company. Chaplin tried again
to get out of the First National contract but realized that the only
way to be free was to make the bloody films and leave. Desperate
for an idea that would set one of the entailed films quickly into
work, Chaplin went into his studio's prop room and amid all the
clutter found some old golf clubs. The tramp—and golf clubs—an
unlikely combination, thus a comic combination.

So was born *The Idle Class* which was, for Chaplin at this stage
of his development, somewhat old-fashioned. He plays dual roles,
Charlie, an alcoholic socialite, and Charlie the Tramp. The best
gag in the film is another surprise reversal. Charlie the Socialite is
looking sadly at his wife's photograph: she has threatened to leave
him because of his drinking. He turns from the camera as if
ashamed to show us his sadness, his shoulders moving convulsively. He turns shortly and we see why he was so moved. He
pours out a well-shaken cocktail. Inevitably Charlie the Tramp is
taken for Charlie the Socialite by the long-suffering wife to the advantage of the tramp. There are pleasant but inconsequential high
jinks on the golf course, during which Charlie the Tramp has another dream, this one in the vein of Jimmy the Fearless of Karno
days. Charlie the Tramp finds high society not to his liking, and
we share his feelings.

The Idle Class, slight though it is, is a winning film, a farcical
Jekyll and Hyde conundrum whose title asks which is the idle
class—the idle rich or the idle poor? The dream sequence shows
how persistently this device surfaces in the Chaplin canon. It also
appears in *His Prehistoric Past* (for Sennett), *The Bank*, *Shoulder
Arms*, *Sunnyside*, *The Kid*, and in films to come. In all of them
Charlie has a romantic adventure and awakes to the antithesis of
romance—this dusty world. Chaplin, as an indelible romantic,
would just as soon not be here.

Chaplin had begun work on a comedy featuring Mack Swain
and himself as members of one of the world's richest professions,
plumbing, when he suddenly decided that he must go on holiday
to England. In seeing him and Carl Robinson off, Sydney had
only one order to the publicity man: "For God's sake, don't let
him get married."

In New York Chaplin met Doug and Mary Fairbanks and went with them to a lively party. Playing charades at the affair, Doug and Mary were one of the great hits of the evening. Posed on a table top, she was a streetcar passenger and he as conductor called out a long litany of station stops, finally arriving at the passenger and collecting her fare. They hopped off the table, danced about the floor, exclaiming that they were a pair of genuine fairies at brookside picking flowers. Mary fell in the brook, Doug jumped in after her, pulling her up on the banks. Over. Guess as they would, a widely erudite body of guests could not conceive what word the Fairbankses had acted out. Doug finally said, "Fairbanks!" and the guests applauded.[1]

Chaplin and Madame Maurice Maeterlinck, a distinguished actress, topped that however by enacting the death scene from *Camille*, during which her racking tubercular cough infected him and instead of her dying in his arms he succumbed in hers, his coughs like the barking of a great Dane.

The next morning Chaplin sailed on the S.S. *Olympic*, the ship which ten years before had brought him from England for his second tour of the United States. On that trip he went tourist class and was given a guided tour through the first-class cabins. Now he occupied the finest of those elaborate cabins and reveled in it. His chief companion on the trip was playwright Edward Knoblock, a genial man and fellow Englishman. At Southampton old friends came aboard: Donald Crisp, the actor, then directing films in England; Chaplin's cousin, Aubrey Chaplin; Tom Geraghty, Doug Fairbanks' scenarist; and an old stage companion, Arthur "Sonny" Kelly, Hetty's brother.

Chaplin was particularly anxious to tell Kelly that not long before sailing a letter had arrived from Hetty saying that she was married, living in London, and hopeful that Chaplin would look her up when he arrived. That indeed was one of the reasons Chaplin wanted to visit England. After boarding the train for

[1] Typical of the little contradictions between something Chaplin said early and his later version of it is the charade story as told here, according to his *My Trip Abroad* (1922). In *My Autobiography* (1964), Chaplin has the entire party shouting out "Fairbanks!" I pick the earliest version because it was told a year after the incident.

Waterloo, Chaplin mentioned Hetty's letter. Kelly looked at him oddly and said, "Hetty died, you know." He did not know and the shock was profound. Although in love several times since his brief liaison with Hetty, he had not forgotten her. She was the first love of his life, a typical unattainable ideal of beauty any young romanticist treasures. Her features were always to remain the standard of feminine beauty for him.

But the depth of Hetty's loss did not touch him immediately. He was caught up in the excitement of the London arrival when thousands greeted him at Waterloo Station and later at his hotel, The Ritz. On the balcony of his hotel suite he was called out time after time to wave to the crowds, "like royalty," he said proudly. What Chaplin did next that day was to become an important pattern of action the rest of his life, revealing a deep-seated need. He changed clothing and left the hotel from a side door to go as quickly as possible to the scenes of his childhood, Lambeth and the Kennington Road. The places where he lived and agonized as a boy: 3 Pownall Terrace, the garret he, Sydney, and Hannah occupied; 287 Kennington Road where he and Sydney lived with his father and Louise; Kennington Park where he once saw Hannah on a park bench bowed in tears; Baxter Hall where he went to see magic lantern slides for a penny. (That penny also gave him a cup of coffee, a piece of cake, and a religious card.) To Kennington Oval where he had walked with Hetty; to a barbershop where briefly he was a lather boy. Seeing all these filled him with deep emotion.

This emotion was not, as Somerset Maugham described it, a "nostalgia of the slums." It was the feeling of a highly sentimental, deeply romantic artist returning to his first sensibilities, his first stirrings, to the place where it all began: the visions, the resistance to injustices that deterred him, the self-doubts conquered by resolve. At the time of this return in 1921 Chaplin said, "I want to shriek with laughter at the joy of being in this same old familiar Kennington. I love it!" When he was eighty-five, after continued return trips, he could say in a fierce vein of reminiscence, "The Workhouse gates are still there—one of the few places that don't let me down when I revisit these childhood scenes."

Chaplin continued his 1921 visit to London with much celebrity hobnobbing. Those who detect in Chaplin one who dearly loves a lord or anyone of high degree are technically correct. Understandably Chaplin has always been engrossed with his own rags-to-riches story. As an inveterate romanticist, it would fascinate him, the people he had aspired to be among would fascinate him. When added to this is the sense of accomplishment in breaking the social barriers in caste-ridden England, one cannot easily fault Chaplin's delight in the company of the titled. One may not share it but who can really fault it?

Shortly after they arrived in London, Knoblock gave a party at his suite in The Albany, climaxed by an opportunity for Chaplin to vent both his sense of high farce and deep drama. Knoblock in conversation said Chaplin's career was at its peak. Tom Geraghty, made profound by several whiskies, agreed and said solemnly that to go on living after reaching such heights was anticlimax. To die at apex was surely the only fitting end for Chaplin.

He made such a point of this that Carl Robinson and Knoblock got Chaplin on the side with an idea for a practical joke. During the party a heavy rainstorm had come up. Lightning was flashing and occasionally a severe thunderclap crashed. Chaplin decided to take advantage of one of the thunderclaps at the proper time. He returned to the company and carefully shocked the Catholic Geraghty with several virulent blasphemies. Chaplin went to the window, opened it, and hurled defiance at the Deity, daring Him to strike him dead. Chaplin timed his outburst until one thunderclap climaxed, then screamed in agony and fell. Geraghty dropped his drink and shouted, "My God, it's happened!" Chaplin was carried into the bedroom and Donald Crisp, in on the joke, emerged a few moments later to say solemnly that their great friend was dead. Geraghty in a seizure of sorrow and despair was walking to the window to jump out when Chaplin tripped into the room wearing a sheet for a tunic and pillowcases over his arms for wings.

Chaplin's most enjoyable visit in London was with H. G. Wells. They shared a common origin, both lower class boys who won vast renown despite formidable odds, and, eccentrics both, they recognized not only that in each other, but the realization that they were both extraordinarily sensitive and shy, something they both had pretty much hidden from the world.

Increasingly Chaplin found it difficult to escape the London crowds and perpetual press attention. He went impulsively to Paris but the crowds were not less and the celebrities wanting to meet him were as numerous as in England. Cami, the French satirical cartoonist, had been in correspondence with Chaplin for years, each deeply admiring the other's work. They met and talked for hours with gestures only. "It did not occur to me that he did not speak French," Cami said. Chaplin also went on to Berlin, a place he had never seen and did not now enjoy except for a somewhat fateful meeting with the then reigning queen of German cinema, Pola Negri. Chaplin could speak no German and Miss Negri's English was limited to the enigmatic phrase, "Jazz boy, Charlie!" which she kept repeating to him. The Negri-Chaplin friendship was to be extended elsewhere, later.

Chaplin returned to Paris for a charity performance of *The Kid*, then back to London where he renewed a slight acquaintanceship with Thomas Burke, author of *Limehouse Nights*. Burke, a shy, introspective man, took a long rambling walk with Chaplin through the London streets. Chaplin again felt impelled to visit the scenes of his boyhood, and during the walk spoke at great length to his new friend.

Burke, writing shortly after, saw Chaplin as a naturally tragic figure, the loneliest, saddest man Burke had ever met, shy and quiet, a man who "inspires immediately not admiration or respect, but affection." During their memorable six-hour walk through Cockney London, Burke realized why their comradery had begun so naturally. They both had experienced bitter boyhoods in London streets, and Burke noticed that, like himself, Chaplin loved those streets. Chaplin found in them a Gypsy-like beauty, a beauty that moved him to ecstasy after so many years of the bright, straight-angled cities of North America. He told Burke that he owed little to England and its rigid caste lines. He knew that if he had stayed in England he would not have moved out of his "rude station in life." As Chaplin explained it, the operative questions in England were "Where do you come from?" "Who are your people?" and "What is your school?" In the United

States one was asked only "What do you know?" and "What can you do?"

Chaplin also told Burke that he preferred living in the United States because it was freer. (The mind is tempted to leap forward to 1952.) Chaplin's essential personality eluded Burke because he believed Chaplin did not know himself: ". . . this strange, elusive, self-contradictory character . . . The world has discovered him but he has not yet found himself. But he has discovered the weariness of repeated emotion, and he is a man who lives on and by his emotions. That is why I call him a tragic figure—a tragic comedian."

When Chaplin returned to Los Angeles he knew that his partners, Doug and Mary, were bound to complain again that their financial burden with United Artists had to be relieved. Yet there was the matter of the three films still due First National. By dint of persistent parleying about both the length and the cost of the films, Chaplin got First National to agree that a two-reeler and a four-reeler would count as three films.

Pay Day was the two-reeler, completed early in 1922, a jolly film, with Charlie as a construction worker facing both his workaday world and his domestic stresses. The film is pre-*Bringing Up Father*, with the flavor of Jiggs and Maggie before he came into his fortune: Charlie as a virtuoso bricklayer at work and at play in his local saloon, and coming home at night to his money-hungry dragon of a wife.

As a world institution in 1922, Chaplin found the foreign press just as avid in writing feature stories about him as their American counterparts. Fortunately he had two first-rate writers and press men in his organization, Jim Tully, the well-known hobo novelist, and Carl Robinson. With great tact they stood between their boss and story-hungry reporters, largely telling the truth but aware that the truth was not very entertaining. Chaplin was simply a hardworking comedian, and his principal interest in life was making people laugh. That was all the truth there was to tell and it did not make for inspired reading. Chaplin no longer needed publicity as Berton Braley, who so fervidly lamented the Chaplin inundation seven years before was now relieved to know. This was a different world and Braley saw why the comedian had become so

inextricably a part of American life. Writing for a nationwide
newspaper syndicate, Newspaper Enterprise Association, he made

AN APOLOGY

Charlie, there once was a time that I sneered at you,
Doubted your right to your widespread renown;
Gazed at your antics, then stridently jeered at you,
Said you were nothing at all but a clown.
Shoulder Arms showed your vast versatility,
Brilliant indeed was the work that you did;
Then came that splendid proof of ability,
You were a wonder indeed in *The Kid*.

So, though I sneered in your "earliest period,"
I can see I was far, far from wise;
You were an actor who clowned for the myriad,
Dodging with genius some thousands of pies!
Master of pantomime, comic in attitude,
How we all watch your adventures unfurled,
Conscious we owe you a great deal of gratitude—
You start the laughter that's heard round the world.

So, though the bulk of the movies may weary us
(Duller than anything else on the earth)
Always there's you who can drive us delirious,
Making us drown all our troubles in mirth.
Charlie, your figure is one of benignity,
I now recant all my olden time scrawls;
Charlie, here's to you! or, phrased with more dignity,
"Kid, you're a wonder—I'm strong for you, Charles!"

With *The Pilgrim*, his final effort for First National in work
during the last months of 1922, Chaplin was beginning to feel un-
fettered, which may account for the film's basic plot line: a man
escapes from prison.

The Pilgrim is Charlie, who in escaping finds a minister's
clothes and dons them as effective disguise. He flees to a little
town, Devil's Gulch, and is mistaken at the railway station for
their new minister by a little congregation come to meet him. Unable to resist this and having quashed a telegram explaining the
real minister's delay, Charlie is taken to the church where he

delivers a sermon on David and Goliath. In this, the best scene in the film, Charlic crafts a charming pantomime. IIe lifts his hand high to indicate Goliath, assumes a Charles Atlas stance, strokes a long mustache, and shakes his sword. Checking with the open Bible on the podium for further details, Charlie shrinks down into the midget-like David, then again becomes Coliath swinging his hefty sword. He looks down threateningly to his right, then becomes David, who looks up and to the left. David puts a stone in the sling and throws it. Charlie as Goliath receives the stone through the forehead; it falls out behind. Goliath collapses prodigiously. David, after counting Goliath out on the mat, saws off his head forthwith and fastens it genteelly on the end of a sword. After displaying this victorious token, David lets it slide casually off the sword over his shoulder and back-kicks it blithely away.

In the rest of the film Charlie foils a crook but is caught himself as an escaped convict. The sheriff must reluctantly take Charlie away, and he does, not to jail but to the scrub country just outside town, the Mexican border. With something obviously in mind, the sheriff orders Charlie to pick some flowers, which, Charlie being Charlie, he does happily, giving them proudly to thc sheriff. But the sheriff doesn't want *these* flowers; he wants the ones over there—on the Mexican side. Charlie goes over and the sheriff rides away quickly. Charlie runs after him with the flowers and the sheriff exasperatedly kicks him over the border. Charlie now understands; the sheriff goes off and Mexican bandits nearby shoot at each other. Charlie is now free to go either unfriendly way, so he runs straight down the border toward the horizon, a foot in each country. Once again Charlie doesn't belong. He has just begun another pilgrimage.

With *The Pilgrim*, Chaplin's connection with First National ended. Despite his personal difficulties with the studio, his maturity flowered in these films. They are longer than the Mutual films, thus allowing more scope for characterization and depth of content. They are more realistic than the Mutuals and they have less frantic, concentrated comedic drive. The twelve Mutuals stand as splendid films, easily the funniest films Chaplin ever made purely as comedies. They have a pungent joyousness unequaled in thc entire Chaplin work, and as such they are to be treasured. But he had to go beyond them in the First Nationals to mature the tramp.

In films like *The Kid* and *The Pilgrim*, some of Chaplin's own inner quality was showing. Bertram Higgins of the London *Spectator* speaks of the "hard-pressed shyness" in *The Kid*, of "bewildered courage in the face of unexpected and huge obstacles, mainly human. The interpretation of this attitude is the essence of Chaplin's comic talent: he makes timidity exquisitely funny, attractive, sometimes even beautiful."

It has always seemed to me [said Stan Laurel] that Charlie as a performer and as a person, too, was a wonderful mix—a shy, timid man, who kept getting up courage to do the most wonderful, adventurous things. Jimmy the Fearless. He can mix with anybody in the world when he wants to. Then he retires to shyness again. This kind of up-and-down thing all his life. Two men, two very different men, in one.

10

A WOMAN OF PARIS

A bright, amoral, and intriguing blonde show girl named Margaret Upton left her native Virginia during World War I with a single ambition—to be a millionairess before she was thirty. She made it handily. Changing her name to the jollier-sounding Peggy Hopkins, she quickly discovered that as an actress she had one severe professional disability—she had no talent. But she had beautiful eyes and exquisite legs and an unerring sense of where the money was. Her first husband, Stanley Joyce, a Chicago millionaire, paid a million dollars to be quit of her in a divorce settlement after he discovered that her occupation could be summed up in four words: men—and more men.

Peggy Hopkins Joyce went to New York and inevitably became a Ziegfeld girl. It was in this capacity that a Hearst newspaper reporter first saw the tattered old shoebox she carried with her constantly. She showed him its contents, well over a million dollars' worth of gold and diamonds harvested from five husbands and numerous boy friends. The reporter, much moved by the sight, coined a word for Peggy that went into the language, "gold-digger." Peggy came to Hollywood in 1922 with the vague idea of having her current boy friend finance her motion picture debut. Marshall "Mickey" Neilan, an old friend of hers, was commissioned to direct the film but two problems vexed him: Peggy was constitutionally unable to act and Peggy's boy friend was suspicious of the director's friendship with her. Hoping to get the entire problem out of his bailiwick, Neilan resolved to introduce Peggy to Chaplin in the hope of a romance, leaving Neilan free.

Driving Peggy and Colleen Moore to the Chaplin studio, Neilan talked at length about Chaplin's wealth. When they met Chaplin, Peggy dazzled him with her best smile and a carefully casual show of her thighs. On their trip back to town alone, Neilan laughed and told Colleen, "I knew it would work. How I'd love to see the look on her face when she finds out there won't be any diamonds coming forth from him."

The thrifty Chaplin, as Neilan anticipated, was not in the habit of giving diamonds to girl friends and Peggy Hopkins Joyce, it turned out, was by far the biggest donor in the relationship. She gave Chaplin the idea for his next film. Recently returned from Paris where a young man, to her somewhat pleased horror, had committed suicide over her, Peggy had also known there, in several senses, Henri Letellier, a famous French publisher. Letellier's worldliness was to be the theme of the new Chaplin film. Another influence shaping the film was a Chaplin commitment made to Edna Purviance months before. He had promised her the leading role in a straight dramatic film.

Chaplin and Peggy Hopkins were only briefly an item in the Hollywood gossip columns. After having been snubbed by Mary Pickford, Peggy left for New York, returning to Hollywood in 1926 to make an unmemorable film, *The Skyrocket*, and in 1931 to star with, of all unlikely people, W. C. Fields in *International House*. She looked very pretty in both films. Peggy died of throat cancer in 1957, sixty-four years old, with her sixth husband at her bedside, rich beyond her childhood dreams.

Against all evidence, Peggy had insisted to Chaplin that she was a country girl at heart, a simple soul who longed for the duties of hausfrau and mother. Chaplin accepted this incredible premise and, in *A Woman of Paris*, authenticated it.

Marie St. Clair (Edna), described in a title as "a woman of fate, a victim of the environment of an unhappy home," lives in rural France with her restrictive parents. Slipping away one evening to be with her art student sweetheart, Jean Millet (Carl Miller), Marie is locked out by her irate father. Tearfully apprehensive, she is consoled by Jean, who assures her of his parents' good will toward her, but that proves not to be so. Angrily Jean goes away with Marie to the railway station, determined to alter the pattern of their lives. Giving Marie money to buy tickets on

1. Fred Karno troupe on American tour, 1911, Sullivan-Considine Circuit. Farthest left: Charlie Chaplin; in back row with monocle, Stan Laurel. To his right: Albert Austin.

2. The tramp appears for the first time. Chaplin's second film, *Kid Auto Races at Venice*, 1914. Frank D. Williams, cameraman; Charlie Chaplin; Henry "Pathé" Lehrman, director.

THE HOKUM - FIEND !

*Mirthfully yours,
Stan Jefferson
THE - KEYSTONE - TRIO*

3. Stan Laurel, using his own name, Stan Jefferson, as a Chaplin imitator, American vaudeville circuits, 1915. Text (in his own hand) reads: "The Hokum Fiend! Mirthfully yours, Stan Jefferson, THE KEYSTONE TRIO "

4. Keystone days. Standing: Phyllis Allen, Mack Swain; seated: Mabel Normand, Charlie Chaplin. *Getting Acquainted*, 1914.

5.   Essanay days. Chaplin and Frank J. Coleman, *His New Job*, 1915.

6.   Mutual days. Charlie and Eric Campbell, *Easy Street*, 1917.

7.   Charlie Chaplin's studio, Hollywood, 1921.

8.   Chaplin and Lita Grey as the angel, dream sequence, *The Kid*.

9. Tom Wilson as the cop, Chaplin and Jackie Coogan, *The Kid*, 1921.

10. The key members of United Artists Chaplin, Mary Pickford, Douglas Fairbanks.

11. Hannah Chaplin in California, 1927.

12. Sydney and Charlie Chaplin, Jr., c. 1930.

13. Left-handed violin virtuoso.

14. Chaplin in test pose as Napoleon, a role he dearly wanted to play.

the Paris-bound train, he dashes home to pack. In the station a clumsy porter (Chaplin) bounces a heavy trunk from his back onto the floor.

Jean returns home intending only to get his bag but his father is stricken, and before Jean can explain this satisfactorily on the telephone to Marie she hangs up angrily. Walking out on the platform, the lights of a passing train flickeringly illumine her embittered features. Jean calls the station moments later but she has gone.

"A year later," a title says. "Paris the magic city, where fortune is fickle and a woman gambles with life." Marie has become the friend of Pierre Revel (Adolphe Menjou), the wealthiest man in Paris, a charming voluptuary. He ambiguously designates his bedroom his office and indeed he does keep a ticker tape there for occasional use. Bored with looking at the tape, he leafs through a magazine and sees the announcement of his engagement to a wealthy socialite. Pierre's secretary asks him if this will not compromise his situation with Marie. Pierre telephones her and asks if he can see her tonight and she agrees. Clearly she has not heard the news.

At Marie's expensive apartment, her friend Paulette enters to find Marie and a mutual friend, Fifi. In an aside Paulette asks Fifi if Marie "knows." Paulette has no idea. Marie asks what the matter is and Paulette shows her the announcement. Trying to hide her anger, Marie says with bravado, "Well, such is life." It is her first intimation that such a trauma might well be a life pattern. Her friends assure her all will be well and they go out, chattering. Marie seizes the magazine desperately and reads the wedding announcement.

That evening when Pierre comes by for Marie, he establishes very simply for us his relationship with her. He goes into her bedroom, opens a bureau drawer, and takes out one of his handkerchiefs. Kissing her in proprietary fashion, Pierre offers her a drink but she is too depressed. Seeing the magazine, Pierre says, "You're not worried about that? It will make no difference." She weeps and he says he will see her next day when she is in a better mood.

Later, at a Latin Quarter party, Pierre telephones Marie to come. As he is talking to her a coquettish beauty nuzzles him, and responding to Marie's "What's going on?" Pierre says, "Oh, just a quiet little party with some friends." He tells her the studio address but is not sure of its location within the building. The party slips into high gear as a man carries in a girl wrapped only in a veil which she turns to unwind, another man acting as the spool. Then a close-up of her bare feet pattering away.

Marie arrives at the studio building but cannot find her friends' apartment. She knocks instead on another studio door, which is opened by her old love, Jean, now an art student in Montmartre. He invites her in and when Jean's mother emerges from the kitchen there is acute tension. (Eddie Sutherland, Chaplin's new directorial assistant for A Woman of Paris, thought Marie's meeting Jean again this way was too much of a coincidence. "Do you think it's convenient?" Chaplin asked. "Not particularly," Sutherland replied. "Good," Chaplin said. "I don't mind coincidence—life is coincidence—but I hate convenience.")

With great reserve Jean's mother serves tea while Marie explains why she left for Paris. During this strained interlude the film cuts back to the madcap party at the studio. Back at Jean's, Marie smooths out her napkin and finds several holes in it, an embarrassing statement of Jean's poverty. She talks him into painting her portrait on commission. He walks her to Pierre's limousine and, as it rolls away, Jean realizes bitterly what Marie's life has become.

Next day Jean visits Marie's apartment to begin the painting, and as she shows him some of her rich gowns for the portrait, one of Pierre's collars falls out on the floor. Jean lifts up one of the gowns and for the first time Marie sees the mourning band on his arm. He tells her his father died the night she left for Paris.

Pierre is announced by the maid and Marie goes into the outer room to see him. He jollies her about the man she undoubtedly has in the boudoir and when she tells Pierre he wouldn't understand her explanation, he says, "You jump at conclusions. I understand perfectly." Smiling, Marie tells Pierre he is too clever. They kiss and Pierre, warning her to be careful, pats her almost patronizingly and leaves. Jean has made his choice of her gowns, and he goes—after a handshake.

Weeks later the portrait is almost done. It has been a strain, posing in her best formal dress and elaborate headdress, but Marie is satisfied that she has done something worth while for Jean. He has not let her see the portrait but now she insists. To her astonishment, the portrait is of her in country dress, as she used to be. When she asks why, Jean says, "Because I knew you better then." Fervidly he declares his love and asks her to marry him and start a new life. His mother, just about to enter the room, stops when she hears this, saddened, appalled. Marie tells Jean there is no hope.

Later in Marie's apartment Pierre assures her that this way of life isn't so bad. "You have everything," he tells her, and begins tootling a little saxophone. "Not everything," Marie says. "Poor little woman," he says. As she goes to the window, he follows her and says that she doesn't know what she wants. As they look below, they see a commonplace domestic street scene—bawling children, a tattered, irritable mother spanking one of them. The lesson is pointed but Marie is still upset, betrayed by an emotion she thought dead. Passionately she tells Pierre she is getting nothing out of life.

In reply Pierre runs his hand over her diamond necklace. Angered, Marie throws the necklace out the window, and a smiling Pierre returns to the comfort of his saxophone. In the street a tramp finds the necklace. Seeing this, Marie turns to Pierre for help but, laughing, he continues playing. Marie rushes out into the street, takes the necklace from the tramp, astonishing a policeman nearby. Pierre comes to the window and, amused, watches Marie suddenly return to the incredulous tramp and give him some money. As Marie runs toward her apartment house she breaks the heel of her expensive shoe, a troubling symbol of her harried, luxurious, and uncertain existence. Finding Pierre genuinely enjoying the little episode, she throws the offending shoe at him. Pierre knows Jean is the likely cause of her despondency and, when Marie admits she loves Jean, Pierre looks skeptical, kisses her, and says he will see her for dinner. She says no, and Pierre suggests she phone him "sometime."

Back at Jean's studio his mother nags him not to marry Marie, and Jean wearily gives in. He proposed, he now admits, "in a moment of weakness." Marie, just coming in the room, overhears and leaves angrily. That evening Jean walks the street beneath Marie's window. Later, Pierre takes Marie to dinner. Then follow quick vignettes establishing the psychological distance between some of

the principals: Jean's mother, waiting up for him, holding a ro-
sary; Jean walking, distraught; Pierre casually reading *La Vie Pari-
sienne* as he sips a drink; Jean coming home in sorrowful desperation.

Next is a superb example of indirection suggesting much more
than a frontal approach would. As Marie is getting her morning
rubdown from an impassive masseuse, her chum Fifi gossips at
length. While the two women prattle, the camera remains principally on the masseuse (Nelly Bly Baker), who works stolidly, her
face mirroring a nice balance of boredom and mild contempt for
the women and their lives.

At this moment Jean is putting bullets in a revolver which he
hides as his mother enters, asking him not to weary himself by
staying out late. Back in Marie's apartment Pierre calls for her
and they leave in high spirits for their usual evening on the town.
Jean follows them. In a balloon-studded café as Pierre and Marie
chat, a note is sent in from Jean saying he must see her "for the
last time." Pierre, reading the note, orders Jean brought to the
table.

When Jean comes, Pierre greets him with a great show of courtesy, but a little touch of Pierre's dominance over Marie—his
stuffing Jean's note into his pocket—infuriates Jean. He tries to
strike Pierre but is taken away by a waiter. In the lobby, waiting
before a fountain encircling the statue of a haughty and beautiful
goddess, Jean stands irresolute, helpless. Inside the café the
merriment continues for a time before it is stilled by the sound of
a shot. We see Jean falling into the fountain, a suicide. A
horrified crowd gathers. Stunned, inconsolable, Marie returns to
her apartment.

Jean's mother takes a revolver and goes grimly to find Marie,
only to be told at her apartment that the girl has gone to Jean's.
As the mother enters the studio, gun raised, she sees the disconsolate Marie beside Jean's body, praying. The mother lowers
the gun and, drained of emotion, sits beside Marie. Eventually she
puts her hand on the girl's.

A title tells us "Time is a great healer, and experience teaches
us that the road to happiness is in the service of others." We see
Marie and Jean's mother in a country cottage caring for orphaned
children. The women are obviously happy and fulfilled. A priest

enters and jocularly asks Marie when she is going to marry and have children of her own. She shrugs, laughs.

The film's last scene begins with the close-up of a milestone: "To Paris, 90 KM." Pierre and a male friend are in a chauffeured limousine as it drives past the sign. A hay cart appears on the road with an accordion player in the rear, Marie and a little boy following on foot. In Pierre's car his friend asks, "By the way, whatever became of Marie St. Clair?" Pierre's shrug says he doesn't know and doesn't care. The accordion player on the hay cart asks Marie and the child to join him. She does so, gaily. Pierre's limousine appears on the road in the opposite direction and speeds past. Marie begins to sing.

Shooting of A Woman of Paris began in January 1923 and took eight months. The film did not, unfortunately, make Edna Purviance a star as she and Chaplin so urgently hoped. Perhaps it was just too late for a woman of her slightly adipose beauty to remain in public favor. This was the era of the flapper and Edna in her best days was never that. In real life Edna was not unlike Marie St. Clair: rural-born, brought into the currents of city life by a dazzling personality who loved her for a time; then, slightly past her prime, moving out of his ken. Edna never married. Chaplin kept her on a comfortable pension for the rest of her life, which was ended by cancer in 1958.

A Woman of Paris was very rewarding to Adolphe Menjou, whose Pierre was indeed the film's best performance. Menjou, although fairly well known in Hollywood before the film, attained permanent stardom as a result. Chaplin too received high praise. His concern with psychological experience, despite the occasional melodramatic posturings of the plot, was warmly received by the critics if not by American filmgoers. A Woman of Paris was caviar for the general.

Stark Young in the New Republic found the film "really stirring . . . stirring because in every place the essential is discovered and set down. They seem strangely essential, these flashes and moments; they are stirring because of their truth, the truth of each moment as distinguished from all other moments."

To find this truth Chaplin urged his actors continually, "Don't sell it! Remember, they're peeking at you!" He made his actors work. In a scene where Jean's body is brought home as his mother

looks on, Chaplin wanted the actress, Lydia Knott, to react not
with standard histrionics of grief but to be stunned, almost immo-
bile, then to begin cleaning the house, and suddenly faint. Chaplin wanted the audience to supply the emotion, said Eddie Sutherland, "not the actress. I can't tell you how many times we shot it.
She kept playing it as a sweet, smiling, courageous old lady. She
was a very fine person, and very determined, so it was tough
going." Chaplin shot the scene over fifty times and, not getting
what he wanted, asked Sutherland to take over. Sutherland shot it
perhaps thirty times, finally getting the old lady so angry that she
swore at them. Bitterly she agreed to do it their way but, as she
said, "it's not the way I am." The scene was shot with her in such
a high temper of resentment that her very repression of anger perfectly suited Chaplin's intentions. The brief scene took a week to
complete. Lydia Knott was, said Sutherland, the only player he
had ever known to argue with Chaplin.

Part of the success of *A Woman of Paris* was due to the expert
and very dependable assistants Chaplin hired. Eddie Sutherland
was an imaginative young director on the brink of a very rewarding career as a comedy director. He was to work with W. C.
Fields and Laurel and Hardy. Monta Bell, who wrote part of the
script, had also written most of Chaplin's 1922 book, *My Trip
Abroad*; and two highly qualified technical advisers were retained,
Jean de Limur, a French army-officer-turned-actor, and Harry
d'Arrast, a French marquis.

All of them talked Chaplin out of the original ending he
wanted—Marie leaving Pierre after Jean's suicide and becoming a
nurse in a leper colony. Reluctantly Chaplin gave way but he did
shoot another ending for the European market where presumably
happy endings were not mandatory. In this one Marie returned to
Pierre. In the present authorized version the happy ending is retained. Still, Chaplin has said, "I cannot tell you with any assurance just what Marie is going to do with her life once she goes
down that country road."

Seen today, *A Woman of Paris* is still good drama, its melodramatic elements made potently believable by the psychological
honesty of its acting and direction. It is just what Chaplin called
it, the first silent film "to articulate irony and psychology." Revived early in 1977 at the Museum of Modern Art in New York, it

won discriminating audiences all over again. It is, said Jack Kroll of *Newsweek*, "an elegantly glittering tale, perversely both chaste and libidinous, of passion, money and art—the trinity that ruled Chaplin's sensibility."

11

LITA

Lita Grey and Pola Negri—for Charlie Chaplin's tastes—had one vital similarity. They were women.

The catholicity of Chaplin's taste in women was always pronounced. As Adela Rogers St. Johns put it,

> . . . the lover's lane Charlie Chaplin has trod . . . is strewn thick with every kind of romance. No man in modern history has loved and been loved by so many beautiful, brilliant and famous women. Paradoxically enough, the great comedian of the screen must be recorded as the Great Lover of the twentieth century. Don't let anybody delude you with the idea that Charlie's amours have been trifles, chimeras of the press agents, unfounded gossip, mere casual friendships.

The range of these many more-than-casual friendships is best exemplified by two of the women he loved—the alluring and fascinating Pola Negri, who looked, sounded, and acted like the glamorous movie star she was, and sweet-faced Lita Grey, young and young-looking, another Hetty Kelly.

When Pola Negri came to Hollywood in September 1922 under contract to Paramount, she renewed a friendship begun with Chaplin the year before in Berlin. She and Chaplin were seen in various Los Angeles cabarets, their engagement was announced in the newspapers, followed shortly by headlines proclaiming that she had jilted Chaplin. Because both Chaplin's and Negri's memoirs treat of their connection it is instructive to note their *Rashomon*-like views of the romance many decades later.

Chaplin gives the impression that Pola sought him out in America primarily for publicity purposes (thus beginning what he termed "our exotic relationship"), and when their engagement was mysteriously announced to the press Pola told him that he should comment on it publicly. Chaplin said any comment had best come from the lady involved; Pola asked what the comment should be. Chaplin shrugged. Next day Pola sent word that she could not see him, then relented by asking him to come and, when he did, languished on a chaise longue, accusing him of cruelty. A day or so later a Paramount executive called on Chaplin to complain that the press stories of the romance were making their star very ill indeed, and would Chaplin please make a statement, a public statement? The executive hinted that the statement might best be a wedding announcement. Chaplin said he did not propose to marry Pola simply to save Paramount's investment. That, as far as Chaplin was concerned, ended the matter.

Pola's version of the Chaplin relationship differs from his as wine from water. In her memoirs she speaks in detail of his fervid wooing dance: daily flowers, a diamond and onyx bracelet ("I was told that there could be no greater indication of the seriousness of his intentions, for he was notoriously miserly"), and much talk of the advantages marriage would bring them both. She gently put him off because she did not find him physically attractive although he was a stimulating conversationalist. Mary Pickford told Pola, "Anybody Charlie loves as much as he says he loves you, we're bound to love too." Gradually Pola's affection for Charlie deepened. She was attracted by the Chaplin quality that Sergei Eisenstein found pronounced. "It was," said Pola, "as if a part of Charlie had never grown up. It was probably why he retained that marvelous child-like wonder and innocence that contributed so much to his genius." (This was also Stan Laurel's considered opinion of Chaplin's essential personality.)

Pola asserts that Chaplin announced their engagement to a reporter from the San Francisco *Examiner*. However, she said, the engagement was soon marred with quarrels. He accused her of having an affair with the leading man in her current film. Pola told him to get out of her life and absolutely "no more tears, no more pleas for another chance." Chaplin took this news interestingly, said Pola. He accepted it with masochistic pleasure. Days later, she goes on, he made peace overtures "but this time they did not move me."

Thus the Chaplin version, the Negri version. Reader's choice.

Lillita McMurray was born on April 15, 1908. Six years later, to the day, she met Charlie Chaplin. Her mother, Lillian McMurray, took her to a Hollywood restaurant for a birthday celebration and, seeing Chaplin at a nearby table, went over impulsively to present her little girl. It was to be another six years before they met again. Chuck Riesner lived in the McMurrays' neighborhood and his son was Lillita's playmate. Riesner suggested that the girl might be suitable for films, and Chaplin later visited the neighborhood and saw the girl playing on her front lawn. Impressed with her piquant looks, he gave her a year's contract and put her in *The Kid*, in which she played the flirtatious angel with some skill. By now her professional name was Lita Grey, a name given her by Chaplin. During the making of *The Kid* she was surprised to find that all the adult actors were expected to call the boss Mr. Chaplin and all the kids were encouraged to call him Charlie.

Lita was a high-spirited young woman with a Spanish-Scotch-Mexican heritage. She was, said Jim Tully, "bold as a pirate and carefree as the wind." After *The Kid* and a bit role in *The Idle Class* her one-year contract ended. Months later, after seeing a newspaper story that *The Gold Rush* was in preparatory stages, she came down to the studio to see Riesner and tell him of her interest in the yet uncast role of the dance hall girl. Riesner was not encouraging but he told Lita and Merna Kennedy, a girl friend with her, to sit at one side and watch the studio activity if they liked. As the girls watched, various actors came by, among them Henry Bergman, who greeted her warmly. She had met Bergman during filming of *The Kid* and enjoyed his avuncular personality. As the Chaplin company's court jester, Bergman was a man easy to like. He asked Lita if Chaplin knew of her presence at the studio and when she said no he assured her Chaplin would be along. "He doesn't miss a pretty face!"

When Chaplin saw her he was astonished to see how she had grown. He proudly showed the girls the three-walled cabin set which played such a vital part in his new film, *The Gold Rush*. The cabin, as he demonstrated, set in an intricate pulley system, was able to move up or down by lever. The upshot of Lita's visit

was that Chaplin agreed to give her a screen test. After the test
Chaplin asked Jim Tully what he thought of the girl. Tully, needing his job, countered by asking Chaplin what *he* thought of her.
Chaplin thought she was marvelous. Lita then came into the
room and asked Chaplin how he liked the test. "Not bad," he
said, and offered her a contract at $75 a week. She would play the
dance hall girl. One must record that Lita promptly said, "Goody,
goody!" and clapped her hands. Chaplin soon began to meet her
after studio hours, making sure Mrs. McMurray did not know. He
took Lita on dinner dates with Thelma Morgan Converse to divert attention from his real interest but Mrs. Converse caught on
soon enough and disappeared huffily from Chaplin's life. He again
began to meet Lita secretly, the mother still unaware. Lita knew
Mrs. McMurray would be displeased at any liaison between the
thirty-five-year-old Chaplin and her sixteen-year-old high school
sophomore. Lita understood Chaplin's strong frustration because
she shared it. She did not consider their relationship a guilty one
however furtive it seemed. She found purity in it, and although
the age difference was striking, she called their love "as ugly and
perverse as a sunrise."

The foregoing and subsequent statements by Lita in these pages
are from her *My Life with Chaplin* (1966), a candid account of
the love affair and marriage. All that Lita Grey Chaplin says in
this book may be true but unfortunately there is no balancing version of their connection from Chaplin. In his autobiography he
does not even mention her by name and dismisses their marriage
in three sentences. He does not go into detail, he says, because of
their two grown sons, "of whom I am very fond." It is important
then to remember that many of the following details about the
Grey-Chaplin marriage come from one of the parties only.

Shortly before meeting Lita again, Chaplin had built a new
house in Beverly Hills on a six-acre plot just below Pickfair, the
Pickford-Fairbanks mansion. Designed by himself, Chaplin's yellow boxlike structure of plain stucco with a tile roof was a combination of Basque and "modern Spanish" architecture. Inside, the
forty-room house was invincibly English. It had a spacious high-
ceilinged living room with a large pipe organ and lavish movie
projection equipment. It was to this house that Chaplin, after several private afternoons there with Lita, brought the girl and her

mother to an afternoon party to meet the Chaplin inner circle of friends. Mrs. McMurray was the guest of honor and, quiet soul that she was, this flustered her considerably. Chaplin planned the party to flatter her and to subdue increasing motherly suspicions about the closeness between the pair. At the party Mrs. McMurray met such close Chaplin friends as Mr. and Mrs. Alf Reeves, and the next-door neighbors, Dr. and Mrs. Cecil Reynolds. Reynolds was a fascinating man. A distinguished brain surgeon, his principal interest in life was acting. Brain surgery, he told Chaplin, attracted him because of its sheer drama. (Reynolds can be seen briefly in *Modern Times.*) Mrs. McMurray was overwhelmed by all this attention, particularly by Chaplin's graciousness and charm.

Toward the end of the evening Mrs. McMurray became violently ill. She had experienced painful abdominal spasms like this before but she was not, in her words, one who liked "to fuss with doctors." Dr. Reynolds after a brief examination insisted that she be put to bed. He gave her a sedative and ordered that next day she submit to X-ray examination. She was placed in a comfortable room in the Chaplin house and went to sleep. Elated at this opportunity to be alone with his charming little ingenue, Chaplin took her to his bedroom where they made love several times. As they were lying in each other's arms, the door opened and Mrs. McMurray walked into the room.

Later Chaplin tried to convince her that he intended to marry Lita, but the distraught mother wanted the relationship to cease instantly. The contract for *The Gold Rush* would be honored, she said, but beyond that Chaplin was not to see the girl. Mrs. McMurray said this despite the clear evidence that Lita was now very much in love with Chaplin. But the plan for the girl to leave Chaplin was soon forgotten. She was pregnant. The McMurray family insisted he marry her and he agreed, reluctantly. Lita was removed from *The Gold Rush.* Georgia Hale, who had won some attention in the recent Josef von Sternberg film, *The Salvation Hunters*, was given the role of the dance hall girl Lita had been playing for five weeks. At first Lita thought she had been replaced out of revenge, but Chaplin said that would be imbecilic. He was, he assured her, a businessman. The film would take another six months and by that time Lita's pregnancy would be obvious. Thus Lita's version of the events preceding their marriage.

To fool the press, Chaplin announced that he was expanding the locale of *The Gold Rush* to Mexico, a rather extreme expansion, it seemed to some reporters who sensed a story. Chaplin evaded most of the newspapermen as he took Lita together with her mother and Chuck Riesner to Empalme, Mexico, in the state of Sonora. There, on November 24, 1924, Chaplin and Lita were married. On their return to the United States, Lita says, she overheard Chaplin telling one of his aides, "Well, this is better than the penitentiary, I guess, but it won't last." Chaplin later denied saying it.

Theodore Huff, who had talked to Chaplin about the marriage, was able to present something of the comedian's version of these events. Huff states that Chaplin agreed to the marriage on the threat of Lita's lawyer uncle, Edwin McMurray, to sue him if he did not. It was a simple case of history repeating itself, says Huff. Chaplin once more found himself with a totally incompatible young bride, but this time one with a domineering mother. Because of Lita's youth, Mrs. McMurray moved in with the Chaplins and took over control of the household. The Beverly Hills mansion became the stamping ground of the McMurray clan and their friends. Huff adds that it was given out to the press "that Lita Grey had retired as leading lady of *The Gold Rush* because she preferred to devote all her time to being Mrs. Chaplin. Approaching motherhood may have had something to do with it; but still more was Chaplin's resolve to return Lita to oblivion and frustrate his ambitious mother-in-law."

Whatever resolve dominated his personal life at the time, it was insignificant with his by now urgent resolve to make his next film an epic, the greatest of his career. He did.

12
THE GOLD RUSH

On a weekend at Pickfair, Chaplin was looking casually at stereopticon slides, among them some views of the Klondike. The most engrossing was one of Chilkoot Pass, the pathway into the gold country which thousands of prospectors traversed in the agonizing rush of 1898. He imagined Charlie on that snowy slope, and gags began to proliferate. Then Chaplin read a book about the Donner party, snowbound in 1846 in the Sierra Nevada passes until they were reduced to cannibalism.

To realize his expressed intention of making an epic for the tramp employing the themes of cannibalism and human greed against the Yukon fierceness was, on the face of it, formidable. But Chaplin never lacked artistic courage. Following his usual pattern of not worrying about a detailed story outline before shooting, he built several sets—rock-salt snow paths and fields, a dance hall. These scenes he wanted first and a number were completed before Lita left the cast. He reshot the ones needing Georgia Hale and he was very pleased with her sensitivity and ability to project loneliness, a primal theme of the film.

With many of the interior shots finished, Chaplin took his company (together with Chuck Riesner, Henry Bergman, Harry d'Arrast, and Eddie Sutherland as assistants) to Truckee, California, for the spectacular opening shot of the film, the climb of an endless line of prospectors up the pass. Although a very brief part of the film, Chaplin wanted this shot to be spectacular, "the greatest ever made," he told his assistants. Five hundred hobos were hired in Sacramento at the rate of five dollars a day and meals. A special train was hired to take them to Summit, California, for a march to the base camp three miles from town. After they arrived, Chaplin spoke to them through a large megaphone, explaining the procedure of the march up a narrow two-mile pass between two mountains. The hobos listened attentively and cheered Chaplin when he finished his instructions. With the cameras properly situated, he gave the order for the trek to begin and the men walked over and over before the cameras, repeating until Chaplin got what he wanted, by which time the men were authentically tired—and very, very proud.

The following summary of *The Gold Rush* details the action of the film in its original form, the 1925 release, now generally available for purchase. Unaccountably, someone in the Chaplin organization allowed the film's copyright to lapse in 1953 and *The Gold Rush* is in the public domain, now being sold widely for nonprofessional showing. In 1942, Chaplin re-edited the film, removing about fifteen minutes of footage without altering the essential 1925 structure, adding original music and a commentary written and spoken by himself.[1] Because the latter is presumably his considered opinion of the film's spirit and content, I have used its judgments to flavor this evaluation of the 1925 release.

Chilkoot Pass, 1898, the steep snowy ascent up which are climbing hundreds of prospectors going over this last barrier to the Yukon gold fields. Charlie, the loneliest of all those lone prospectors, appears on a narrow snow ledge, unaware of a huge bear following him. Charlie slips and slides down precipitous rocks to the very bottom where, leaning on his functionless but inevitable cane, he falls as it sinks into the deep snow. With profound optimism, he takes out a map and, scrutinizing it from several angles, determinedly follows the North arrow.

Meantime Big Jim McKay (Mack Swain), swathed in a fur coat making him resemble an amiable grizzly, is working on his

[1] *The Gold Rush*, 1925 version (silent), may be purchased from Blackhawk Films, Davenport, Iowa 52808. The 1942 sound version can either be rented or leased for the usable life of the print through August 1, 1991, from rbc films, 933 North La Brea, Los Angeles, California 90038. Blackhawk has a similar lease arrangement for the sound version.

claim in the frozen waste. He sees a huge nugget and exults: he has found a mountain of gold.

A great snowstorm comes up and Charlie slogs through it to find refuge in the cabin of Black Larson. This scoundrel, true to his name, orders Charlie out into the raging elements but the wind won't let him leave. As Charlie turns to walk out, the wind roars through the cabin, forcing Charlie to run in place. The wind blows him out the back door and he crawls back. The wind has another victim—Big Jim, who is blown into the Larson cabin.

Persistently inhospitable, Black Larson, using his rifle as leverage, orders both newcomers to go. Big Jim grapples with Larson for the gun, inadvertently turning it to every corner of the cabin where Charlie tries to hide. Grabbing the gun, Jim looks at the famished Charlie, gnawing a bone; Charlie with a sweet smile gives it to Jim and embraces him in what he hopes is a winning fashion. Charlie now becomes Jim's shadow. Hunger haunts the isolated cabin.

Jim determines that one of the three must go out and seek food. Cards will be cut and low man will go. This is Black Larson, who departs in an effusion of good wishes from Charlie. Larson goes into the white waste and in his wanderings encounters two police officers who have been searching for him. Callously, he murders them.

Time drags on, and as Thanksgiving Day dawns, Charlie and Jim are ravenous enough to eat one of Charlie's shoes, which he cooks lovingly in a big pot. With casual elegance, as if taking a crown roast to the table, Charlie sets down the thoroughly parboiled boot before his companion. Charlie sharpens his knife briskly and, separating the upper from the sole, places it on his own plate, leaving the sole to Jim. Jim, operating on the theory that because he is bigger he is most entitled, reverses the plates. Charlie is not dismayed: the sole takes on the quality of filet mignon for him as he suitably addresses it with fork and knife. He expertly entwines the shoelaces around his fork like spaghetti and eats them. The boot nails are like succulent chicken bones and he sucks off their meat appreciatively. Finding one of the nails bent like a wishbone, he holds it out hooked on his little finger in the hope that Jim will pull the other end. Jim's enjoyment of the boiled shoe is considerably less than his companion's. (As was the case during the shooting of the scene—which perfectionist Chaplin typically did many times over. Twenty-odd pairs of the shoes were made from licorice by a confectioner, and the shoes were all consumed in several days' shooting. Mack Swain, to his great discomfort, found that licorice is decidedly laxative in effect. He later told a friend that he would have preferred the leather.)

Charlie goes out looking for food but comes back, defeated, and warms his rag-wrapped foot in the oven. He offers to put his other shoe in the pot but Jim recoils as if threatened by cholera. Jim becomes delirious with hunger and he now sees Charlie as a fat chicken scratching and puttering about the cabin. When his sanity returns, Jim laughs maniacally, telling Charlie of his delusion. As Charlie bends over the stove he again seems a chicken to the hunger-maddened Jim, who chases him out of the cabin with a knife. Jim picks up a gun, shoots, and the sound restores his sanity. Charlie foresightedly buries the rifle in the snow. Inside the cabin Jim's delusion begins again and he picks up an ax while Charlie scurries out to find the gun. The door bar falls, knocking Charlie out; Jim falls into bed raving. A short scene is intercut here showing Black Larson stumbling onto Jim's mountain of gold.

The following morning in the cabin an uneasy truce prevails, destroyed presently by Jim's reaching for the gun and Charlie's spirited struggling for it. Jim tries to smother Charlie with a blanket but a bear wanders in and Charlie, mistaking him for Jim, wrestles the beast's leg. The bear flees and Charlie fires the rifle after him. Their famine is ended. Days later Jim and Charlie take affectionate farewell of each other, and Jim goes to his gold mountain where he finds Larson in possession. They fight and Jim, hit over the head by a shovel, wanders off, an amnesiac. Larson enjoys his victory only momentarily: he is swept down a great crevasse in an avalanche.

A Yukon town. In a saloon we meet Georgia (Georgia Hale), a spirited dance hall girl, much sought after and by no one more ardently—or impudently—than handsome Jack Cameron (Malcolm Waite). Georgia is attracted by him but she resents his insouciant style of wooing. Georgia has been showing some pals a recent photograph of herself. Jack grabs it kiddingly, and it rips, falling to the floor.

Charlie, more lone and forlorn than ever, comes to the town
and heads for the fount of good companionship, the dance hall.
As he comes in, the aesthetics of the camera placement are memorable. Stanley Kauffmann describes it:

> The harmonics of the picture—light tone against dark, light tone
> arising *out* of dark—are enriched by the Tramp's first entrance into
> the boom-town dance hall. Chaplin, the director, avoids the con-
> ventional sequence: showing us the bustling saloon, then showing
> us the Tramp looking at it—looking at the camera, in fact. He shoots
> past the Tramp, from behind, to the saloon interior. Charlie is in
> outline: the brightness is beyond him. He watches from the edge,
> and we watch from an edge even farther behind him. Yet because
> we see the Tramp from slightly below eye level, there is something
> strong—almost heroic—in his pathos, and, simultaneously, there is
> something comic in his silhouette. It is the classic, quintessential
> Chaplin shot.

Charlie is looking, fascinated, at the dance hall girl. Georgia turns,
sees an acquaintance also named Charlie standing next to our
Charlie. Georgia says, "Charlie!" smiles, and advances to meet her
friend. Our Charlie, happily incredulous, smiles but she walks past
him to her friend.

Enjoying a drink lifted from the tray of a passing waiter, Charlie sees Georgia's torn photograph and picks it up admiringly. He
is brought to high euphoria when Georgia, told by Jack, "Me and
you are going to dance," shows her contempt for him by picking
out the sorriest-looking patron of the hall as partner. As she and
Charlie dance, his pants begin to fall down and not even his indis-
pensable cane can hold them up. He uses a rope on a nearby table
as a belt, not seeing that it is a rude leash for a giant dog. The dog
spurts away to chase a cat and Charlie's dance comes to a disastrous end. He crashes to the floor and borrows a knife to free himself. To further anger Jack, Georgia gives Charlie a rose, and Jack
is stung into confronting Charlie. Charlie tries to kick his way out
of trouble but Jack offers his hand and Charlie is fooled. Jack
pulls Charlie's derby over his eyes; Charlie accidentally hits a post,
knocking a large clock down on Jack, who falls heavily. Charlie is
delighted; he hadn't known his own strength.

Close to the dance hall is the cabin of portly Hank Curtis

(Henry Bergman). Walking by, Charlie peeks in to see a pot of beans bubbling merrily on the fire. Charlie lies down in the snow, assuming the rigidity of one frozen, just before Hank comes out. Hank hauls him into the cabin to thaw, which Charlie does hungrily. Later, Hank leaves to prospect, Charlie promising to take good care of the little home and feed Hank's mule. Meanwhile, Big Jim has come to town, recovered, but still unable to remember the gold mine's location.

Georgia and three of her fellow dance hall girls are out for a romping snow fight and Charlie, opening the cabin door to watch them, gets a face full of snow. Excitedly he invites them inside and as he goes out for firewood Georgia accidentally discovers her torn photograph under his pillow. The girls laugh at this, but laugh, Chaplin's voice-over says, "perhaps in order to hide their pity." On return Georgia politely hopes he will ask them all again, and when he asks her if she means it, she says they will come for New Year's Eve dinner. The girls go out, barely able to suppress their laughter; Charlie leaps into exuberant gymnastics, swinging from a roof beam and throwing a pillow ecstatically until it breaks into white patches of pure joy. Georgia, forgetting her gloves, returns to find Charlie, deeply embarrassed by the feathers, now still, scattered on the floor.

Needing money for the dinner, Charlie goes out to shovel snow, piling it on the sidewalk of his customer's neighbor, then approaching the neighbor for a removal job.

New Year's Eve. Charlie has made the barren cabin a festive delight with an elegantly cut newspaper serving as a tablecloth, pretty party favors and place cards guarding each plate; there is a plump roasting chicken in the oven. A noise at the door, and Charlie opens it in high anticipation—only to discover Hank's unfed mule, marching in to eat the favors before being chased away. Charlie waits. And waits.

The scene dissolves to the dinner party at its height. The girls all open the little favors, exclaiming happily over each, and they call on Charlie for a speech. He stammers that he cannot do that but he will do a dance—a dance of the rolls. He sticks two forks into rolls, then bringing his head forward over them until he seems to be a Mardi Gras grotesque—giant head and tiny stick legs wearing plump sabots—his fingers manipulate an enchanting dance. As the legs skitter about (the Chaplin music for the sound version is an exuberant music hall dance chorus), Charlie's face reflects the legs' vital, high-kicking sauciness. The legs not only do cancan and Rockette kicks but jump sideways, do the splits, slide and "shuffle off" to side stage, returning for the encore bow. The girls are delighted. Georgia is so enraptured she kisses Charlie and he slides to the floor in ecstatic swoon.

The scene dissolves again, and sadly we see Charlie asleep at the gaily bedecked, untouched table. The dream has ended and it is almost midnight. Back at the dance hall Jack and Georgia are warmly companionable, although she has a faint memory of a forgotten promise. She stands on the bar and shoots off a pair of revolvers to announce midnight. The guns arouse Charlie to the pain of that forgotten promise.[2] After all in the saloon sing "Auld Lang Syne" a vigorous reel is danced—and Georgia suddenly remembers. "Let's go up and visit the Little Fellow!" she says. (On the voice-over commentary, Chaplin usually refers to Charlie as the Little Fellow.) With Jack and the girls she goes to the cabin, and her heart goes out to Charlie as she sees the party decorations. Jack's persistence in demanding attention for himself causes her to slap him.

The Recorder's Office. Big Jim is trying to map his fabulous gold claim for the officials but he cannot remember the location. The officials are convinced of his lunacy. All Jim can recall is that it was "near the cabin." Dejected, Jim goes out into the street, not seeing an equally unseeing Charlie hurrying by.

That night Charlie visits the saloon looking for his love and is gladdened by a note the bartender gives him. In it Georgia apologizes and asks for the chance to see him again, and explain. Charlie's happiness is compounded by another—the appearance of Jim in the hall. Jim is ecstatic at seeing his old friend. He tells Charlie that if he can take him to the old cabin Charlie will be a million-

[2] Wee Georgie Wood, prominent British music hall artiste, knew Chaplin as a boy actor. Wood recalls an incident in Oldham when Chaplin invited a number of Wood's company, playing at a rival theatre, to after-performance tea. Chaplin went to much trouble but no one appeared. Their manager had forbidden the young people to travel across town at that time of night. No one troubled to inform the host. Chaplin clearly remembered the incident.

aire in less than a month. Charlie finds Georgia in the hall and says he will be back.

After an exhausting trek, Charlie and Jim find the cabin and the well-provisioned pair settle in to rest, Charlie doing so by devoted attention to Jim's capacious liquor flask. Charlie carries in a huge side of beef, complaining that it is a mighty heavy lamb chop. Rest, and sleep, planning to find the gold mountain in the morning. During the night a great storm comes up, moving the cabin to the very edge of a precipitous cliff. Almost half the cabin projects out over an abyss. Charlie wakes with a horrendous hangover. He cannot see out of the frosted window. As he walks about the cabin it veers and tips but Charlie is not surprised. Simply a liver attack, he thinks. Jim asks if he feels the rocking but Charlie assures him it is just stomach trouble after last night's very full supper. The cabin continues to teeter in every direction Charlie walks. Jim gets up and walks about in opposite directions from Charlie, unknowingly counterbalancing his friend's movements. The floor squeaks and Jim suggests they walk to the other side of the room to see how far it will go over. It veers.

Jim tells Charlie not to get excited, not to move, not to breathe. There is a tremor. Jim accuses Charlie of breathing. Claiming that something must be missing underneath, Charlie after some effort opens the door, steps out—to find that the earth has disappeared. He swings out over the abyss, hanging onto the door, kicking the air frantically to swing the door back to the cabin. This done, Jim hauls him in and Charlie faints on the floor.

The cabin is now at almost a forty-five-degree angle, dangling over the vast ice canyon. Jim and Charlie are desperately hugging the floor. The cabin tips further over the edge; the only thing that keeps it from crashing down far below is a rope, tied to the cabin, that is caught between two rocks on the landward side. Now stretched out on the floor at the forty-five-degree angle, Charlie gets a bad case of hiccups. The cabin shivers. Charlie scrambles up over Jim in an attempt to reach the other door, but he slips, slides down the slope right out the open door over the canyon, and is caught just in time by Jim's ham fist on his collar. Charlie is hauled back inside.

Jim directs Charlie to give him a lift up the slanted floor by cupping his hands as stirrups; Jim crawls up this way and attains the precious opening on land side but the door swings in toward him and hits his head. He lets go and slides down the incline out the chasm door only to be quickly grabbed and hauled back by the Little Fellow. Jim climbs up again to the landward door, getting through it at just the moment when the audience's nerves insist. Jim clambers to the ground and finds there the marker for his gold mine. He rejoices, temporarily forgetting Charlie, who calls out plaintively. Jim drops a rope to him, Charlie walks up the steep floor and jumps clear of the cabin. At that second the cabin tips down, the securing rope broken, and speeds with a crashing roar into the valley far below. Charlie reels about and falls beside the claim marker as Jim shouts to the heavens that now they will be rich.

Beyond the dreams of avarice. Aboard a steamer going back to the States, attired in expensive bearskin coats, they are figures of considerable affluence until Charlie forgets his new status and dives for a fat cigar butt. Jim gently reprimands him, offering him a Havana from a gold case. Reporters besiege them for a story and photographs. But Charlie feels Georgia's loss keenly; he still treasures her photograph. Georgia, it happens, is on the same ship, down on the steerage deck, where she overhears an officer directing a search for a stowaway.

In response to a reporter's request for his rags-to-riches story, Charlie agrees to resume his old clothing for photographs. Posing on top deck, he steps back at the photographer's direction and falls into a coil of rope near Georgia in the steerage. "You!" she says. "I thought I'd never see you again!" The officer finds Charlie and is about to charge him as the runaway when Georgia intervenes, saying she will pay Charlie's fare. The reporter and the captain come down and the officer identifies Charlie as Big Jim's partner, "the multimillionaire." The reporter asks who Georgia is, Charlie whispers in his ear, and the reporter is impressed. He congratulates Charlie, assuring him that this will make a great story because it has a happy ending. "And so it was," Chaplin's voice affirms on the sound track. "A happy ending!"

Some critics have questioned the need for that happy ending, calling it a distortion of reality. If one is searching for reality in

The Gold Rush, consider this: Charlie got his millions, as any number of people did on the Klondike fields, by accident. He got his millions—and a prostitute. As Stanley Kauffmann says, what else can she be? What are the odds on this girl bringing him happiness? The pathos of Charlie's position in life persists beyond the "happy" ending. Or looking at it in full confidence that it *is* a happy ending, one might look at the laws of probability so utterly defied in another great work of art—in the person of Wilkins Micawber, Esquire, for whom something rather splendid did turn up—and no one has much objected to that. Best perhaps just to let us savor the happy ending of *The Gold Rush*. It may not *be* right but it emphatically *feels* right.

Like most great artifacts, *The Gold Rush* was constructed largely at the expense of great sweat. Chaplin's most frequently repeated direction in this and most of his films was "Let's do it again." Eddie Sutherland remembers the constant repetition and Chaplin's assurance that the shot just finished could be done better. He remembers, too, Chaplin's tremendous patience.

At times Chaplin was accused of stealing ideas from others at the studio but Sutherland calls this unfounded. He instances the teetering of the cabin over the abyss, an idea he suggested after Chaplin first thought of the storm blowing the cabin away from the foundations. Chaplin rejected Sutherland's teetering gag as too obvious. Days later Chaplin came to him excitedly and said he had found a climax for the cabin-wind-blowing gag: it comes to the edge of a cliff and teeters. Chaplin did not steal the idea, Sutherland said. "I planted it in his mind. He probably didn't hear it consciously. But subconsciously it stuck there."

The Gold Rush gives us Charlie for the first time in sustained apex, Charlie at full gamut. We are here with him alone enough and often enough to discover an elemental truth about our relationship with him. That simple truth is experienced by almost everyone who sees the film, by almost everyone who knows Charlie through constant viewing of his lesser works too. We marvel at him, relish him on the first level of sheer comedic joy. But the underlay of our enjoyment is ultimately more satisfying. Our empathy as we watch him is total because this commonplace-looking fellow is us. Us—in the finest of our daydreams.

Charlie, says Stanley Kauffmann, in the main "compensates for the shortcomings, social and physical, of our lives and beings. In his movement and in his code, even in his cunning, he is what we feel we ought to be."

15. Pros and non-pros on the tennis court. Groucho Marx and partner Ellsworth Vines met Chaplin and his partner, Fred Perry, 1937. Chaplin and Perry won, 6–1, 9–7. (Wide World Photos Inc.)

16. Supervising the opening shot of *The Gold Rush*, Truckee, California. Rollie Totheroh behind the camera, 1925.

17. Opening shot, *The Gold Rush*.

18. With Mack Swain in the teetering cabin, *The Gold Rush*.

19. Virginia Cherrill and Charlie with elaborate boutonniere, *City Lights*, 1931.

20. Work-crazed Charlie, *Modern Times*, 1936.

21.   Charlie's daydream of a bountiful life in suburbia includes Paulette Goddard as helpmeet, *Modern Times*.

22.   Chaplin directing the loading of the big gun, *The Great Dictator*, 1940.

23. Douglas Fairbanks visits Reginald Gardiner and Chaplin on *The Great Dictator* set.

24. Henry Bergman, Alf Reeves, and Rollie Totheroh with the bound scripts for the fourteen Chaplin films from A *Dog's Life* through *The Great Dictator*, 1940.

25. Chaplin, Oona O'Neill, and Charles Boyer visit the Stork Club.

26. In distinctly unuxorious mood, contemplating the temporarily subdued Martha Raye, *Monsieur Verdoux*, 1947.

27. Buster Keaton and Chaplin as superannuated vaudevillians on the comeback trail, *Limelight*, 1952.

28. As King Shahdov, between Joan Ingram and Dawn Addams, *A King in New
York*, 1957.

29. Accepting his special Academy Award "Oscar," Hollywood, 1972.

13
CARRY ON

With a pregnant wife, there was little for Chaplin to do about his forced marital situation but hope. He did not know for what: it could hardly get worse. The marriage was doomed because two more different personalities could not have been joined together under more trying circumstances. Lita came to believe this in time, using the word "ridiculous" to characterize the union.

Despairing of what he had done to himself, Chaplin would leave the Beverly Hills mansion for weeks at a time. Their first Christmas together he got weavingly drunk, something no one who knew him had ever seen before. It was the most convincing proof of his desperate unhappiness.

Sydney Chaplin was to some degree able to serve as intermediary between his brother and sister-in-law. Sydney told Lita that, among other things, Chaplin was worried about the health of the coming baby. For some reason Chaplin had taken on himself the blame for his infant son's death in 1919 and was tremendously apprehensive about the current pregnancy. Lita asked Sydney why her husband had not confided in her about it. Sydney explained that this was always Charlie's way. He was a hard man to live with, Sydney told her, but most "of Charlie's instincts are good. It's just that he doesn't understand himself very well."

Lita for her part tried to understand him but it was extraordinarily difficult not only because of her age but because beneath all the obvious disharmony was her jealousy. She was in love with her husband and it galled her immeasurably when he vanished

from home, supposedly to work and sleep at the studio. She
thought of him constantly in the midst of a grimy amour somewhere. Actually he was usually too busy for these love games, according to Sydney.

When *The Gold Rush* premiered in New York on August 16,
1925, at the Strand Theatre, Chaplin came and gave a short
speech of thanks for the rousing reception it received. The critics
and public alike gave it the highest praise. Edmund Wilson spoke
of Charlie as a "mythical hero, now a figure of poetry, now a type
out of the funny papers." St. John Ervine, speaking for most English critics and certainly for the British public, observed in *The
Living Age* that Chaplin's pathos in the film did not dissolve the
audience in tears; it was not so cheap a pathos. It was instead the
pathos "that suddenly seizes the mind and alters its direction,
compelling those who are bent on cruelty to be as bent on kindli-
ness. . . . *The Gold Rush* is the funniest film I have ever seen. It
is probably the funniest film that anyone has ever seen."

Time has verified that opinion. *The Gold Rush* decades later
won from the International Film Jury the rating of second
greatest film of all time, *Potemkin* just edging it out. Put another
way, *The Gold Rush* is probably the best comedy film of all time.
Chaplin could now ignore the plea of critics like Stark Young,
who said prior to *The Gold Rush* that the tramp, as one of the
great clowns of all time, was a finished creation, unable to touch
the more profound life themes. *The Gold Rush*, if it did nothing
else, proved that Charlie had a soul.

During the making of *The Gold Rush*, Chaplin met Marion
Davies. Chaplin, who like many had been bored by the all-out
publicity campaigns William Randolph Hearst had begun for his
mistress, had already seen a Davies film, *When Knighthood Was
in Flower*. He was impressed, as many eventually were who saw a
Davies film. She was not only pretty but projected a remarkably
radiant and perky charm. She was funny, too. In his autobiography Chaplin speaks of the great friendship that began between them. Lita Grey Chaplin is unambiguous in saying that
the friendship was actually an off-and-on love affair with little emphasis on love. "Marion Davies' sometime boy friend" is Lita's description of her husband.

Whether or not this is true, Marion Davies and William Randolph Hearst became Chaplin's close and lasting friends. Of all the people Chaplin met in his life, Hearst was unequivocally the personality he found most memorable. Chaplin was intrigued by the man's extraordinarily complex nature—the shrewd strength, the viciousness combined with kindness and geniality, the vast wealth and the compelling unaffectedness. Hearst for his part thought Chaplin the most talented man he knew.

Chaplin spent much time at San Simeon with Hearst and Marion; he visited them frequently at the Davies home in Beverly Hills. He was also reputedly a guest on the Hearst yacht, *Oneida*, the third week of November 1924 when the prominent producer, Thomas H. Ince, was supposedly murdered. Much mystery has been attached to this rather prosaic event, prosaic, that is, to all the participants save Mr. Ince. Gossip through the years has inflated Ince's natural death to the dimension of a major scandal. The persistent story is that Hearst caught Chaplin and Marion *in flagrante delicto* and in chasing his erstwhile friend around the deck, Hearst accidentally gunned down Ince. Hearst, the surmise runs, then made great payoffs to maintain secrecy, the largest of these a commitment to Louella Parsons that she become a queen bee of the Hearst empire.

The facts are unremarkable. Chaplin was not aboard. Louella Parsons was in New York. Ince, who suffered from both stomach ulcers and heart trouble, was under doctor's orders not to drink alcohol or eat anything that might irritate his stomach. He did both, drinking champagne lavishly in response to birthday toasts directed to him and munching salted almonds, a particular passion of his. He paid heavily for these excesses, vomiting incessantly during the night. Ince was removed from the *Oneida* at San Diego early next morning. Mrs. Ince met the boat and took him to their Beverly Hills home where the family doctor diagnosed gastric upset and a heart attack. Ince died a day later.

Chaplin has unwittingly contributed to the confusion surrounding the Ince affair by stating in his autobiography that he, Hearst, and Marion went to see Ince two weeks after the attack, the stricken man telling them he would soon be well. But Ince died the day after being removed from the *Oneida* and Chaplin was photographed by newsmen at Ince's funeral three days after the incident. Chaplin's statement in the autobiography is typical of

his vagueness on chronology there. Likely Chaplin confuses this
with a time when he, Hearst, and Marion visited Ince some weeks
before when the producer had also been ill.

In addition to Hearst and Marion, Chaplin spent his time away
from Lita with his old chum, Doug Fairbanks, at Pickfair. The
Chaplin relationship with Mary Pickford was always a trifle ambiguous. They liked each other but both were intense people,
greatly interested in money and especially the ways to make it and
keep it. Prickly in temperament, they were to have quarrels over
business matters within the United Artists framework. Chaplin
was amazed and, to use his word, "saddened" at Mary's ability to
grasp and use the jargon of corporate finance. In her autobiography, Mary described Chaplin as, "That obstinate, suspicious,
egocentric, maddening, and lovable genius of a problem child."

When Colleen Moore signed as a feature player for First National it was close to the time Chaplin left the organization. Although unhappy with the First National management, Chaplin
was intrigued by the company's widely publicized acquisition in
1924 of Giovanni Papini's best-selling *Life of Christ*. First National proposed to film the book in 1925 with an awesome budget.
Chaplin invited Colleen and several First National bigwigs to
lunch at his studio. He asked Robert Leiber, president of First
National, if it was true the company had bought the Papini book.
Leiber admitted it, and Chaplin said urgently, "I want to play
the role of Jesus."

Everyone was stunned. "I'm a logical choice," said Chaplin. "I
look the part, I'm a Jew, and I'm a comedian." He amplified that
by saying that good comedy and good tragedy were a hairline
apart. "And I'm an atheist, so I'd be able to look at the character
objectively. Who else could do that?" His auditors were still in
mild shock when Chaplin reached his arms up above his head,
clenched his fists, and shouted, "There is no God! If there is one,
I dare Him to strike me dead!"[1] The visitors sat congealed. These
Robert Ingersoll histrionics, unlike the 1921 episode at Edward
Knoblock's rooms in London, were seriously consummated.

[1] In time Chaplin's atheism seems to have softened to a hopeful agnosticism.
In his autobiography he speaks of the need to live by faith, and the King
James version of the Bible became a bedside book in his later years.

During the return drive from the studio, one of the men said, "He's the greatest actor alive, and he'd give a historical performance, but who of you would have the nerve to put in lights on a theatre marquee: Charlic Chaplin in *The Life of Christ?*" Mr. Leiber, whose offices were in the Midwest, said, "It would be the greatest religious picture ever made, but I'd be run out of Indianapolis."

Jim Tully and other close Chaplin associates left his employ during or after *The Gold Rush*. Harry d'Arrast, Monta Bell, Eddie Sutherland, and Chuck Riesner simply went on to greater opportunities elsewhere. Tully quit, he was the first to admit, because of the unconscious clashing of two strong egos, and he faulted himself primarily. He and Chaplin had been particularly close, Tully felt, because they had both come from the lower depths of society and were innately suspicious of mankind. Above all, they were both unpredictable eccentrics, according to Harry d'Arrast. D'Arrast's favorite story of Chaplin's eccentricity was of a story conference when Chaplin kept slapping at a fly buzzing around his head. Calling for a swatter, he swung several times but missed. Then the offender settled down before him and Chaplin lifted the swatter for the death blow. Suddenly he paused, looked carefully at the fly, and lowered the swatter. "Why didn't you swat it?" he was asked. Shrugging typically, Chaplin said, "It wasn't the same fly."

Chaplin's moodiness under the pressures of his unhappy marriage increased, growing to the point where he even shouted at his own brother. Trying to discourage any publicity about the extent of his youthful poverty, Chaplin was outraged at an interview Sydney gave saying that at times in their boyhood he and Charlie actually had to eat from garbage pails. Chaplin raged at Sydney for such a slur on the family name.

One tension of the Chaplin marriage was lifted by the birth of a boy on May 5, 1925. This is the date given by Lita Grey Chaplin in her autobiography, claiming that the birth date of June 28, 1925, on Charles Chaplin, Jr.'s birth certificate was there because of Chaplin's insistence that fathering a six months' baby would end his career. Lita says the attending physician argued with Chaplin that the correct date must be put on the certificate—but was persuaded to alter it for the sum of $25,000. Lita was secluded in a

160

specially rented house for the baby's birth and on June 28 Chaplin announced the birth of his son. Charles Chaplin, Jr., was a name Chaplin disliked. He predicted, quite accurately, that the name would be a burden to the boy, but Lita prevailed. In her memoirs she says that, following Charlie, Jr.'s birth, she was consumed by a physical desire for her husband which was unlike anything she had ever experienced. She sought him out and shared his bed frequently. For three months they were united, quite satisfactorily united, physically. In August 1926, Lita became pregnant again, and it was because of this, she said, that the Chaplin marriage was doomed. He felt trapped and accused his wife of having deliberately engineered the entrapment. Sydney Earle Chaplin was born on March 30, 1926, five weeks prematurely. Like his brother, he was a healthy and handsome boy, and Chaplin grew to love them very much, a love that grew through the years.

The underlying discord between the Chaplins climaxed one evening when, coming home very late from the studio, he went to bed and was aroused a few hours later by the arrival of Lita and noisy guests. Lita, thinking that Chaplin had planned to sleep over at the studio, was unaware of his presence. Chaplin came to the head of the stairs and shouted down to her that the guests must leave at once, adding, "What do you think this is, a whorehouse?" The guests were hustled out.

Toward the end of November 1926, Lita and Chaplin were separated. She retained her lawyer uncle, Edwin T. McMurray, to represent her in a divorce suit filed January 10, 1927. In later years she regretted it, coming to realize that expedience was her uncle's chief tactic: "I was still very young . . . but I can't use that as an excuse. I must have had some awareness that they were going to work to hurt my husband, and I didn't stop them." They "hurt" him in just about every sense of the word. The fifty-two-page document filed by McMurray at the county clerk's office was full of what were for the time highly scandalous allegations. Because it was a public document, it was available for anyone's scrutiny and the next day a line of would-be readers formed in the clerk's office leading down out of the building and around the block. Someone obtained access long enough for a copy to be made and by January 12 mimeographed copies of the entire document were being hawked for sale on Los Angeles streets. Thousands were sold.

In legal but clear phraseology, the complaint variously accused Chaplin of stinginess, absence from home, disbelief in marriage, suggesting to his wife that she kill herself, refusal to meet her friends and guests, spying, changing of house locks, asking her to have an abortion, and other fairly mild transgressions. But the juiciest part of the charges were two other items: first, that Chaplin really loved "a certain prominent moving picture actress," and, second, that Chaplin had urged his wife to submit to and perform "acts" for the gratification of Chaplin's "degenerate sexual desires, as to be too revolting, indecent and immoral to set forth in this complaint . . . the act of sex perversion defined by Section 288a of the Penal Code of California."

The unnamed movie star was quickly conjectured to be every actress in the Hollywood pantheon but Mary Pickford. Section 288a was assiduously researched by numerous amateur law scholars who found the section proscribed oral sex and authorized a prison sentence for those convicted under the specification of up to fifteen years. At the time, Section 288a forbade the participation of "any person" in an act of oral sex, causing one legal scholar of the day to guess that under that provision quite a few thousand perfectly respectable married folk in California were liable to fifteen years in the pokey. (Section 288a has only recently been revised, eliminating oral sex as a crime except when perpetrated on certain minors or by force.)

Chaplin filed a cross complaint on June 2, 1927, denying all of Lita's charges and accusing her of "unwomanly, unseemly" conduct.

It was a time when troubles came not single spies for Chaplin. Lita's lawyers were demanding that the Chaplin community property (which they estimated to be more than $16 million) be restrained from sale, and the Internal Revenue Service filed against Chaplin for failure to pay $1,133,000 in back taxes. To top this, Chaplin's lawyers, ignoring a court order that Lita be paid temporary alimony of $3000 a month, made the mistake of offering her a permanent income of $25 a week. Lita's lawyer uncle announced this to the press with thundering eloquence and women's clubs across the country rose in shocked indignation, a number of them offering to contribute to the upkeep of the Chaplin children. The beleaguered Chaplin, who had fled to New York with his butler, Kono, hastily ordered the $3000 alimony sent to Lita at once.

It was too late, however, to prevent a wave of deep revulsion against Chaplin from sweeping the country. Not only women's clubs but editorial writers everywhere denounced Chaplin for allowing his children "to go without milk." The public outcry against him was so strong that H. L. Mencken, who admitted to being no Chaplin fan, wrote, "The very morons who worshipped Charlie Chaplin six weeks ago now prepare to dance around the stake while he is burned."

Professionally Chaplin was having his troubles too. Before the divorce suit he had begun work on *The Circus,* now hastily put into abeyance at great expense. He was worried about Edna Purviance as well. Unhappy that *A Woman of Paris* had not helped her reputation, he wrote a scenario for her, *The Sea Gull* (or *A Woman of the Sea*) and assigned Josef von Sternberg to direct. A tale of love in a Monterey village, it was according to John Grierson, who saw it being made, a "strangely beautiful and empty affair—possibly the most beautiful I have ever seen—of net patterns, sea patterns and hair in the wind. When a director dies, he becomes a photographer." Von Sternberg at this point in his career may not have been unwilling to accept the designation. Making the film was agony. He said of *The Sea Gull* and of Edna:

> One of the stars consigned to my care in a film that never saw the light of day was the most willing woman that ever faced my camera. But unfortunately, when the camera turned, her face disintegrated, her eyes became helpless, and her body trembled like the leaf of an aspen. The only remedy for this condition was alcohol, which had caused it, and this was unsuitable. I called for a pair of kettledrums, and the timpani distracted her long enough for her to play her part. It was her last film and almost my last.

Chaplin saw the completed film and ordered it burned.

As Lita's suit approached something of a standoff, with Chaplin refusing to settle out of court, Lita's uncle decided drastic action was the next best strategy. She had told her uncle of a scene between Chaplin and herself in which he boasted of adultery with Edna, Merna Kennedy, and Marion Davies among others. McMurray convinced Lita that going to Marion and threatening to involve her in the suit was the only way to resolve it. Presumably Marion got the word quickly to Chaplin because he shortly announced his willingness to settle. These events, as recounted by Lita, may be true but, again, Chaplin's lack of comment on the matter leaves his side of the story untold.

The divorce was granted on August 22, 1927, with a property settlement for Lita of $650,000 together with a $200,000 trust fund for Charlie, Jr., and young Sydney. Chaplin also paid court costs and legal fees, $950,000, a sum exclusive of his own attorney's fees. Some newspapers titled Lita's victory *The Second Gold Rush*.

This was the first of several periods in Chaplin's life when tearingly adverse public notice of him surfaced in striking contrast to the adulatory press of previous years. There was, it seemed, no middle ground. As the years went on, Chaplin was either ludicrously overpraised or absurdly excoriated. As in most things, the truth was somewhere in between. Chaplin was not beyond criticism as an artist; neither was he an old lecher bent on rending society's fabric.

In his personal life, Chaplin continued his pattern of charming and astonishing his friends. Piquant Louise Brooks, still a Ziegfeld girl and not yet a film star, was briefly close to Chaplin during the period when he visited New York for the opening of *The Gold Rush*. She tells of their numerous evenings on the town; of a time when he walked apprehensively down Fifth Avenue looking back occasionally, insisting that Hearst was having him shadowed; of his incredibly astute flights of mimicry among his friends. He danced as Isadora Duncan in a trailing veil of toilet paper, did John Barrymore picking his nose during a somber Hamlet soliloquy, swished ludicrously across the room in a Follies girl walk— which Louise realized she must abandon forthwith. It was for her an enchanting time and decades later, as she read his autobiography, she wondered if his failure to mention those eventful weeks except perfunctorily was evidence either of her dullness or of some bitter memory of the time. But no, Louise Brooks decided. One always faces an intrinsic difficulty in defining the Chaplin personality: "I wondered . . . realizing how hopeless it was to ponder the motives of a faun."

14
THE CIRCUS

In the traumatic days of the divorce suit, Chaplin was working—
or trying to work—on an idea that had long intrigued him, Pa-
gliacci in a modern circus setting. When he began the first scenes
of *The Circus* he had little reason to imagine that his personal life
would become Pagliaccian with a vengeance. He began the film
with confidence. His leading lady (Lita's old girl friend, Merna
Kennedy), although no Georgia Hale, looked pretty enough and
wore her circus costumes charmingly. She was not called on to do
much more in the film. The script Chaplin was able to fashion
with the help of a friend, Harry Crocker, witty newspaper columnist and former Hearst aide.

Hearst was much on Chaplin's mind as production on *The Circus* began. Rollie Totheroh, who knew more about what went on
at the Chaplin studio than anyone, is emphatic in saying that
word of the Chaplin-Davies dalliance finally reached Hearst, who
came roaring down to see Chaplin. Chaplin hid in a studio attic
while *The Circus* crew kicked footballs around the yard. Lawyers
came to talk secretly while Hearst walked angrily up and down
outside the dressing rooms. Chaplin fled briefly to New York
where his lawyer advised him to settle with Lita and Chaplin returned to Los Angeles.

The day he decided to take his lawyer's advice and give in to
Lita's demands was a particularly difficult one on *The Circus* set.
The combined mental and physical anguish within the span of a
day and a night turned Chaplin's pepper-and-salt hair completely

white. Henry Bergman, the first to see him at the studio the morning after it happened, thought at first Chaplin was wearing a wig. "I was shocked, profoundly shocked," Bergman said. "My God, if ever anybody wanted proof of what Charlie had been through, there it was."

During these agonizing times Chaplin was faced with a tremendous task he had set for himself—making a comedy as good as *The Gold Rush*. This was inevitably foredoomed—one can't do better than best—but *The Circus* is a good film notwithstanding and, considering the conditions under which it was made, a marvel.

A fourth-rate circus, steadily losing patronage, is displaying its bedraggled wares: some tired and pathetic clowns and an inexperienced young bareback rider (Merna Kennedy) who is beaten by her stepfather and boss of the circus (Allan Garcia) for her performing failures. He denies Merna supper as added penalty.

Charlie comes as part of the crowd before the funhouse. A pickpocket, lifting a wallet and watch from an old man and realizing that he is suspected, stuffs both articles into the pockets of the unsuspecting Charlie. At a nearby stand Charlie, desperate for food, sees a little child leaning over his father's shoulder, biting contentedly into a hot dog. Charlie charms the little one into giving him several bites as the father, oblivious, chats with a friend. Charlie even manages to add a touch of mustard before taking another bite. The pickpocket returns and as he is trying to regain his loot a policeman nabs him with his hand in Charlie's pocket. The wallet is "returned" to Charlie, who ecstatically orders a dozen hot dogs. He is about to enjoy them when the pickpocket's victim spots his watch on Charlie. A cop now chases the pickpocket, another cop chases Charlie, and as the miscreant and the innocent spurt along side by side, Charlie tips his derby to the thief.

Charlie escapes into the hall of mirrors at the funhouse where he collides with his image several times, insistently tipping his hat politely to himself. He is next confronted by many images of the crook, who has entered to demand the stolen goods. Charlie, now pursued by a cop, flees to the outside of a Noah's Ark funhouse where he fools his pursuer by assuming the rigid posture of one of the wooden figures in front.

He is discovered and runs away straight through some tents into center ring of the circus during performance. There his inadvertently comic actions as part of the magic act (*he* appears in the magician's box instead of the Vanishing Lady) are wildly applauded. Charlie runs out of the tent directly into the pickpocket and the cop, and gladly surrenders the loot. The circus audience meanwhile is vociferous in its demands for Charlie, the best of all the clowns they've seen. The boss, finding Charlie asleep in a chariot, wants him to come back in the morning to audition.

Next day, still on the lot, Charlie is preparing to cook an egg over a rude fire when the starving Merna, not seeing him, snatches a bread crust from the ground and eats. Charlie chides her gently and in sharing his little meal warns her not to eat fast lest she hiccup. She hiccups at once and, in perfect sympathetic response, Charlie gets such a bad case of them that she has to finish the egg alone.

At his audition, among the routines Charlie is asked to do is a barbershop gag in which clowns over-lather a customer with gobs of white suds. Trying it, Charlie is so bespattered he cannot see and lathers the boss thoroughly. He is fired, but the head property man, dismayed by lack of help, hires Charlie as assistant.

Handed a pile of dishes, Charlie is going about his duties when an unsocial donkey chases him into the ring during performance and Charlie crashes spectacularly into the plates, falling into a lady's lap, thence into a barrel. The audience roars. Unaware of it, Charlie is the hit of the show. The boss sends him out every evening with the dishes, followed by the mule—and Charlie's disastrous antics soon make him the audience's favorite. He has no idea of this.

The boss makes Charlie a janitor and stagehand's assistant. Charlie, nothing loath, does his work so thoroughly that he even wipes off goldfish in a bowl, and when told to blow a large golfball-size pill down a horse's throat, gathers breath only to have the horse blow first, shooting the pill deep inside Charlie. Charlie's enemy, the donkey, chases him into the lion's cage, where he is accidentally locked in.

Fortunately the lion is snoozing and Charlie is in a bad way trying to get out quietly when Merna happens by, sees him—and faints. Charlie throws a pail of water on her to no avail, the lion wakes up, walks over to Charlie and, finding him a bore, lies down again. When Merna wakes up to let him out, Charlie advances in heroic pose to the lion, whose loud roar of disdain sends Charlie flying out of the cage high up a pole. Charlie descends, flapping his hands like wings, to assure Merna that the pole trip was just a full-fashioned bird imitation.

The head property man catches Charlie relaxing and arse-kicks him for malfeasance of duty, thus bringing up the horse pill. Hotly Merna tells Charlie that he need not take this, indeed he is the real hit of the circus. Overhearing, the boss is about to beat her when Charlie, now in confident control, says he will quit if she is touched. Charlie also demands and gets a raise. He becomes the feature attraction with a dressing room next to Merna's, and one night when he hears a fortuneteller assure the girl of marriage with "a dark handsome man who is near you now," Charlie is joyous.

The dark man is actually a new act, Rex the tightrope walker (Harry Crocker), and Merna falls in love with him. Charlie buys an engagement ring but, overhearing Merna speak of her love for Rex, Charlie's heart is broken. Yet, bravely, he continues to go out every show and get huge laughs. For a time. Sadness begins to alter his work, the laughs diminish. Jealously he begins to practice tightrope walking—on the ground. When Rex is suddenly indisposed, Charlie is called on to substitute for his rival, but Charlie secretly bribes a prop man to secure him safely with wire and halter. Now supremely confident, Charlie goes up to the high wire despite Merna's pleas that he stay below. He does death-defying stunts with cool and graceful recklessness. Below, the prop man tries to warn him that the halter has come loose but Charlie goes on blithely—until he sees the halter dangling above him.

Mid-walk on the wire, his fears are now compounded by three escaped monkeys who swarm over him and rip off his pants. Charlie falls but catches the wire, easing himself to a high platform where he mounts a wire-riding bicycle and zooms down, missing the catch below, roaring into a shop across the street. He returns, staggering, for his bow. Remonstrating when his boss is vicious to Merna again, Charlie is fired.

Charlie resumes his vagabondage but Merna follows him, saying she has run away from the circus. Charlie returns her to Rex, gives him the ring he bought for Merna, and sees them safely married in a rural church. When they return to the circus Rex forestalls the boss's bullying of Merna by saying she is his wife. The boss perforce makes up with the couple but he will not shake Charlie's hand. The newlyweds say they will not perform unless Charlie is rehired. The boss relents. Rex and Merna ask Charlie into their wagon for a nuptial party but he shoos them inside.

The circus leaves, and Charlie in the empty ring watches the wagons on the go. Finally alone, he sits on a box in the deserted circle. At his foot he finds a torn piece of tissue paper on which is printed a star. It is a scrap from the hoop through which Merna jumps every performance. Charlie crumples it up, kicks it away with his heel, and walks spiritedly down the road.

The Circus still engrosses, particularly with a recent sound track of Chaplin-composed music, including a simple little song, "Swing, Little Girl" sung by Chaplin himself. The film's critical reception in 1928 was generally good, most of the reviewers understanding that this was not *The Gold Rush*. Stark Young was a bit disturbed by the "conscious and elaborate pathos" of the film's last shot but, like Robert Sherwood, who found no contrived pathos at all, he agreed that it was very funny. And so it is, but under the burden of one major implausibility—the sequences in which Charlie is sent nightly into the ring followed by the mule. Night after night he does this and arouses noisy hilarity. A cluck (Webster's: "a dull or stupid person") could do this but the mature Charlie is no cluck. One may speak of the willing suspension of disbelief, and this is quite acceptable in the paper moon world of Mack Sennett, but not in the realm of the older Charlie to whom we give our mind as well as our heart.

The film won a special Academy Award for 1927-28, with a citation, "For his versatility and genius in writing, acting, directing and producing *The Circus*." Chaplin did not attend the banquet, the first of its kind, at the Hollywood Roosevelt Hotel on May 16, 1929, saying that he thought the entire idea of Academy Awards foolish. Yet he always kept the special Oscar in an honored position among his household gods.

In the months just before *The Circus* was filmed, Chaplin's mother had suffered several gall bladder attacks. Her doctor was optimistic because she seemed of hearty stock and was only sixty-one. She was overweight but mainly seemed in good health. Then she was stricken severely and taken to Glendale Hospital. When

Chaplin went to see her he assured her she would be well. "Perhaps," she said, squeezed his hand, and lapsed into unconsciousness. The following day while Chaplin was working on the *Circus* set, a phone call came from the hospital to say she was dead. When Chaplin entered her room her expression in death was troubled. He sat with her for a time, and when the cruel memories of their early life flooded in on him—of their afflictions and of her courage—he wept. It was an hour before he could regain composure. In his autobiography Chaplin speaks of her life as "tragic" and "wasted." Tragic doubtless, but a woman who gave a major comic artist to the world, a woman who strongly helped to shape that talent, hardly wasted her life.

Hannah Chaplin died August 28, 1928. Sydney, ill in Europe, was unable to attend the funeral. After a brief Episcopalian ceremony, she was buried in Hollywood Cemetery.

By 1929, in the fifteenth year of his film work, Chaplin the man and the artist was ripe for a searching appraisal by a major critic. He received it in an article by Waldo Frank for *Scribner's* magazine, September 1929, a deeply felt and sensitive assessment of a man most Americans had come to recognize as a major artist.

Frank summed up Chaplin as a man who both saw and felt too much, an intense loner who was yet far from being a recluse—a man unused to giving himself and one who rarely took from others. Frank saw that the London slums were in Chaplin's heart of hearts, and that his half-Gypsy mother gave him yet another world within himself, "a world of meadows and irresponsible laughter." This is a Chaplin who is so close to life that, paradoxically, he cannot give himself over to it. He loves the world, yet despises it, remaining in a curious equipoise between all the forces of the world.

As to his work, Frank found that the theme of the Chaplin film ultimately is "Chaplin himself, in relation (opposition) to the world. He journeys through it, immeasurably roused, solicited, moved—yet aloof, yet intactly alone."

This was the man and the artist to be seen vividly drawn in the most dramatic and what he finally came to consider the finest of his films—*City Lights*.

15
CITY LIGHTS

Chaplin knew instinctively that Charlie was a child of the silences, a myth who would forever destroy himself if he opened his mouth. What voice, what words, could match that exquisite, sublimely graceful gamin? Yet, as Chaplin well knew, sound film in 1930 was not only here, it was to prevail. Charlie dared not speak but how could he not speak in the sound era? Chaplin gradually came to realize that talk need not be the prime element of the talkies, and he said so in an article for the New York *Times* in which he conceived of sound "as an addition not as a substitute." There was, of course, the problem of the sound camera, which had an undeviating speed of twenty-four frames per second. Rollie Totheroh, on Chaplin's precise instructions, would at times "under-crank" the silent camera to eighteen, sixteen, or fewer frames per second to speed up screen movement for humorous purposes. The sound camera could not accommodate to this, or so it seemed at first, and in consequence a realistic tempo of movement for any Chaplin film seemed mandatory. (Chaplin would solve this problem in *Modern Times*.)

Chaplin also had a casting problem. He wanted a beautiful girl who was capable of portraying blindness with a natural charm. One Friday evening at the American Legion prize fights, his invariable weekend diversion, he met a beautiful blonde with an engaging smile. Virginia Cherrill was resting in California after a strenuous divorce suit in Chicago and her interest in Chaplin's proposal for a screen test was not strong. But she filmed well and

Chaplin said she looked blind "without being offensive." She was not inclined to work very hard, however, and Chaplin let her go, trying Georgia Hale in the role. He was then romantically interested in Georgia and had strong hopes she would do. Rollie Totheroh warned Chaplin that Georgia was simply not photographing "blind," and reluctantly Virginia Cherrill was brought back. She was now totally co-operative.

City Lights begins in a large city where a crowd has gathered for the dedication of a large statue, "Peace and Prosperity," three supremely bland figures, a seated woman and two male figures, one with sword uplifted, standing below. As the notables address the crowd, the sound track offers a mindless gabble as of a fourth-grader at his saxophone. (This is also a gentle kidding of the talk in most current talking pictures.) The statue is unveiled with great ceremony to reveal Charlie sleeping soundly in the seated figure's lap. Shocked, the dignitaries shout at him, and the Little Fellow wakes up and clambers down, impaling his pants on the raised sword. The band plays the national anthem and he strains miserably to remain erect. Scrambling away, Charlie gets into a position where he is unknowingly cocking his snook with one of the statue's raised hands. Charlie jumps over a fence and is away.

That afternoon, after being bedeviled by a nasty newsboy, Charlie escapes torment by looking at a beautiful nude statue in the window of an art shop. He stands out front admiring the fair lady, not noticing the sidewalk elevator descending behind him periodically. As he steps back to gain the proper perspective view of the statue, the elevator providentially rises to meet his tread; as he goes forward for a closer view, it descends. But he is finally caught, taken down, and climbs back onto the sidewalk, scolding the operator below who, coming up with his elevator, turns out to be a giant. Charlie runs.

Avoiding a cop by walking through a limousine parked at a curb, Charlie encounters a lovely flower girl (Virginia Cherrill) who, hearing the car door open, offers a bloom for sale to the affluent arrival. Charlie discovers her blindness when she gropes for the flower he has accidentally knocked from her hand. He gives his only coin to her, then sits nearby just to enjoy her exquisite face. The girl cleans her bucket at the corner fountain and throws the water at the enthralled Charlie. She returns to her neat but poverty-stricken room which she shares with her grandmother.

That evening on a river embankment a stupefyingly drunken millionaire (Harry Myers) has tied a weighted rope around his neck and is about to hurl himself into the water when Charlie, flower in hand and savoring a memory of beauty and hope, stops him. He lectures the millionaire spiritedly on life's charms; the man implacably places his rope about both their heads but fails to tie himself in. The rope and rock are hurled riverward and Charlie is plunked in alone. The millionaire rescues Charlie extravagantly until he needs to be rescued himself; finally the two stand on the river's edge, cold and dripping.

Exhilarated, the millionaire takes Charlie home for a drink but after they have settled in and the butler tells his boss that his wife is leaving him, the millionaire tries to kill himself with a gun, Charlie insistently trying to talk him out of it. Persuaded, the millionaire takes Charlie with him on a kill-care night club tour. They drink heartily, Charlie to the point where, thinking the menu a hymn book, he rises to sing. The millionaire keeps weaving back and forth with a cigar Charlie finally succeeds in lighting for him, but the cigar is thrown on a lady's seat and her gown ignites. Charlie thoughtfully douses it with a seltzer bottle. In eating spaghetti, he intertwines paper streamers descending from the ceiling and chews far upward in the process. Gallantly he tries to rescue the girl member of an apache dance act and then, maddened by the dance music, he swings across the floor with a lady passing his table. He changes partners with a tray-carrying waiter who falls, dishes unbroken. Charlie is tired and the millionaire drives them home erratically. He is surprised at one point to learn that he is driving. Charlie admires the car; it is given to him instantly.

Arriving at the mansion, they see the flower girl walking by and Charlie is given money to buy her wares. He buys all she has and later drives her home in his new car. He is entranced; she promises to "see" him again.

Later, sobered, the millionaire has no memory of Charlie and orders him barred from the mansion. Nonplused and wanting a cigar, Charlie gets into the limousine and drives until he sees a cigar smoker throw away his butt. Charlie jumps out of the Rolls-

Royce and scrambles for the butt, utterly baffling an old bum who hoped for it. Charlie returns to the mansion; the millionaire comes out, does not even look at his erstwhile chum, and drives away in the gift car. Charlie is incredulous.

Later in the day Charlie again encounters the millionaire who, now under the full steam of several drinks, recognizes his old pal, embraces him heartily, and throws a party for him at the mansion. In taking a toy whistle as a party favor Charlie inadvertently swallows it and develops hiccups which at every spasm force out a piercing blast, thereby enraging a concert singer hired to perform. Charlie gets into the garden where his involuntary whistling summons in turn a taxi and a pack of dogs. The morning after the riotous party, the millionaire awakes to find Charlie in bed with him. Revolted, he orders the little stranger away.

Bewildered, Charlie goes to the flower girl's corner, finds her missing and, eavesdropping outside her room, hears a doctor say she needs special care. To get money for her, Charlie becomes a street cleaner but is terribly daunted by a gala parade of circus animals including an elephant. He is able, however, to bring the girl food as well as news about a Viennese surgeon who may be able to cure her. The girl is thrilled because it means she will be able to see Charlie; his heart sinks as he realizes she pictures him as suave and wealthy. The girl and her grandmother threatened with eviction, Charlie promises to bring the needed money next day. Late for work, Charlie is fired, and a boxer, seeing this, asks him if he would like to make some easy money.

A fight arena. Charlie is prepared to split a purse fifty-fifty with his new friend by taking a dive. Charlie whispers to his friend, who points to a door. Charlie goes, comes back to have his gloves taken off, leaves again. We see his destination—a drinking fountain.

Charlie's boxer pal, getting word that police are hot on his trail, leaves quickly and a new fighter (Hank Mann), a rough and tough one, is substituted. By his dressing-room demeanor, this boxer is clearly not privy to the fifty-fifty arrangement. He is out for blood. Charlie tries to ingratiate himself with winsome looks at Hank. Hank suspects Charlie's virility. A black boxer rubs himself with a lucky rabbit's foot; Charlie borrows it for similar use. Minutes later the black boxer is brought back unconscious and Charlie tries to rub off the good luck.

Once in the ring Charlie is aggressively a coward. He clinches when he can and ducks blows eloquently. Charlie makes the referee an active participant in the battle, usually as a shield or buffer, and at one point—by dexterously stepping out of the battle radius—as a substitute for himself. If the footwork in this scene seems to have the flavor of expert choreography, that would be right. It *was* choreographed, in thirty days of rehearsal. And it is beautiful: Charlie walking backward as Hank advances, the referee equidistant from them in perfect tandem walk; then when Charlie gets behind the referee and remains in perfect step, using him as a shield, Hank gets into the pattern of the movement and the effect is of three fast-walking crabs sidling to nowhere. Charlie is knocked out.

Passing a theatre, the millionaire, now again happily sozzled, sees Charlie and boisterously hails his sometime pal home. Cheerfully he gives Charlie the money for the girl's eye operation, but crooks hiding in the house knock out the millionaire and chase Charlie. The robbers flee and when the police come Charlie is accused of theft by the butler. The revived millionaire does not know Charlie, who grabs the money, switches off the lights, and runs. He goes to the girl, tells her she must have the operation, and leaves her, promising to return one day. Caught, he is taken to jail but there is a heavier punishment—two fears: a fear that he won't see the girl again, and a fear that he will, when she is able to look at him for the first time.

The girl has a successful operation and opens a charming flower shop. Every handsome, well-dressed young man who comes into her shop is—she hopes—her benefactor, her gallant knight, but he never comes. Meanwhile Charlie has been released and, unable to find the girl, shuffles along the street in all his ragged despair.

Several newsboys tear what little dignity he has left by shooting peas at him. Watching this from the window of her shop, the girl is deeply amused at the tatterdemalion little fellow. Turning away from the boys, Charlie sees her and is heart-struck. So intense is his look that the girl, amused, says to her grandmother, "I've made a conquest!"

To compensate for the rudeness of her stare, she holds out a coin and a flower to Charlie. He starts, and walks away in confusion, but she comes out and calls after him. Uncertain, he stops; she puts the flower and money in his palm, and folds his fingers over them. At that touch, she knows that her handsome young Lochinvar is this disreputable little tramp.

"You?" she asks. He nods, smiles shyly.

"You can see now?" he asks.

"Yes, I can see now."

She does not know what to say; he does not know what to say. She is stunned, happy, unbelieving, disappointed to the heart, moved to the heart. He looks at her timidly, smiling in tender pain. He is hopeful, yet he dare not hope, yet he dare not fail to hope. As he watches her eyes, the camera moves in to him for that rarity in Chaplin films, a close-up. The scene fades.

Of that last scene in the film James Agee says, "It is enough to shrivel the heart to see, and it is the greatest piece of acting and the highest moment in movies." Amen.

City Lights is not a silent film. Very much not a silent film. Use of sound effects is awkward but its pervasive musical track is excellent. Theodore Huff has counted ninety-five musical cues in the film. Except for "La Violetera" ("Won't Somebody Buy My Violets?"), used as theme for the flower girl and three or four other pieces of music briefly used, all the music—at least twenty different themes—is Chaplin's. Unable to read music, he had to hum his tunes to professional arrangers, a necessarily tedious job. From *City Lights* on, music was to be integral to every Chaplin work.

In some ways, after 1931 music was to be his primary artistic interest. He spent much time and energy composing and conducting his music. The music has mostly a robust theatricality derivative of his earliest music hall days when he wrote ballads for various performers. It is *by itself* very slight music, and Chaplin has never made any claims for its quality. Slight though it is, it is perfectly right for the images it serves. "Strange how potent cheap music is," said one Noel Coward character—speaking of a slight Coward song now grown timeless.

As the director of *City Lights*, Chaplin followed his set pattern of explaining and acting out movement to his actors. One of the pea-shooting newsboys in the last scene, Robert Parrish, grew up to be a prominent film editor and director. In his *Growing Up in Hollywood,* he describes Chaplin explaining the pea-shooting sequence. He supervised the boys' make-up, told Rollie where to set up the camera, went through Charlie's movements for the boys, then acted out Virginia Cherrill's actions. This he capped by becoming the two newsboys. According to Parrish:

> He would blow a pea and then run over and pretend to be hit by it, then back to blow another pea. He became a kind of dervish, playing all the parts, using all the props, seeing and cane-twirling as the tramp, not seeing and grateful as the blind girl, peashooting as the newsboys. Austin [the other newsboy] and I and Miss Cherrill watched while Charlie did his show. Finally, he had it all worked out and reluctantly gave us back our parts. I felt that he would much rather have played all of them himself.

City Lights opened in New York on February 6, 1931, at the George M. Cohan Theatre on what is now known as a road show policy of advanced prices. Gilbert Seldes in the *New Republic* spoke for the critical majority who loved the film. He called it a masterpiece and cited Chaplin as the only artist whose films "always give the impression of being created before your eyes, with this extraordinary result, that when you see them, you can't believe that they have ever been shown before. . . ."

Konrad Bercovici had not seen Chaplin for five years when they met again during the making of *City Lights.* Five years before, Bercovici had known a haunted man with a face liberally lined. Now the lines had gone, he looked much younger, and significantly Chaplin did not once mention money during a two-hour chat. How had Chaplin found his new self?

Chaplin put it in a word—tennis. He played tennis every day for several joyous hours, and in consequence his prime fears had gone, he said. The thing Chaplin loved most about tennis was its form, its grace. For him it was really not important if you hit the ball as long as you moved gracefully and in *form.* Tennis was dance: that was why he loved it, he said, and it had become for him both recreation and a search for beauty. Vitally, it had destroyed all his inhibiting tensions.

Bercovici was also intrigued by Chaplin's speaking the Gypsy tongue with some fluency. The words kept coming back to him,

Chaplin explained: every day he remembered more and more. He said that when he was born all Hannah's relatives with that blood had arrived at their home in exotic caravans from many places. It was something of a neighborhood scandal because Hannah had always kept that part of her blood a secret. "Miri prala, miri prala," Chaplin said jubilantly to the half-Gypsy Bercovici. "Dear brother, dear brother."

That evening as Bercovici was walking down the slope from the Beverly Hills house, he heard Chaplin playing a piercing Gypsy melody on an accordion. Pierrot, thought Bercovici, the Pierrot of the world.

16
INTERLUDE

Chaplin's first return visit to England, for all the surging crowds and great applause, had been at base a disappointment. Hetty Kelly's death had robbed him of a precious confrontation, the outcome of which he dared not guess at, but a confrontation he needed to complete something yet in his spirit. Whether this was his unrequited love needing redress or a proud display of himself on a see-what-you-missed-getting basis was not clear to him. What was certain after her death was that suddenly his visit had no real purpose, outside of seeing his childhood streets, and that it was unrewarding to depend on people who grow up and pass out of your life.

During his 1931 trip abroad Chaplin was under no such burden. He wanted to see the scenes of his childhood again, to enjoy all he could of the best and hobnob with the nobs. In 1931 Chaplin saw much of the nobs. He went to the London premiere of *City Lights*, again visited the scenes of his childhood, went to Berlin, Vienna, and Paris.

During the Paris stay Chaplin met King Albert of Belgium in an unintentionally comic episode. When he was ushered into the august presence Chaplin found the chair assigned him disturbingly low, His Majesty's excessively high. Chaplin was just a little over five feet, Albert of the Belgians six feet three. As they talked, Chaplin's nose was roughly on the level of the king's knee. Nor was the king very talkative. As he frequently did when embarrassed and at a loss for words, Chaplin prattled on endlessly, looking desperately for a topic they might share. He seemed to have found one in flying; it had been noted in the press that Albert had flown to France. Chaplin praised flying volubly, said he enjoyed flying very much, repeated the statement, and went on to say that flying was thrilling, flying was exciting. He then looked out of the window in genteel agony and confided to His Majesty that flying was here to stay. Albert looked solemn at this information.

Realizing that the topic had been a little overdone, Chaplin smiled desperately and said, "I suppose you are a busy man these days?" then wondered if he had been too familiar in calling the king "man." On reflection, however, it occurred to Chaplin that he could not very well have said, "I suppose you are a busy king these days?" The conversation died.

But it revived because Albert was a man of many interests and he proved stimulating on them all. When Chaplin left he remembered that at the British court one backed out of the royal presence but in a simple embassy room this seemed excessive. He compromised by walking crablike to the door, bowing impressively.

Chaplin visited brother Syd, then in retirement in Nice, had a potent love affair with May Reeves, a beautiful Czech brunette, and at Douglas Fairbanks' urging joined his old friend in Switzerland.

It is amusing to hear what Chaplin thought of Switzerland in 1932, twenty years before it became his last home. In his long article "A Comedian Sees the World" (ghostwritten by his secretary, Catharine Hunter), Chaplin says, "I've never been intrigued by Switzerland. Personally I dislike all mountainous country. I feel hemmed in and isolated from the rest of the world." It can, of course, be reasonably conjectured that by 1952 Chaplin was happy to be isolated from the rest of the world.

Sydney joined his brother in Switzerland and, deciding a trip to the Far East would be educational and diverting, they went to Ceylon, Singapore, and Bali. Then to Japan, for which Chaplin had a special feeling. He knew Lafcadio Hearn's *In Ghostly Japan* with its vivid images of the gentle and beautiful life there. Chaplin had always employed Japanese for personal servants. His Beverly Hills home was completely run by them under the efficient hand of Toraichi Kono, Chaplin's combined valet-chauffeur-amanuensis. A tall man who spoke toneless but impeccable English, he was born in Hiroshima of a wealthy family. Disliking the formalistic rigors of traditional Japanese life, Kono broke with his family and emigrated to the United States where he found work in domestic service. He had a wife and a son but they came second. Kono was devoted to Chaplin and showed it every working day of his life.[1]

It was Kono who alerted Chaplin during their trip to Japan in May 1932 to the fact that the assassination of Premier Tsuyoki Inukai, which occurred during their visit, had been meant to include Chaplin. The Black Dragon Society, the group of militaristic terrorists who killed the Premier, believed that killing so popular a man as Chaplin would bring a war with the United States. The plan was aborted when a projected tea for Chaplin by the Premier was rescheduled.

Although Chaplin enjoyed the cultural ambience of Japan, especially the Kabuki theatre with its emphasis on strong stylized movement, he was glad to sail for the States with Kono. Syd left for Nice. On the trip to Seattle, Chaplin began making notes for a new film, a film that would very indirectly reflect his growing interest in economics. He was aware, too, that some of his recent work had been criticized for being old-fashioned.

At least the title of his new film would reject the past—*Modern Times*.

---

[1] Kono ended his job with Chaplin by government fiat. Together with many other Japanese-Americans, he was hustled away during World War II to the disgraceful relocation center at Manzanar, California.

17

MODERN TIMES

Paulette Goddard met Chaplin aboard Joseph Schenck's yacht when she was doing bit parts for Hal Roach. Born in New York City in 1911, Paulette, nee Pauline Levy, made her stage debut in a 1926 Ziegfeld revue, *No Foolin'*, followed it the next year with a role in *Rio Rita*, and went on to Hollywood where she appeared fleetingly in several Laurel and Hardy shorts and other Hal Roach films. She had been married briefly before meeting Chaplin. When she and Chaplin began seeing each other in 1932, the twenty-two-year difference in their ages was business as usual with Chaplin. The ageless master actor could become any age he liked, as all younger women who knew him soon discovered. But most women palled for Chaplin after a bit because they lacked his lively and inquiring intelligence. This he found in Paulette together with the quality he valued most in the world, a sense of discerning humor. Buying up her contract from Roach, he tutored her in acting and, not incidentally, in life. Eager to learn, mature for her years, and invincibly pretty, she was an ideal companion.

Chaplin was particularly pleased at her adaptability in making Charlie, Jr., and young Sydney a part of her life. When she moved into the Beverly Hills mansion the boys were usually weekend guests. Charlie, Jr., said that he and his brother "lost our hearts at once, never to regain them, through all the golden years of our childhood." Paulette, he said, was at once a mother, sister, and friend. Even Lita liked Paulette. She described her successor as "utterly without affectation or guile." Paulette gave the boys joyous companionship and at times was a buffer for them with their father when he was out of sorts.

Modern Times was a long while gestating. In 1901 Chaplin had a temporary job as a printer's devil in a plant dominated by an enormous Wharfdale printing machine. When the foreman took the twelve-year-old Chaplin to it, the machine loomed up forbiddingly, intimidating the boy. To operate it, he stood on a platform five feet high, and as the foreman started the machine, Chaplin watched in horrified fascination. It began to grind, roll, grunt. "I thought it was going to devour me," Chaplin said. That fear was to be fantasized comically in one of the best scenes in *Modern Times*.

The film also derived from a conversation Chaplin had with a young reporter who described the assembly line in Detroit auto plants and its debilitating effect on healthy young workers. Additionally, Chaplin saw a miniaturized version of the factory-belt system in a Los Angeles restaurant. An endless rubber belt took the dirty dishes from the dining room to the dishwashers, and as Chaplin and a luncheon guest watched it in fascination, the guest said that surely everything was becoming mechanized. The idea took hold.

Modern Times has a theme-heavy opening: first, a title saying the film is "the story of industry, of individual enterprise—humanity crusading in the pursuit of happiness" (which the film is not about at all), and then the film's first scene, a juxtaposing of shots of running sheep and workers pouring out of the subway. The right mixture of slapstick and satire comes in the next scene where Charlie has become a semi-automaton in a factory, tightening nuts on double bolts passing on a relentless conveyor belt. Holding two wrenches with arms muscle-locked in scissors position, he pecks down on the bolts as they speed along, convulsively tightening them. When he misses a nut, he must pursue it down its inexorable path, knocking over workers beside him, even jumping on the belt itself as it rumbles on. The plant boss (Allan Garcia) in his elegant office, bored with his jigsaw puzzle, orders Charlie's section to be speeded up and the conveyor belt increases its savage tempo. Charlie's entire body is consecrated to the nut-turning. He finally takes a work break, going into the washroom to sneak a cigarette; just as he is enjoying the first drag, one wall of the lavatory becomes a giant television screen. The indignant boss appears and tells him to quit stalling and get back to work.

Hoping to eliminate the lunch hour by getting the men to eat on the job, the boss allows a worker-feeding machine to be demonstrated with Charlie as guinea pig. Strapped into the unit, he is confronted by a revolving turntable which pushes food into his mouth, pours soup down his gullet, and offers him a revolving cob of corn. After each transaction an automatic mouth-wiper, looking like a large nail buffer, gently but firmly comes forward to do its work. All works well for a few minutes until a short circuit causes the entire machine to speed up. Steel nuts fly loose and are pushed into Charlie's mouth, soup is poured on his lap, and the corn-on-the-cob holder rotates against his mouth like a grindstone. The machine self-destructs.

Charlie returns to his conveyor belt and the nut-tightening. The boss orders another speed-up of the belt. (This speed-up and many action segments of *Modern Times* are shot at various silent speeds to accelerate the motion and regular sound track is added. Thus Chaplin gets the best of both worlds.) By this hour, Charlie's reflexes have set his arms into an automatic spasm. A secretary comes into the plant wearing a dress with ornaments like the nuts Charlie has been turning. Berserk from hyperactivity, he dangles his wrenches as earrings, sees the ornaments, and chases her out on the street. He attacks a hydrant bolt with his wrenches; a stout lady walks by also wearing nutlike gewgaws on her bosom. He stares, she runs, he follows, and a policeman chases him back into the plant. Now completely frenzied, Charlie pulls all the plant's control levers, altering the assembly line speed, seizes an oil can and squirts every face in sight, breaking into an ecstatic dance of freedom from work. He leaps on an overhead pulley and squirts oil on the boss.

Hospitalized for a time, he is cured of his nervous breakdown and walks the city streets looking for a job. A red warning flag from a truck falls off and Charlie, picking it up, waves it after the departing machine. As he does, Communist demonstrators turn the corner and march behind him. He is mistaken for their leader and put in jail. A drug addict trying to hide his cocaine puts it in a salt cellar which Charlie uses innocently, doubling his strength and allowing him to quell a prison break. He has a splendid, well-

appointed cell and enjoys prison life. But he is "rewarded" with
freedom and goes reluctantly into the world.

Meantime a hoydenish gamine (Paulette Goddard) has stolen
bread and bananas for her starving family. She flees from juvenile
officers who take her two sisters into protective custody after the
shooting of their father in a labor battle. Charlie encounters Paulette and they lift each other's spirits. When she is apprehended,
he decides jail is really home after all and seeks to return by ordering a huge restaurant meal he cannot pay for. On his way to the
patrol wagon Charlie executes one of his joyous little mimetic non
sequiturs that advance nothing in the film but our admiration of
him. In the restaurant he picked out an expensive cigar and now
in police custody still savors it, inhaling luxuriously. The cigar is
snatched away from him. Charlie grabs at the air with cupped
right hand, pats the top of his derby, then while twisting his right
ear exhales the cigar smoke. It is a cheeky little joke, done so expertly and with such good-natured panache that one longs to du-
plicate it.

Charlie encounters Paulette in the patrol wagon and they con-
trive to escape. Footsore, they rest on a curb and see a housewife
kissing her husband good-by. Charlie now projects both Paulette
and himself into a most vivid daydream where they become a suburban pair: she watching the roast as he calls the family cow to
the kitchen door for milking. While Charlie waits for the milk, he
sucks at grapes gracefully bending down for him from the doorway. It is another dream of success by Jimmy the Fearless.

Dream over, the two finally discover an empty shack on the wa-
terfront and move in, Charlie taking care to sleep in a little ad-
joining kennel. When morning comes he goes briskly for a swim,
dives gracefully—into eight inches of water. He gets a job as night
watchman in a large department store and sneaks Paulette in,
wrapping her in an ermine spread and letting her sleep in a downy
bed. Putting on roller skates to reach his time stations more easily,
he also entertains Paulette by a skating exhibition which almost
ends in catastrophe as he skates backward in a great swooping arc
to a hairline away from a broken balcony railing. Former factory
workmates of Charlie break into the store and he grants them access to the liquor section. Next morning Charlie is blamed for the
break-in. Jail once more.

While he is there, Paulette gets a job singing in a café and at Charlie's release she prevails on the kindly owner (Henry Bergman) to give him a waiter's job. Charlie discovers the job is perilous. On one order he must carry a roast duck lifted high on a platter above a crowded dance floor while he is borne hither and yon by the surge of revelers. The duck is pierced by the chandelier and remains suspended as Charlie struggles forward with empty tray. A featured singer at the café does not show up and Charlie is asked to substitute. To help remember the lyrics, Charlie has Paulette write them down on his cuffs. As the vamp music for the song begins, Charlie "shoots" his cuffs and they fly offstage. He is forced to ad-lib lyrics (to the tune of "Titine"), a wonderfully weird collation of nonsense syllables and foreign-sounding phrases. Thus, for the first and last time, Charlie the Tramp's voice is heard:[1]

> Se bella pew satoré, je notre so katoré,
> Je notre qui kavoré, je la ku la qui la kwa!
> Le spinash or le busho, cigaretto toto bello,
> Ce rakish spagoletto, si la tu la tu la twa!
> Senora pe le fimah, voulez-vous la taximeter,
> Le zionta sur le tita, tu le tu le tu le waah!

And on for six more lines of similar absurdities counterpointing Charlie's pantomime of an exuberant flirtation. He sees a curvaceous girl who acts coy at his advances. But Charlie persists, becomes bolder, twirls his mustache with a villainous grin, puts his hand out to grab her, tries to kiss her, pleads with her to go away with him. Finally she does and they go off together in a taxi.

This action is clear enough but we have no idea what the words of the song are about, fittingly. What song or statement that Charlie makes now can appropriately honor the event of his speaking? Better for him to retain his elemental mystery. James Agate said, "Half the secret of that wistful tramp, that pilgrim of eternity in a finer sense than Byron ever knew, lies in the fact that he has walked the silent screen guessed at by all the world, yet never wholly revealed."

[1] I most emphatically do not believe the barber in *The Great Dictator* is Charlie. Charlie an amiable run-of-the-masses sort? Hardly.

The café crowd is properly enchanted with the song and a career for Charlie as a comedy tenor is indicated. But the juvenile officers come seeking Paulette and she runs away with Charlie. They are downcast initially but brighten to say, "We'll get along." They walk down a sunlit road, hand in hand.

Modern Times was greatly liked by the public, a bit less so by the critics, some of whom were expecting *The Gold Rush* again or at least *City Lights*. There were valid critical complaints that the film had too many titles, thus slowing action, and a charge of discontinuity was valid. Otis Ferguson claimed the film was really several two-reelers, *The Shop*, *The Jailbird*, *The Watchman*, and *The Singing Waiter*. Some critics, inferring from the film's title and opening shots that social comment was its underlay, were put out when little of it occurred. Chaplin then and throughout much of his career said that social significance played no part in his work, but in some quarters he was simply not believed. In Russia (where Eisenstein was later to proclaim that in *Modern Times* Chaplin saw "the new era of our day") the reception for the film was cool. The red flag there was hardly a comedy prop and the conveyor-belt scene, probably the funniest in the film, was puzzling to many Russian workers, who had just been urged by Stalin to speed up assembly line production. Why does Comrade Chaplin laugh at such a thing? Conversely, *Modern Times* was banned in Fascist Italy and Germany as Communist in tone. Brooks Atkinson put it judiciously when he said that if *Modern Times* was offered as social philosophy "it is plain that [Chaplin] has barely passed his entrance examinations, his comment is so trivial."

Modern Times is simply misnamed. If it had been given the title Alexander Woollcott used to describe his beloved tramp, *Charlie As Ever Was*, critical reproaches might have been muted. After all, as Mark Van Doren said of Chaplin in the film, "his line is laughter. And I for one am glad that he has kept to it. . . . The film as a whole means no more than Charlie Chaplin means." There could hardly be higher praise.

With *Modern Times*, the tramp disappears forever. Not counting several cameo film appearances as himself, Chaplin made eighty-two screen appearances. Of these, seventy were in the traditional tramp facial make-up, with a variety of costumes, the tramp's of course predominating. The general division of these seventy falls into three categories: first, a tramp or vagabond, a derelict; second, an employed or self-supporting person, definitely not a tramp; and third, a person who could be either one. Number two includes various drunks with money of their own, suitors, a boardinghouse resident, a waiter, flirtatious men about town, a confidence man, a fight referee, married men, a dental assistant, a property man, an actor, a bath chair attendant, a janitor, a piano mover, a paper-hanger, a shopper, a fireman, a tailor's assistant, a carpenter, theatre patrons, a handy man, and a laborer. Of the three categories in the seventy, the second is by far the largest—forty-five such roles. Of number three, the indefinite category, there are twelve appearances, and of the fabled tramp—the penniless gentleman of the road—there are only thirteen. Charlie was a bit more like us bread-winners than is perhaps realized.

Modern Times' fadeout shot of Charlie and Paulette walking down to the sunset bid fair for a time to be the pattern of their real lives. Chaplin says that loneliness was the principal cause of their union, which to this day shows no official record of a marriage. Charlie Chaplin, Jr., who should know, said that sometime in 1936, during a vacation in the Far East, Chaplin and Paulette were married in Canton, China.

Returning to Beverly Hills, the Chaplins settled down to domestic life, although a number of women's clubs were making public inquiries as to Paulette's marital status. Since Chaplin, properly, thought it was none of their damned business, he did not tell them.

Following the successful release of *Modern Times* in France, Films Sonores Tobis, producers of René Clair's *A Nous la Liberté*, sued Chaplin on the grounds that *Modern Times* plagiarized Clair's film, notably the production line sequence which was one of the highlights of the French film. The suit was later dropped and Clair said graciously that, if Chaplin had indeed borrowed from him, he was honored and flattered. "God knows," said Clair, "I have certainly borrowed enough from *him*."

As her success in *Modern Times* receded in memory, Paulette's professional situation was unsettled. Chaplin had been toying with several story ideas for her but there was little tangible for them to sit down and discuss. During this period David O. Selznick announced his nationwide search for a girl to play Scarlett O'Hara in *Gone With the Wind*. He asked Paulette if she would be interested in a test. Excitedly she asked Chaplin for approval; she was not only his wife but a contractee of Chaplin Studios. Chaplin did not approve. He was working on a script for her which he thought had possibilities.

Paulette was upset; Chaplin was even more upset because the script he had been fashioning was not taking form.

Then a friend mailed him a press clipping saying that Hitler had banned all Chaplin's films from Germany because of the tramp's physical resemblance to the Fuehrer. Some time before, Alexander Korda had casually suggested a Chaplin-Hitler film, and Konrad Bercovici had approached Chaplin with a similar idea. Why not, said Bercovici, make a film as Hitler's double? Chaplin pondered the idea and vetoed it. It was, he thought, too grim.

18
THE GREAT DICTATOR

Paulette was put under short-term contract by David O. Selznick in 1938. She appeared for him in *The Young in Heart* that year and was greatly appreciated by her new producer. The search for Scarlett O'Hara was nearing its climax in 1938, when Paulette made two screen tests for the role, the last winning from Selznick the comment that each time he saw it he was more and more impressed. In a memo to an aide, Selznick admitted that Paulette had "plenty against her in the way of the public's attitude" but he was not going to let clubwomen's concern over her stand between him and his choice for the best female role of the decade. There is evidence that Paulette would indeed have played Scarlett had not Myron Selznick found Vivien Leigh.

Signs of a growing estrangement between Paulette and Chaplin grew. He did not like the idea of her working for someone else even on a temporary basis. To gain perspective on their marriage, early in 1938 he went alone to spend a brief holiday with a new friend, Tim Durant, at Pebble Beach on the California coast. The holiday lasted five months. Durant seemed an unlikely friend for the socially rebellious Chaplin. Durant was conventional of manner and a conservative temperamentally. But he was an excellent tennis player, a man who listened intelligently and was stubbornly loyal. Chaplin dubbed him "the irreconcilable Yankee" and grew to consider him his best friend.

After his long visit with Durant, Chaplin returned to Paulette and the old closeness was resumed for a time. He had a new script almost completed that would feature his wife and Gary Cooper. Cooper had shown interest and some preproduction planning was in work—but the Hitler concept kept intruding on Chaplin's thoughts. Recent conversations with Konrad Bercovici both at Beverly Hills and at Pebble Beach had stimulated him to reconsider the possibilities. Moreover, an English-Jewish friend, Ivor Montagu, had sent him a Nazi propaganda book that included a picture of Chaplin captioned "This little Jewish tumbler, as disgusting as he is boring . . ." It was a strong temptation to make a comedy showing the Nazis as both. The war tensions in Europe became another factor: would not a satire on Hitler help show up this ridiculous man?

There was a particular suitability about the idea. It was commonly said in Berlin of the early 1930s that the reason Hitler chose a toothbrush mustache (cut down from his original handlebar) was because he thought a resemblance to Chaplin increased his acceptability as a politician. And now with Chaplin mimicking Hitler, the whirligig of time would indeed bring in his revenges. Chaplin began to write.

A provisional script, *The Dictator*, was copyrighted in November 1938, but Paramount claimed it owned the name because the Richard Harding Davis farce of that title was their property. Chaplin asked what they wanted for the title, and when they told him, he was outraged. "I can't spend $25,000 for two words," he said.

The provisional script of *The Great Dictator* placed stronger emphasis on the sufferings of Jews in Germany than the final version. It was also more insistently farcical than the final script—the dictator, "Furor" Hynkel, for instance demanding a universal salute on his appearance, even to dachshunds raising their legs. The Mussolini counterpart is Mussemup of Ostrich, another supreme egotist who stops traffic when he wants to tell a dirty joke. However, as shooting began on September 9, 1939, one week after World War II erupted, Chaplin realized that his laughter would have to be considerably more purposeful.

During the summer of 1939 he had found just the man for the Mussolini role. This was Jack Oakie, rotund and extroverted, who was honored at the choice but felt a bit dubious about a Scotch-Irish actor playing Mussolini. He asked Chaplin why an Italian wasn't cast, and Chaplin's reply was to the point: what is funny about an Italian playing Mussolini? The growing seriousness of Chaplin's approach to the film is evident in the name changes of the Oakie character from Mussemup, to Benzino Gasolini, to Napolini. Chaplin had always wanted to do a Napoleon film, thinking initially of himself or James Cagney in the role, but there were always other things to do. The name Napolini was the sole remnant of that dream.

Chaplin coached Oakie and Paulette very carefully during the shooting. He had amply prepared for his own role by running Hitler newsreels over and over, and he found a single quality in Hitler to admire—his tremendous acting ability. "That guy's a great actor," he said. "Why, he's the greatest actor of us all." Reginald Gardiner recalls that when Chaplin was playing the Jewish barber he was his usual amiable self on the set but the morning he appeared as the dictator in smartly severe uniform the Chaplin personality altered. He was cool and crisp, and later in the day, driving with Gardiner to a new location, he spoke contemptuously of the passengers in a car blocking their way. Immediately, Chaplin broke into laughter and reminded Gardiner of something said at lunch days before when Chaplin claimed that the very wearing of a uniform makes one feel speciously superior. Of his rude remark about the people in the car, Chaplin said, "Just because I'm dressed up in this darned thing I go and do a thing like that."

The Great Dictator begins in World War I when the state of Tomania is on the losing side. One of the reasons is a little Jewish barber who has been drafted to serve as artilleryman on a gigantic cannon aimed far afield. This little fellow resembles Charlie, even does some of the things Charlie might do, but he is pleasantly commonplace—a decent little chap epitomizing all decent little chaps caught up in the maelstrom of war and international power struggles. The barber is an inadequate gunner; the first shell he sends forth destroys an outhouse, and the second just plops out of the cannon and lies there. When he is sent to check its fuse, it comes alive, spinning around sputteringly toward him.

A Tomanian pilot, Schultz (Reginald Gardiner), injured in a forced landing, is saved by the barber taking over his plane. Despite flying upside down most of the time, the barber gets them safely out of the active war zone until the plane runs out of gas, dumping them severely in a mudhole. The barber, suffering amnesia from the crash, is sent to a hospital where he remains for years, unaware of the passage of time and ascent to power of Adenoid Hynkel, dictator of Tomania, leader of the Double Cross Party, and a dead ringer for the barber. Hynkel, in addressing a party meeting, speaks in a vulgar German-English patois which an urbane radio announcer/translator sanitizes. When Hynkel rasps, "Democratia shtunk! Libertad shtunk! Frei sprachen shtunk!" the announcer purrs, "Democracy smells. Liberty is odious. Free speech is objectionable." Beamingly, proudly, Hynkel says of the two aides at his side, the obese Herring (Billy Gilbert) and the saturnine Garbitsch (Henry Daniell): "Herring shouldn't schmelten fine from Garbitsch, and Garbitsch shouldn't schmelten fine from Herring."

As Hynkel gets progressively heated in his oration he goes into a coughing fit, followed by a plea for more babies to raise as soldiers, and concludes in a risingly violent harangue that escalates into gibberish shattering the radio wires. The translator explains that Hynkel has just referred to the Jewish people. After the speech, Garbitsch tells him his attack on the Jews was too soft, that assaults on the Jews would keep the Tomanian people from thinking of their empty bellies. Hynkel agrees; the ghetto has been too quiet lately. As Hynkel's party drives away from the speaker's stand, the statues raise their arms in salute.

In the Tomanian ghetto, storm troopers throw tomatoes at the orphaned Hannah (Paulette Goddard) carrying her fresh laundry. (Chaplin here memorializes his mother in the name of the sweet and spunky character Paulette plays.) As Hannah tries to clean up her basket, she shouts defiantly at the roistering troopers. The little Jewish barber has just returned from the hospital to open up his barbershop, unaware of the passage of years. When he cleans it out he is astounded at the number of cats that escape and the dust that is everywhere. As he tries to stop storm troopers from painting "Jew" on his window, he is arrested but Hannah helps him by hitting some of his assailants over the head with a frying pan. She accidentally hits the barber, who staggers dazedly down the street like a drunken tightrope walker.

Hannah is winning but new troops appear and prepare to hang

the barber from a street lamp. The aviator Schultz, now a high-ranking party official, driving by, recognizes his old benefactor and saves him.

At Hynkel's palace a proud inventor of a bulletproof suit stands before the dictator, who tests the invention by shooting the man. He dies on the spot and Hynkel observes cagily that the suit was far from perfect. Herring brings in a man who has invented a parachute hat. The inventor heils and jumps out of the window to demonstrate. Hynkel leans out of the window, looks down, and says, "Herring, *why* do you waste my time like this?"

Hynkel needs money to invade neighboring Austerlich and because this means borrowing from the prominent Jewish financier, Epstein, contemplated onslaughts on the ghetto are suspended. When Hynkel is brought word that the leaders of a strike have been shot, he orders all the workers shot as well—until it is pointed out that he needs them for production. Commenting that the permanently chastised leaders were brunettes, Garbitsch says peace can never come to the world until blue-eyed blonds rule—with Hynkel as dictator of the world. Ecstatic at this vision, Hynkel climbs up a window curtain, and in his lofty dominance demands to be left alone.

As the Prelude to Wagner's *Lohengrin* counterpoints his grandiose dance of self-intoxication, Hynkel takes the world globe on his desk and, after examining it carefully, lifts it lovingly, spins it on one hand, bounces and kicks it gracefully as it soars—now a balloon and the tangible metaphor of his one abiding lust. He bumps the world into the air with his head, his hand, his foot, his bottom, with every part of him that can move. He is Atlas without strain, the prime and only mover of the universe. Unable to restrain himself, he embraces it fervidly and when it bursts Hynkel sobs bitterly on his desk. The world should never have done that to him.

In the little barbershop an elderly customer (Chester Conklin, twenty-six years after Keystone) sits in the chair while the barber shaves him in precise time to Brahms's Hungarian Dance No. 5. (Chaplin needed no instruction on how to act as a barber. All his adult life he cut his own hair—with a pair of scissors, hand clippers, and two mirrors. He did this simply because barbershops took up too much of his time.)

At the palace, Epstein's refusal to make the loan puts Hynkel into a rage and he orders a pogrom to begin. Schultz protests, is arrested, but escapes into the ghetto. Hannah and the barber watch the barbershop burned by the troopers, and Schultz exhorts the little fellow to join a conspiracy to blow up the palace. To choose the agent for the job from among five of the conspirators, Hannah is asked to place a coin in one of the cakes the men will eat. Disliking the plan, Hannah puts a coin in each cake, and four of the men quickly pass their cakes to the next man. The barber receives three coins in this fashion and quickly swallows them. The oldest conspirator proudly announces he has found the coin, which prompts Hannah to reveal her ruse. The barber hiccups out all his money.

Because Schultz and the barber have been identified as part of the underground, they are hunted, caught, and taken to a concentration camp. Hannah flees to a lovely farm in Austerlich.

About to launch his invasion of Austerlich, Hynkel is shocked to hear that his fellow dictator, Napolini of Bacteria (Jack Oakie), is prepared to do the same. He invites Napolini for a conference and both men try to outface each other, all in a great show of friendship. They vie for the best place in news photographs. Hynkel, primed by Garbitsch to create situations in which his rival must literally look up to him, arranges for Napolini to sit on a low chair looking up to Hynkel (shades of King Albert!) while a glowering bust of the Tomanian dictator looks down on him. It is planned for Napolini to be further intimidated by making him walk in from the far end of a long room. Napolini defeats all this, however, by entering from a door near the desk, backslapping Hynkel off his chair, taking a high seat near the desk, and looking even more belligerent than the Hynkel bust—on which he scratches a match.

The dictators decide to get a shave together (one of the barbers is Leo White, back in Chaplin's employ) and, in trying to dominate each other, jack up their chairs in spurts higher and higher until Hynkel hits the ceiling and crashes down. At a ball that night Hynkel is also bested—by protocol, which forces him to dance with the huge Signora Napolini, who forces his back into a curve. At the buffet supper later, the boastful dictators mix food and the invasion treaty they propose to sign into a literal mess.

Each satisfied he has dominated the other, they embrace. To distract international attention, Hynkel goes duck hunting until time for the invasion.

Meanwhile the barber and Schultz steal Tomanian army uniforms and escape from the concentration camp. Hynkel, in Tyrolean garb rowing on a nearby lake, capsizes and must swim ashore where he is apprehended as the barber. The barber, running into Tomanian troops, is hailed as Hynkel and drives into Austerlich a conqueror. Roadside posters proclaim that the ghetto has been overcome and Jewish property confiscated.

In the Austerlichan capitol all is ready for the words of the victorious dictator, words that will set the tone and the terms of the capture. A vast audience is assembled. The barber is terrified of speaking but Schultz, now his aide-de-camp, tells him it is their only chance. Garbitsch goes to the microphones to deride democracy and to commit every man to total service for the state. The barber goes to the microphones and, at first quietly, says that he does not want to rule anyone, that he wants to help everyone to be as free as they should be. Greed, he says, has replaced feeling; kindness and gentleness are needed badly. To the millions of people listening, he would say not to despair, that hatred will pass, dictators die, and the power of the people now taken from them will return to them. But at a price. Men must not fight for brutes but for liberty. The kingdom of God is within all men as well as the power to create beauty and happiness. For democracy's sake, that power should be used to fight for a unified new and decent world. Lying dictators have promised these things but they enslave instead.

"Now," the barber says exultingly, "let us fight . . . to free the world, to do away with national barriers, to do away with greed, with hate and intolerance. Let us fight for a world of reason—a world where science and progress will lead to all men's happiness. Soldiers, in the name of democracy, let us *unite!*"

Then, as the camera takes us to Hannah in her country retreat where she lies on the ground, beaten by Tomanian soldiers, she hears the barber's voice on the radio calling on her and those like her to look up, for a bright new world is coming, a glorious future that belongs to them both, "and to all of us. Look up, Hannah, look up!" Hannah looks up intently, then smiles bravely, heartened by his words.

The Great Dictator took six months to film and, after another six months scoring and editing, opened at the Astor and Capitol theatres, New York, on October 15, 1940. The first audiences were pleased but a bit puzzled, particularly by the last speech, a six-minute peroration, which some critics found banal to the point of suffocation. Mary Pickford, among others, regretted that the tramp had gone, perhaps for good. Chaplin had lost her, was the Pickford comment. The public apparently did not agree because The Great Dictator grossed more than any Chaplin film up to that time.

In England where Hitler was not exactly a remote figure the reception of The Great Dictator was uniformly warm. The New Statesman and Nation called it not only Chaplin's masterpiece but "the best heartener we could have, with war standing still or going for or against us." Basil Wright, himself a skilled film maker, said in the Spectator that in these perilous days there was no convenient sunrise toward which Charlie could walk, this concept surely informing the film. Wright saw the final speech as poorly written but so well and sincerely spoken that it became true and moving in spite of itself. He also found the film uneven in mood and construction and far too long. "But," he said, "it has an undeniable greatness, both in its pure comedy and its bold contrast between the small people of the ghetto or the slums and the big people of the Fascist chancelleries, equating both in terms of fantasy and in terms of the adored Chaplin himself."

Chaplin won the 1940 award for best actor of the year from the New York Film Critics Circle. Angered, hurt, Chaplin refused it. The well-meaning critics had said in effect that only Chaplin's acting was memorable. "Many hurtful things happened to Chaplin all through his life," said Albert Margolies, Chaplin's publicity man at the time, "many more than he deserved. But I doubt whether any caused him more pain than to be regarded as a mere actor."

Seen today, The Great Dictator does not wear its age especially well. As Hynkel, Chaplin is very funny at moments—his schmaltz-clogged speech to his party and his challenges to Napolini are fine, and he is exquisite in the globe-balloon rhapsody. But otherwise the dictator is a rather dull dog, and stupid to boot. As the Jewish barber, there are good moments when Chaplin encounters the big artillery gun, when he is conked on the head by the frying pan to cavort like a booze-struck Charlie, and again when he shaves Chester Conklin so eloquently. But the ghetto scenes are not consistently interesting and they take place in settings so cheerfully antiseptic that they look like the work of department store window dressers. Nor does Chaplin hesitate to trot out again his very oldest gag, that by now terribly fatigued and fatiguing gag, arse-kicking. For bad measure, the film is twenty minutes too long.

The last speech, despite its strident clichés, is ultimately moving not only because it is beautifully acted but also because, like any good homily, it makes sense. And more. It is in retrospect a haunting reminder that because there was no little Jewish barber to deflect them Germans set forth to erect Auschwitz, Buchenwald, and Treblinka. It is worth listening quietly for six minutes to remind ourselves of that.

Had he known of the actual horrors of the concentration camps, Chaplin said, he would never have made *The Great Dictator*. As it was, he made the film for the Jews of the world, for "the return of decency and kindness." That intent, honorably realized, and the fun that does enrich the film periodically make it, despite its defects, worth viewing.

An engrossing footnote to the film's history is Adolf Hitler's connection with it. There is proof that Hitler was seriously disturbed when he heard Chaplin was at work on the picture, and in the fullness of time Hitler actually saw the film. Chaplin was told this by an agent who fled Germany after working in the film division of the Nazi Ministry of Culture. The man told Chaplin that Nazi agents bought a print of *The Great Dictator* in Portugal during the war and took it to Germany. Predictably, when Goebbels saw it he raged, denounced it, and decreed it must never be shown. Hitler, however, insisted on seeing the film—alone. The next night he saw the film again, and once more alone. That is all the agent could tell Chaplin. Chaplin, in telling this story to friends, added, "I'd give anything to know what he thought of it."

While working on *The Great Dictator* Chaplin said he felt so close to Jews that he was sure he must be Jewish. His comments

on his real or presumed Jewishness make an interesting and contradictory picture. Chaplin's predisposition to Jews and Jewishness
certainly stemmed from his love for Sydney, his half-Jewish
brother. Mack Sennett, not citing evidence, believed that Chaplin's father was part French, part Jewish, a statement made in the
Sennett autobiography, King of Comedy. In 1916, Chaplin told
interviewer E. H. Smith of McClure's magazine that he was "of
Jewish extraction," and Smith so reported in a biographical account of the comedian.

To counter this, Rollie Totheroh, the member of Chaplin's production staff who knew him best over many years, said that "a lot
of people thought Charlie was Jewish but he's not." In Chaplin's
account of his 1921 trip to London, he speaks of chatting with a
little Jewish girl on the return voyage. She asked him if he
thought Jewish people were clever, and Chaplin replied that all
great geniuses had Jewish blood in them. He added quickly that
he was not Jewish, but with a qualification: "I am sure there must
be some somewhere in me. I hope so."

This wish became certitude in 1924 when Chaplin confronted
Colleen Moore and the First National executives with the possibility of his playing Christ. "I'm a Jew" was his unequivocal asser-
tion. In a long article on Chaplin for the Atlantic Monthly in August 1939, Alistair Cooke, who had talked at length with his
subject, in speaking of the Hitler role foreclosing on German and
Italian income, said, "Chaplin has scorned to publicize the simple
error these countries make in identifying him as a Jew." In a
Collier's article a year later, another perceptive reporter, Kyle
Crichton, quotes Chaplin as saying directly, "As a matter of fact,
I'm not Jewish. Haven't a drop of Jewish blood. I've never
protested when they said I was Jewish because I'd be proud of it if
I were."

On the other side of the ledger was a comment in a 1953 issue of
Commentary, the Jewish magazine of current affairs. Commentary, in reviewing Limelight, was immediately struck by Chaplin's
Jewishness: "And for once Chaplin's Jewish heritage is visible, in
the sweet and contemplative old man's style, in the self-pity and
self-mockery, in the idea of sacrificing the old for the young."
Nine years later Harold Clurman, himself Jewish, visited Chaplin
in Switzerland to discuss, among other things, The Great Dic-

tator, and William Randolph Hearst's opposition to the film. Hearst had asked Chaplin why he disliked Hitler so much, then, stopping himself, said, "Oh, I understand. It's because you're Jewish." As Chaplin was telling this story, Clurman interrupted him, "But you're not Jewish." Chaplin gave Clurman a quizzical look and went on, " 'That,' I said to Hearst, 'has nothing to do with it: I am against Hitler because he's anti-people.' "

Ivor Montagu, who had sent Chaplin the Nazi propaganda book that was one of the stimuli for doing *The Great Dictator*, and a man intensely aware of his own Jewishness, saw nothing of it in his friend:

> Charlie is not a Jew or of Jewish origin. He attributes his curly black hair in youth to a Spanish strain. But he has rigorously refused ever to deny publicly that he is a Jew. He says that anyone who denies this in respect to himself plays into the hands of the anti-Semites.

In the late 1940s the screen writer Alvah Bessie had a conversation with Chaplin in which the comedian specifically denied being Jewish. He never contradicted anyone who called him Jewish, he told Bessie, because to do so would remove his comradeship with the victims of Nazism.

What is one to make of these contradictions? One clue may lie in something Chaplin told Konrad Bercovici in 1915. Chaplin was fulminating against a then popular writer when Bercovici interrupted him with some surprise, pointing out that Chaplin had said exactly the opposite to a reporter a few days before. "Did he put that in the papers?" Chaplin asked. "Well, I lied to him." He thought for a bit, then went on, "And maybe I did not lie. Maybe in his presence I just felt like telling things differently." Bercovici said of this, "Knowing the chameleon-like nature of Charlie, I am never surprised when I see him being a hundred different persons in the presence of a hundred different people." When Chaplin the total actor wanted to become someone, he did, and totally.

As to his final word on his Jewishness, real or presumed, it will serve to set down his last recorded comment on the matter. In 1964 he told Peter Steffens that relatives on his father's side living in Africa looked extremely Jewish, some even having Jewish names, so there was a likelihood of his being part Jewish. As far as he knew, he could be "part French, and Jewish, or German."

What Chaplin seems to be saying in these contrarieties is simple: he would like to be part Jewish. Who is to deny him?

19

JOAN BARRY

Chaplin's professional accomplishments by 1941 had been spectacularly successful but his personal life boasted only one success —marriage to Paulette, and that was now winding down. To understand Chaplin it is vital to know that his creative work was by far the dominant force in his life. His personal interests—women, friends, intellectual commitments and goals, indeed everything else—ranked far below his professional concerns. It was the reverse of John Barrymore's situation when asked if—in comparison with his stage career and other interests—his screen career was of primary or secondary importance. Barrymore replied that his screen career was of *tertiary* importance. For Chaplin everything other than his films was not in the running. He was terribly interested in women, he said, but knew nothing at all about them:

> I am a very hard person to live with. Every artist must be. I must find a woman who understands that creative art absorbs every bit of a man. When I am working, I withdraw absolutely from those I love. I have no energy, no love to give them.

Chaplin's first two wives testified amply to that. Paulette was an exception because she was able to share both his personal and his professional lives.

By 1941 Paulette was on the threshold of a most rewarding career. An informal estrangement with Chaplin begun during the making of *The Great Dictator* extended itself into a separation in 1941, and a Mexican divorce followed in 1942. There were regrets on both sides but a key problem seemed to be that so skilled and ambitious an actress as Paulette could not be expected to remain indefinitely sequestered at the Chaplin studio. And there was no doubt that Chaplin's relationship with young women inevitably took on the nature of *maître* and *protégée*. Virtually at the end of the Chaplin-Goddard relationship he met, through Tim Durant, a voluptuous redhead, Joan Berry. Miss Berry, having stage ambitions, had altered her name to Barry on the grounds that it was visually more agreeable.

Chaplin, lonely, was attracted physically and intrigued professionally by her hearty Irish appearance. A few weeks before he had taken an option on the screen rights to Paul Vincent Carroll's play, *Shadow and Substance*, whose leading lady, Bridget, was a simple Irish girl of deep spirituality. Miss Barry's spirituality was not perhaps immediately evident to anyone but Chaplin; still, there is no doubt the girl was very presentable. She reminded Tim Durant of a respectable Brooklyn stenographer. Chaplin was in any case intrigued both by her and by the play. *Shadow and Substance* with its strongly Catholic orientation he did not at all understand but, when asked by Al Hirschfeld why he bought the property, Chaplin answered simply, "Because it's great." He trusted his instincts, said Hirschfeld, instead of his intellect.

He sent Joan to Max Reinhardt's acting school for several months. A screen test showed she photographed beautifully; and her reading of Bridget was excellent. She and Chaplin became lovers but soon Joan began to fret under the highly disciplined regimen of study he had projected for her. She started drinking and, according to Chaplin, their relationship ended in February 1942. She began to come around to the Beverly Hills house at late hours, smashing windows when Chaplin would not answer her phone calls. He kept her on the payroll, however, giving her an adequate living stipend.

Meanwhile Chaplin had taken a deep interest in the raging terrors of World War II. Horrified by the carnage on the eastern front when Germany attacked Russia, he was sympathetic to a request from the American Committee for Russian War Relief to substitute for the indisposed Joseph E. Davies, former Ambassador to the Soviet Union, at a San Francisco rally in May 1942. In his speech Chaplin specifically disavowed any Communist affilia-

tion and said he was speaking on behalf of all opposed to the
Nazi horror. He spoke for forty minutes, ending with a strong plea
that a second front be opened at once. He began the speech with
the salutation "Comrades! And I mean comrades!" He intended
"comrades" in the literal or non-Communist sense, a meaning not
credited by Westbrook Pegler and several newspaper columnists,
who found in Chaplin the very model of a pinkish fellow traveler.

Two months later Chaplin spoke via telephone to a CIO-spon-
sored rally in Madison Square Garden, again urging a second
front, pointing out the Russian need for relief and asking what to
some was an extraordinarily naïve question: "But can we afford to
wait until we are sure and ready? Can we afford to play safe?"
Leading military strategists thought we could hardly do other
than be sure and ready. In October on a visit to New York,
Chaplin made two more addresses, pleading for the second front
and for the curtailing of anti-Communist propaganda in order to
maintain harmonious relations with our Russian allies.

This was bait for eager sharks. Westbrook Pegler in his quaintly
titled column, "Fair Enough," attacked Chaplin unremittingly,
speaking of his "decided partiality to Communism" and his fatal
alliance "with the pro-Communist actors and writers of the
theatre and the movies who call themselves artists, but are mostly
hams and hacks." It was Pegler who began the meaningless accu-
sation, persisting in some quarters to this day, that Chaplin, after
his long residence in this country, "failed" to become a United
States citizen. Another variant on this theme is that Chaplin "refused" to become a citizen, as if he had received serveral urgent in-
vitations through the years to do so. Pegler and his ilk apparently
were and are unaware of the hundreds of Americans living in England for decades—frequently to their financial advantage—who are
not regarded there as reprehensible blackguards because they do
not become British subjects. Stan Laurel, who proudly retained his
British passport from his arrival in California in 1910 to his death
there in 1965, was never accused of "failure" to become a United
States citizen, and it irked him considerably to read the press attacks on Chaplin in this respect.

As for Chaplin's pleas for a second front, they were utterly sincere, and militarily most naïve. That a second front in 1942 would
have been strategically disastrous has been the most carefully considered professional military opinion since that time.

When Chaplin went to New York in October 1942 to give the last of his second front speeches, he had been preceded there by Joan Barry. In September she told Chaplin that since work on *Shadow and Substance* seemed to have stopped she wanted to go to New York—"perhaps I'm really not cut out to be an actress." Chaplin paid train fare for Joan and her mother, and cut her salary to twenty-five dollars a week. She went to New York on October 5, checking into the Waldorf-Astoria Hotel and leaving there on October 10, went to the Hotel Pierre on that date, in the company of an unidentified man who was present as she signed the register. (The Pierre was owned by J. Paul Getty, who had known Joan in Mexico before she met Chaplin. Getty, according to Rollie Totheroh, was her "boy friend.") Chaplin arrived in New York five days later, staying at the Waldorf-Astoria. He saw Joan a few nights later at the Stork Club dancing with the man who had checked her in at the Pierre. That night Chaplin took her to his rooms at the Waldorf in the company of Tim Durant. Chaplin denied any intimacy with Joan on this occasion, saying he listened to her plea of poverty and gave her $300.

Chaplin left New York on October 27. Neither Chaplin nor any Chaplin employee paid Joan Barry's hotel bill. The details of the New York meeting are important to know because the $300 given the girl became the basis of a Mann Act charge subsequently filed against Chaplin.

After he returned to California, Joan followed him, using her $300 for this purpose. She called him persistently on the telephone and when he refused to see her she bought a gun, broke a window in Chaplin's study one night, entering the house. She found Chaplin and held him covered with the gun for an hour and a half while she talked to him. He pleaded for the gun; she gave in. They were intimate and she picked up the gun, went to another bedroom, and spent the night. Next morning Chaplin agreed to give her some money and she surrendered the gun.

This incredible story, told by Joan Barry in court during the Chaplin Mann Act trial, was corroborated by Chaplin and became for his lawyer, the well-known Jerry Giesler, absolute proof that Chaplin had not transported her to New York for immoral purposes. Who would take the young lady to New York when he could have her at home for the price of a bus ride?

A week later she came to the house again and Chaplin called the police. Given a suspended ninety-day sentence, she left the courtroom to be met by a representative of Chaplin Studios who gave her a ticket to New York and $100. She did not leave Los Angeles. A month later she broke into the Chaplin home once more and was arrested. She spent thirty days in jail on a vagrancy charge, part of which was spent in a hospital. She continued to harass Chaplin, at times soaking herself fully clothed in the sprinklers on his lawn and occasionally driving a car at high speed around the Chaplin circular driveway.

Early in 1943 Joan Barry became pregnant. According to Giesler, the girl accused Chaplin of paternity a few weeks later but said she would not press charges if he gave $65,000 to her mother and set up a $75,000 trust fund for the baby. Chaplin refused, and a paternity suit was filed against him, on Joan's behalf, by her mother, Mrs. Gertrude Berry.

The irony of finding the supreme happiness of his life at the time of his greatest public agony has never been lost on Chaplin. Kenneth Tynan is the source for a story that Orson Welles, intrigued with Eugene O'Neill's darkly beautiful daughter Oona, took her to a night club on their first date and after only two hours' acquaintance read her palm and predicted, "Within a very short time you will meet and marry Charles Chaplin." Oona, a debutante with a vague interest in acting, had left the East to visit her father and stepmother. Through an agent, Minna Wallis, Oona was introduced to Chaplin as a possible Bridget in *Shadow and Substance*. His personal interest in her was quickly reciprocated.

As the Chaplin-Oona courtship progressed, the newspapers took up Joan's now public declaration that Chaplin was the father of her unborn child and blazoned it in portentous headlines. Joan appeared one day in Hedda Hopper's office and sobbed out the story that she was carrying Chaplin's child: Chaplin had thrown her out of his house, she told the columnist. Miss Hopper broke the story, the first of many petty, vindictive ones she printed about him in the coming years.

It is a strong tribute to the levelheadedness of seventeen-year-old Oona O'Neill that she was able to see at once the unique fitness of the union between Chaplin and herself. She was precisely what he had been waiting for all these years. They were married on June 16, 1943. Her father was not pleased. A friend of Oona's described her as having an essential stillness: "There's something peaceful about her that makes you know at once why he married her—she's the antithesis of his own frantic antics." But Chaplin described Oona best in an interview twenty years before he met her: "I want a wife who is restful, but who knows that an artist lives more passionately, more deeply, with more seeking for life and truth and beauty than any man in the world—and who can respond to that."

In early October 1943, Joan Barry's child was born, a girl she named Carol Ann. The paternity suit was in abeyance and Chaplin had a period of comparative tranquillity before February 10, 1944, when he was indicted by a federal grand jury on the charge that the trip Joan Barry took to New York in October 1942 was a violation of the Mann Act. Giesler was able to convince the jury that the government's charge of transporting Miss Barry three thousand miles for a single act of intercourse was ludicrous. The jury took four ballots, however, to decide Chaplin's innocence. Giesler said:

> Chaplin was the best witness I've ever seen in a law court. He was effective even when he wasn't being examined or cross-examined, but was merely sitting there, lonely and forlorn, at a far end of the counsel table. He is so small that only the toes of his shoes touched the floor.

The paternity suit against Chaplin under present rules of evidence anywhere in the world would have resulted in immediate dismissal of the charges against him. On February 15, 1944, the result of three physicians supervising a blood test showed that Joan Barry's was A, Carol Ann's was B, and Chaplin's O, thus making it impossible for him to be the father of the child. But the presiding judge ruled that the "ends of justice" would best be served by a "full and fair trial of the issues." Since the key issue had already been medically determined, this thinking would seem to be rather clouded. Chaplin, in any case, was placed on trial, which ended in a hung jury voting seven to five for acquittal. A mistrial being declared, a second trial began April 12, 1944.

Chaplin had retained for his defense Charles A. "Pat" Millikan, a straightforward, no-nonsense lawyer, who was sure that the undisputed medical evidence would acquit his client. Millikan did not count on the presence on the other side of Joseph Scott, a lawyer of the old school. Joan Barry's first lawyer, on hearing the results of the blood test, withdrew from the case, but Scott, a prominent old counselor who had the reputation of putting love of church and country before all else, forgot the former as he nursed the latter in spasms of outraged patriotism.

Scott was yet another who could not understand why Chaplin had "failed" to become an American citizen. In taking up the cudgels for Joan Barry, he was willing to ignore the palpable scientific evidence and attack Chaplin on emotional grounds. Scott turned in a performance that even Chaplin might have envied in other circumstances.

Millikan rested Chaplin's case on the testimony of a Tulsa lawyer who said Joan Barry had told him of her love affair with an Oklahoma oil man during the time of Carol Ann's conception and on a blood-grouping demonstration by a doctor proving that Chaplin could not possibly be Carol Ann's father. Scott accused Chaplin of satyriasis, and in a *coup de théâtre* asked Joan to hold up Carol Ann near Chaplin so the jury could see the resemblance for themselves. Scott roared that Chaplin was a lecherous swine, "just a little runt of a Svengali," and that Joan was a living Magdalene. Scott grew vitriolic, calling Chaplin a "master mechanic in the art of seduction," a "cheap Cockney cad," and a "grayheaded old buzzard." Conceding that Joan was not without fault, Scott said that nevertheless, when she pleaded with Chaplin to marry her, "this reptile just looked upon her as so much carrion. Finally he took her up to the house and read her a script about Bluebeard."

The Scott histrionics won the day. The jury was out for three hours and returned with an eleven-to-one decision against Chaplin. The judge ruled that Chaplin must pay seventy-five dollars a week support for Carol Ann until she was twenty-one. This was done. Joan Barry's subsequent history was sad. After a failed marriage and two children, she was committed to Patton State Hospital after she had been found wandering distraught in Torrance,

California. She stayed in Patton for a number of years and then returned to anonymity.

Emotionally depleted, Chaplin took Oona, now pregnant, to Nyack, New York. They stayed in a quiet house where he could concentrate on that script about Bluebeard.

20
MONSIEUR VERDOUX

When the Chaplins settled in a backwater near Nyack it had been Chaplin's hope to finish his Bluebeard script (bearing the working title, *The Lady Killers*) but it was too quiet. He missed the creative ferment of his own studios. He returned to California and finished the writing project which had been in his mind since Orson Welles suggested to him a film based on Landru, the modern French Bluebeard. Welles thought of it as a documentary; it was Chaplin's idea to make it a comedy, albeit a bitter one. Charlie Chaplin, Jr., thought the film, *Monsieur Verdoux*, as it came to be called, was even more of a mission with his father than *The Great Dictator*, that it "served to objectify for him all the mingled fascination and horror he had felt throughout his life toward violence and the macabre."

Chaplin filmed *Monsieur Verdoux* in the (for him) rapid time of twelve weeks. His leading lady, Martha Raye, was at first incredulous that he wanted her for a role but she quickly lost her reverential attitude and began calling him "Chuck," the only time a co-worker ever called him that. Chaplin as usual was a hard taskmaster, and as usual driving himself more than anyone. One day Martha stopped the action mid-scene by shouting loudly, "One hour!" Chaplin, startled, asked what she meant. "Lunch," she said. "It's two o'clock and we haven't had lunch yet." This had never happened on a Chaplin set and some of the crew were shocked. But the boss agreed readily enough, and thereafter

Martha called time for lunch. Chaplin, true to form, was stimulating to work with; he also had one of the most volatile tempers the players in *Monsieur Verdoux* (almost all new to his studio) had ever encountered. Robert Florey, assistant director of the film and a long-time friend of Chaplin's, gives in his book, *Monsieur Chaplin*,[1] a verbatim record of Chaplin tirades rendered on one shooting day of *Monsieur Verdoux*. "Yet Charlie was no tyrant," said Bernard Nedell, who was in the film. "A hard worker, he expected hard work, damned hard work. And the cast loved him. I remember one day when he was absolutely depleted physically, almost sick with overwork, going endlessly over and over a scene with an actress until it came just right. He had that curious mixture of a hot temper and very great patience."

Under the subtitle, "A comedy of murder," *Monsieur Verdoux* begins with a close-up of Verdoux's tombstone, giving his dates, 1880–1937. Chaplin's voice-over explains that Verdoux was a bank clerk until the 1930 depression when he went into the business of marrying moneyed women and killing them, a business validated by the need to support his family.

We encounter the bickering family of an aging lady, Thelma Couvais, who has suddenly left her family to marry one Monsieur Varnay, emptying her bank account to do so. Thelma's sister Lena is thoroughly suspicious of Varnay's intentions toward Thelma. At a small village in the South of France, Varnay, actually Henri Verdoux (Charlie Chaplin), is seen trimming his roses while at the edge of his property an incinerator pours out ominous smoke clouds. He almost steps on a worm, shudders, and puts it on a leaf. ("Verdoux" translates to "sweet worm" or "nice little worm," perhaps Chaplin's identification of his protagonist as a pleasant little nonentity.) Receiving Thelma's money in the mail, Verdoux counts it with the astonishing dexterity of the professional cashier. This is a businessman.

Marie Grosnay, a wealthy widow (Isobel Elsom), arrives to look over the Varnay/Verdoux house, now for sale. Verdoux is utterly charmed to hear she is a widow. He woos her audaciously, following her around the room, insisting, despite her protests, that it is never too late for love—that, in effect, ripeness is all. As he

[1] *Monsieur Chaplin* also publishes for the first time Chaplin's little-known anti-war short story, "Rhythm."

closes in on her, the real estate agent enters, and Verdoux, pretending to be chasing a bee, swings at it and misses, tumbling out of the window onto the roof. He returns, ruthlessly charming, and gives Madame Grosnay roses for remembrance.

A shot of churning train wheels, used throughout the film to indicate Verdoux's move to another sphere of operations. In Paris he finds his stock market investments in trouble: he must find fifty thousand francs quickly. He visits another aging lady, Lydia Floray (Margaret Hoffman), who is under the double delusion that he has been in Indochina and that she is his wife. By talking of an impending bank crash, Verdoux gets her to withdraw her savings. They retire to bed, she ungraciously. In the morning he prepares breakfast for two, then, recollecting himself, removes one of the plates.

Train wheels. An idyllic scene of Verdoux at home with his real wife (Mady Correll) and their son. This is refuge from the vicious outside world, a world in which he, with a crippled wife, was fired from his bank after thirty years of faithful service. His wife, who knows nothing of his activities, is worried about her husband. She senses another and disturbed personality in him. Verdoux is quietly happy to be with his dear ones ("all I have on this earth") and exults that this charming home is now theirs. He hopes to be able to "retire" soon.

Train wheels. Verdoux visits another "wife," bouncy Annabella Bonheur (Martha Raye), who stubbornly refuses to let Verdoux handle her affairs. From a druggist friend Verdoux learns of an untraceable poison, which he buys. Annabella is on the verge of investing her money in a new firm and Verdoux is determined to stop her, but first he must see if the new poison works. In Paris, after sending roses again to the still resisting Madame Grosnay, Verdoux finds a disconsolate young girl (Marilyn Nash) who might well serve as a guinea pig for the poison. But so touching is her life story (just out of prison, she has been taking care of her recently dead invalid husband) that Verdoux spares her, giving her money instead. A detective tracks down Verdoux, arrests him, and is given the poison in a glass of wine Verdoux hospitably pours out for him. Verdoux is hustled aboard a train by the detective, who dies en route.

Train wheels. The murderer escapes to Annabella's house where his poison bottle, mistaken for peroxide by the maid, is used to bleach the hair right off her head. In the mix-up Annabella is given peroxide in her drink and spits it out indignantly. Verdoux, desperate, tries to do in the apparently indestructible lady by taking her fishing in a boat and drowning her after a thorough chloroforming. But he accidentally chloroforms himself, and on reviving tries to bind Annabella with a weighted rock and pushes her over. He falls overboard himself and the hearty lady rescues him.

Finally Madame Grosnay capitulates to Verdoux's persistent wooing and a wedding date is set. At the wedding reception Verdoux hears Annabella's sharp laugh, and he deserts the celebration. (Edna Purviance can be glimpsed briefly among the wedding guests, matronly but still handsome. She was considered for the Madame Grosnay role and was relieved not to get it.)

A montage of headlines take us through the stock market crash, the rise of Hitler and Mussolini, and the advent of war in Europe. In Paris a worn Verdoux is almost run down by a limousine bearing the young girl whose life he had spared. She takes him to the Café Royale and he learns that she has become the mistress of a munitions maker, the one rising profession in this strife-filled world. It will soon pay big dividends, Verdoux predicts. Verdoux admits to being at life's nadir. Both his wife and son have died, and he is almost penniless. At the café, Lena Couvais and her nephew come in and recognize Verdoux. Realizing he cannot escape, Verdoux says good-by to the girl ("I'm going to fulfill my destiny") and gives himself up to the police.

Train wheels. At his trial his only friend is the girl. She cannot believe Verdoux is a Bluebeard. No more does Verdoux, who blames society for turning him into a murderer. The world encourages mass killing, he points out, and he is simply an amateur in comparison. When the guilty verdict is brought in he says to the court and to the world, "I shall see you *all* soon—very soon." At the death house Verdoux further details his philosophy to a group of reporters, speaking of "Wars, conflict—it's all business. One murderer makes a villain; millions, a hero. Numbers sanctify!"

A priest coming in to offer solace is asked instead by Verdoux what he can do for *him*. When the priest asks if he has no remorse, Verdoux says he does not know what sin is—"born as it is from Heaven—from God's fallen angel." What, he asks the priest, would *he* be doing without sin? "May the Lord have mercy on your soul," says the priest. "Why not?" says Verdoux. "After all, it belongs to Him." Offered rum, Verdoux refuses, then changes his mind. He has never had rum; one should taste life to the very lees. The march to the guillotine begins.

There is only one flash of Charlie in *Monsieur Verdoux*. In the boat scene when Verdoux tries to drown Annabella, she turns suddenly to see him in a murderous stance. Verdoux unclouds, sits as Charlie does, stretching his arms down between his legs in winsome ingratiation, smiling "cutely" at her as he hunches up his shoulders.

But then the film was not meant for Charlie, and it is against its function to judge it in terms of anything Chaplin ever did. An anti-war piece, it argues that the logical extension of unrestrained business is war. One need not challenge this unduly to jib strongly at Chaplin's extension of this theory, namely that Monsieur Verdoux is an inevitable part of this societal structure. The perceptive English critic, Alan Dent, enjoyed the film exceedingly but as to its rationale, he was dismayed: "I shall once again marvel how a man of genius can make the culmination of his film of such little sense and logic—the message that private murder is justifiable in a world which lets itself be dragged into mass-murdering on a wholesale scale."

Monsieur Verdoux for all the charm—and it is considerable—that Chaplin invests in him is not a very nice fellow. It is hard to disagree with Parker Tyler's conclusion that, as a Bluebeard, Chaplin's Verdoux is nothing more than a disguised psychopath.

Yet like anything Chaplin has ever done, *Monsieur Verdoux* so speaks that we, like the wedding guest to the Ancient Mariner, cannot choose but hear. Despite the occasionally bad production work including erratic editing and at least two glaringly inadequate backdrops, the film engrosses because we see a murderer in the skin of a great comedian. An ironic statement of life's inequities, it is not meant to be funny except by the way.

When *Monsieur Verdoux* opened at the Broadway Theatre on April 11, 1947, the critics were—with one prominent exception—bored, antagonized, or disappointed. Some, not understanding the film, felt cheated of laughter; others just wanted Charlie back; yet

others were affronted by its message—whatever that might be, and
there were varieties of opinion on just that.

The one critical big gun on Chaplin's side was James Agee, who
wrote in the *Nation* that he loved the film "as deeply as any I
have seen" and that it was "high among the great works of this
century." For Agee, the film's theme was simple—the problem of
surviving at all in such a world as this. Agee said Verdoux makes
us uncomfortable because he is too much like us, and we resent
the proximity. In a later review, Agee admitted that the film "had
serious shortcomings, both as popular entertainment and as a
work of art." But, Agee emphasized, whatever it lacks, *Monsieur
Verdoux* was not only one of the most notable films in years but
the finest picture Chaplin ever made, certainly the most fascinating.

Dwight Macdonald years later found three films in *Monsieur
Verdoux*: a sentimental melodrama, an old-style Chaplin comedy kidding that melodrama, and a drama with its banal, late-ar-
riving "message"—that a wholesale killer (like Napoleon) is called
a hero while a retail killer (like Verdoux) is denounced as a murderer.

Chaplin's only comment on *Monsieur Verdoux* in retrospect
came in 1974 when he said that, although the film had some
clever dialogue, he now considered it too cerebral and that more
action and pantomime would have served him better.

The public—what public there was—rejected *Monsieur Verdoux* almost out of hand and the film had a very brief New York
run. In some states it was senselessly banned or picketed either on
the grounds that it made a joke of murder or that its maker was
not a very nice man. Some of this stupidity was stimulated by stories written by reporters after a Chaplin press conference held in
New York by United Artists on April 12, 1947, the day after
Monsieur Verdoux opened. It was a debacle. Chaplin, gravely
courteous as always to the press, was questioned rudely and cross-
examined on his patriotism and political connections. He anticipated some of this because he began by saying lightly, "Proceed
with the butchery . . . fire ahead at this old gray head." The
lightness soon vanished.

Asked about his political beliefs, he said he had no political
persuasions whatsoever, had never voted in his life, and was not a

Communist. As to being a Communist sympathizer, he had during the war sympathized with Russia's need for relief on her battle front. One persistent questioner, a reporter for the Catholic War Veterans' paper, was grindingly sarcastic in his self-appointed role as spokesman for all veterans. On their behalf he asked why Chaplin had announced himself a citizen of the world, why he had "no patriotic feelings about this country or any other country." When Chaplin began to answer the question, the reporter rushed on in a tangle of censorious rhetoric: "You've worked here, you've made your money here, you went around in the last war, when you should have been serving Great Britain, you were here selling bonds, so it stated in the paper that I read, and I think that you as a citizen here—or rather a resident here—taking our money should have done more!"[2]

Chaplin quietly defended his patriotism and what he had done for the war effort. His patriotism, he explained, was not to one country or one class, but to the whole world and the common people. And that included people who objected to his form of patriotism.

Chaplin's friendship with composer Hanns Eisler, whose brother was reputed to be a Soviet agent, was questioned. Would it make any difference to Chaplin if his friend Eisler was a Communist? It would not. What was Chaplin's reaction to the reviews of *Monsieur Verdoux?* The one optimistic note, Chaplin said (in the conference's first pleasant moment), was that the reviews were mixed.

Amid accusations that he had stopped being a good comedian since he began making "message" pictures, Chaplin was asked the inevitable: would he state his reason for not becoming an American citizen? Politely Chaplin said he had stated his reason. He was not nationalistic. After a series of questions in which he was asked when he would make comedies for children again and if *Monsieur Verdoux* was irreligious, James Agee, seated in the balcony, could take no more. With voice trembling, he said:

> What are people who care a damn about freedom—who really *care* for it—think of a country and the people in it, who congratulate

[2] A transcript of the entire press conference is in *Film Comment*, Winter 1967.

themselves upon this country as the finest on earth and as a "free country" when so many of the people in this country pry into what a man's citizenship is, try to tell him his business from hour to hour and from day to day and exert a public moral blackmail against him for not becoming an American citizen—for his political views and for not entertaining American troops in the manner—in the way that they think he should. What is to be thought of a general country where these people are thought well of?

Chaplin thanked Agee and gently said he had nothing to say to the question.

The questions wound down. Chaplin was exhausted and depressed and he had reason to be. Picketing and other pressures exerted by the American Legion, the Catholic War Veterans, and other groups caused cancellation of many *Monsieur Verdoux* bookings across the country. Chaplin withdrew the film. In an oppressively nasty column covering the United Artists press conference, Westbrook Pegler warmed to another of his Chaplin attacks, speaking of how the comedian had "seduced a stage-struck girl, who had been beguiled to his mansion, and got her pregnant." Lies of this kind together with a denunciation in Congress by Representative John E. Rankin (stating that Chaplin had "refused" to become a citizen, and that his "loathsome pictures" should be kept from American youth) were intensely debilitating to Chaplin.

He was further upset by news stories that the House Un-American Activities Committee was planning to question him on alleged Communist views. Chaplin wired the committee that he was not a Communist but a peacemonger, and invited HUAC members to see *Monsieur Verdoux*, a statement of his humanistic philosophy. Chaplin was subpoenaed by HUAC to testify but his appearance was postponed a number of times. Finally he received a polite letter saying his testimony would not be needed and that the matter was closed.

One would have thought that the law of averages should by this time be veering back in Chaplin's favor but, at the height of his troubles in 1947, Konrad Bercovici, his old friend, sued him for $6,450,000, claiming Chaplin used ideas of his for *The Great Dictator*. Chaplin wanted to contest the suit but he claims that court pressure for a settlement (the judge wanted to leave and visit his dying father) and the low state of his own popularity in the country forced him to settle. The amount was $95,000.

Finally, as ironic footnote to an ironic film, the alleged Communist sympathizer found his film attacked by the Soviets. *Monsieur Verdoux* was not released in Russia but its scenario was printed in the Soviet literary magazine, *Culture and Life,* which faulted the film strongly for "lack of progressivism." The Soviet critic said that Verdoux need not have murdered: "Socialist optimism and confidence in his own power and in the power of other people like him who didn't like capitalism would have saved him."

This had been the worst year of Chaplin's life.

21

LIMELIGHT—AND EXILE

From the outset, domesticity well and truly agreed with Chaplin. Soon after their marriage Oona told him she was no longer interested in a career, that he had become her career. Oona came to him just in time to assuage the agony of the lawsuits and press attacks and to end a lifelong loneliness. Chaplin had few close friends and most of them had gone. His best friend, Douglas Fairbanks, died during the making of *The Great Dictator*, and jolly Henry Bergman, who boasted accurately that he was Chaplin's mascot and trademark, died during the filming of *Monsieur Verdoux*. Alf Reeves, Chaplin's studio manager who went back to the Karno days, was also gone. Oona became not only Chaplin's greatest love but his best friend as well. Their family grew. The first child, Geraldine, was born in August 1944, followed by Michael in 1946, Josephine in 1949, and Victoria in 1951.

Still stinging from the merciless slating received from critics on all sides in 1947 and 1948, it was probably inevitable that Chaplin should think of his beginnings and the warm world of the music hall where applause came uncomplicatedly and always validly. In a sense *Limelight* is an allegory about Charles Chaplin in time of his deepest trauma—the once wildly popular star brought to disfavor, who, on meeting an enchanting young girl, comes to terms with himself. *Limelight,* for all its flaws, is a film which (to echo Pepys's praise of Betterton) gives us fresh reason never to think enough of Chaplin. In Eric Bentley's words, "The film is at best a glorious failure about a glorious failure."

That failure is Calvero, an old music hall artist who had been one of the great star turns in the nineties. Living in embittered alcoholism in a seedy boardinghouse, he wonders why his magic touch with audiences failed, reducing him to such crushing anonymity. (Frank Tinney, the Broadway comedian whose career sputtered out, served as a model for Calvero.) Coming home one day from the pub, Calvero smells gas in a flat beneath his, breaks down the door, and discovers a young girl, Terry (Claire Bloom), unconscious. The girl is not thankful for the help. She has what appears to be a psychosomatic paralysis of the legs; her future as a ballerina seems hopeless. Calvero chides her, encourages her, tells her that if she wills it hard enough she can really walk. In this process of encouragement, Calvero gives new hope to both Terry and himself. As she begins to dream old dreams, Calvero discovers a few of his own. Perhaps he can make contact with his audiences again.

Putting her up in his room, Calvero nurses her until the glorious day when she takes her first faltering steps. She returns to her dancing, getting stronger daily, and in time goes beyond even her old skills. She finds an interim job at a music shop where she and a young customer, Neville (Sydney Chaplin), are mutually attracted. Neville is abysmally poor and Terry, compassionately giving him too much change, is fired for her indiscretion. Neville's fortunes as a composer grow. He falls in love with Terry and offers her the leading role in a new ballet he has written.

Terry fights the love she feels for Neville. Grateful for what Calvero has done for her, she transmutes that gratitude into a forced love for him. She wants to marry him but he sees the folly of it. Calvero steps out, making a comeback try at a flea-bitten music hall, but it does not come off. Terry gets him a job at the Empire Theatre where she has been engaged. He plays a small clown role in the ballet but does not prove satisfactory. Discovering that he is about to be let go, he wanders out of Terry's life. Terry's impresario, Postant (Nigel Bruce), learning that this commonplace bit actor is actually the once great Calvero, tries to find him, without success.

The war. Months pass and Neville, now in the army, sees Calvero among some street buskers in a pub. (Typical of the muted autobiographical references in the film is Calvero's statement to

Neville about his present job: "There's something about work in the streets I like. It's the tramp in me, I suppose.") Calvero politely says he wants to be left alone. Terry finds Calvero. Postant wants to give him a benefit but Calvero needs only a chance to show that he is not through yet. He has been working on a comedy act he feels is worthy of Calvero.

It is. And fully worthy of a fellow named Chaplin too. Before a large audience at Postant's theatre, Calvero, violin in hand, introduces his partner and comic-accompanist (unnamed in the film), the great Buster Keaton, wearing thick spectacles and looking like a myopic turtle, carrying a thick sheaf of piano music. Buster gropes his way to the piano, sits, strikes a chord, and his music slithers to the ground in cascading folds. As Buster gathers up his music unendingly, Calvero prepares. He wears baggy mid-calf-length pants and from time to time one or the other foot ascends into a pant leg, astonishing him considerably. He can kick out the shrinking leg to normal length but it invariably shortens again, surprising and vexing him in equal measure. Once *both* legs withdraw, making him an instant dwarf, but, inspired, he takes his violin bow, pulls himself up by the crotch, rising to full height.

Buster is now ready, nods; Calvero, violin in hand, nods, wants an A, Buster gives him an A which mysteriously rises in pitch. Calvero keeps tuning, a string pops up, Buster indicates that is *not* the key. Calvero keeps tuning as Buster's note keeps going up in pitch; another string pops up. Buster tries to tune the violin; Calvero takes a tuning rod, works on the piano strings, one breaks. Calvero's violin falls to the ground, Buster accidentally steps on it, it sticks to his foot. The piano innards spring upward one by one, Calvero pulls out a large tangled sleave of piano strings; Buster takes wire cutters and snaps them all off, throwing the entire mess offstage. Calvero does a triumphant glissade on the piano: it's perfectly fine.

Buster sits down; Calvero takes his bow, looks for his violin, discovers it on Buster's right foot, tries to pull it off, making Buster fall off his stool. Calvero reaches in back of himself, pulls out a new violin, and the two men play a smart roulade stirringly, then into a soft lyric that entrances Calvero to the point where he kisses the piano. Buster looks on patiently. Calvero plays now to such a point of lush sentimentality that he weeps piteously; it is too much: he falls sobbing on the piano, Buster too. Calvero pulls himself together and goes into another strain, this one *vivace;* he is almost demonic in his happiness. Buster pounds away so strongly that his stool crashes down but he plays on gamely. Calvero plays on and on, swirling right and then left in his ecstasy— and falls into the orchestra pit. Buster, mildly astonished not to see his friend, plays on. Calvero has landed in the drum and two musicians hoist him painfully to the stage. Calvero is still playing. (Curiously, all during this uproariously funny routine, there is no audience reaction on the sound track. Perhaps Chaplin wanted our absolute attention to the act. He need not have worried.)

The audience now thunders its approval, demands more of Calvero, but he is unable to be moved. Still held up in the drum, he gives a brief curtain speech of gratitude, and is brought backstage. He has suffered a heart attack. Terry does not want to leave his side but he insists she dance Neville's beautiful ballet. Calvero watches her from side stage and dies doubly content—in the knowledge of his final success and of her love for him.

When *Limelight* premiered in New York, October 23, 1952, the critics were unanimous in their relief that the "old" Chaplin was back. The film was very much a family affair with Neville well played by his son Sydney, a brief appearance by little Geraldine, Michael, and Josephine, and other roles filled by Charlie Chaplin, Jr., and Chaplin's half brother, Wheeler Dryden. Claire Bloom was entirely right as Terry and Buster Keaton and Chaplin were superb in the comedy act. Associate director Robert Aldrich kept production values intact and Chaplin's ballet "The Death of Columbine" was exquisitely danced by Melissa Hayden and Andre Eglevsky.

And yet . . . Almost every time the film moves forward it takes a step back. This occurs when Chaplin decides to issue little philosophic bulletins that tell us more than we need to know of things we don't care about. "From the first reel of *Limelight,*" says Walter Kerr, "it is perfectly clear that Chaplin now wants to talk, that he *loves* to talk, that in this film he intends to do little *but* talk." Robert Warshow, also lamenting Chaplin's inability to stop talking, said, "his true profundity is still in his silences."

Of course this may be a reasonable price to pay for, if not our Charlie, at least someone very close to him. For not only did

Frank Tinney serve as inspiration for *Limelight* but so did two
other comedians as well—Chaplin and his father. The alcoholic
comedian who knew better days can hardly be anyone other than
Charles Chaplin, Sr.; the much-married performer who likes
young women, who can no longer make people laugh and who has
been harried by life's turns and buffets, must be Chaplin himself.
Indeed, as Andrew Sarris observes, Chaplin has had the exalted
experience in the film of imagining his own death, "a conception
of sublime egoism unparalleled in the world cinema," since "to
imagine one's own death one must imagine the death of the
world."

Just as, at the height of his supremely successful career, George
M. Cohan wrote a play that projected how it might have been
had he failed, so Chaplin crafts his own *Song and Dance Man:
Limelight*, a nostalgic journey to what might have been.

The press reception for *Limelight*, to use Chaplin's adjective,
was "lukewarm," but over the years the film did very well com-
mercially. Shortly after the film was finished, the Chaplins decided to take a six-month tour of England and Europe. Oona had
never been abroad and was looking forward to the trip with great
anticipation. After a bon voyage barbecue for the Chaplins given
by Tim Durant, he drove them next morning to the Union Station in Los Angeles. In the car Chaplin turned to Durant, eyes
brimming, and said he had a presentiment he would never return.
Durant scoffed but Chaplin insisted his feeling was very real.

Weeks before he had applied for a re-entry permit from the Immigration Department and although there were pointed questions
about his second front speeches and tendency to follow "the
Party line," the atmosphere was friendly and the permit issued.
Chaplin, Oona, and their four children left on the *Queen Elizabeth* on September 17, 1952, and two days at sea, the United
States Attorney General, James McGranery, ordered the Immigration and Naturalization Service to bar Chaplin's return to the
United States under a code denying an alien's entry on grounds of
morals or Communist affiliation. McGranery told reporters the action had been contemplated for some time and that he would not
reveal what the charges were. When asked why not, he made the
curious reply that to do so would tip off Mr. Chaplin. In other
words, Chaplin was not allowed to prepare a defense. A few days

later McGranery was a little less vague but only a little. He said that Chaplin had been "publicly charged" with being a Communist and "publicly charged" with "grave moral charges, and with making statements that would indicate a leering, sneering attitude toward a country whose hospitality has enriched him."

Chaplin, properly stunned at this Lewis Carroll maundering, grew apprehensive about his fortune. His money was in California and if such attitudes as McGranery's existed in other high places —who could guess? Oona flew back to California from London and was able to get the money out of the United States.

The McGranery charges, like *Limelight*, got a mixed press. That astute political analyst and sociologist, Hedda Hopper, was moved to say that, although Chaplin was undeniably a good actor, that did not give him the right "to go against our customs, to abhor everything we stand for, to throw our hospitality back in our faces. . . . Good riddance to bad company!" William Bradford Huie, editor of the *American Mercury*, less ponderously than Miss Hopper scored Chaplin too, accusing him among other things of loathing the poor and loving no one but himself. But, Huie asserted, in the United States one had the sovereign right to be a stinker, and Chaplin was "a genuine, twenty-four carat, ringtailed stinker." The Hearst papers were part of the Hopper-Huie axis.

More than balancing these onslaughts were editorials supporting Chaplin from the New York *Times* and *Life* magazine. Mary Pickford, hardly the darling of the left, called the McGranery move "beneath the dignity of the great United States." Samuel Goldwyn, visiting London, spoke up resolutely for Chaplin, adding, ". . . and if they don't like me defending him—well, they can stop me from re-entering America too." Buster Keaton was indignant, saying that never in the twenty-five years he had known Chaplin had he ever heard him utter a political opinion.

Graham Greene, in an open letter to Chaplin printed in the *New Statesman and Nation*, recalled a visit to the Chaplin home not long before. On that occasion Greene suggested that Chaplin bring Charlie back to the screen. The plot would be simple: Charlie, living forgotten in a New York attic, is suddenly summoned before the House Un-American Activities Committee to account for his past—that is, for his suspicious behavior in the ring in

Modern Times and other films, and "for all the hidden significance of the dance with the bread rolls." Greene pictured the committee members solemnly taking their damaging notes as they watched early Chaplin films.

> You laughed the suggestion away [continued Greene to Chaplin] and indeed I had thought of no climax. The Attorney General of the United States has supplied that. For at the close of the hearing Charlie could surely admit to being in truth unAmerican and produce the passport of another country which, lying rather closer to danger, is free from the ugly manifestations of fear. . . . Intolerance in any country wounds freedom throughout the world.

In London, after the inevitable visit to the scenes of his childhood, this time with Oona, Chaplin arranged for the London showing of *Limelight*, a charity performance with Princess Margaret in attendance. Even though the reviews of the film were not enthusiastic, he had good reason to think that the American public would give the film the same warm welcome as European filmgoers.

The American public never got the chance. Howard Hughes, the American Legion, and other veterans' groups began either pressure tactics or boycotting to discourage showing of the film. By May 1953, when under normal booking circumstances *Limelight* would have already been shown in over 25,000 American theatres, it had appeared in only 150.

Commonweal made an effective summary of the affair:

> But whatever may be one's opinion of Mr. Chaplin's private life and views, the fact remains that he is a very great artist whose contributions to American life and culture have been far in excess of any material reward America could give him in return. His vision of the comedy, pathos and tragedy of human destiny, and his consistent plea for the dignity of human life, are things beyond measuring in terms of material reward. If now, in the midst of controversy, American audiences are denied the opportunity to share his vision and hear his plea, America itself will be the loser.

Limelight continued to receive a few sporadic showings across the United States.

Worried about blocked currency, Chaplin decided that Switzerland with its superb banking facilities and ideal tax base would make a likelier residence than London. The Chaplins found a beautiful twenty-room house, the Manoir de Bain, in the village of Corsier, just above Vevey. The stately but not lavish home was on thirty-seven acres of land, a part of which the Chaplins used to grow all their vegetables including the corn on the cob he had cherished from his first days in the States.

Oona, in helping her husband settle into his last home, made the commitment to him total by giving up her American citizenship and becoming a British subject. Chaplin had found, after years of almost uninterrupted personal turmoil, the perfect wife.

Chaplin's personal and professional lives had been the converse of each other: the former, an extension of failures ending in a superb success; the latter, a long run of successes trailing away badly. It is tempting to take this reverse symmetry of a failed private life and a supremely successful career and find in these opposites a psychological underlay to explain it tidily. But that would be mostly guessing. We do not know why it happened nor is it terribly important that we do. Certainly Chaplin was deeply distressed over the press's unremitting attention to his so-called escapades. One sensible speculation about the conditioning factors of Chaplin's failures in the public eye comes from Roger Manvell, who believes that there is a strong dichotomy in Chaplin's nature, as well as a dichotomy "within the period in which he has lived, and within the public who have both over-idolized and over-persecuted him. The idolization sprang from the extraordinary speed of the worldwide recognition of his genius, which could only have been effected by the rapid, universal dissemination of his image through the cinema. . . . The persecution arose with almost equal rapidity because the mass-circulation press . . . was able to exploit wide-scale public interest in the scandals which came to be associated with his name. But the dichotomy was deep in [Chaplin] himself. At one and the same time, he exploited and resented his phenomenal fame. He both gloried in it and loathed the results of it. What neither he nor anyone else could be expected to understand at the time was the price that had to be paid for this sudden fame."

The most galling of the penalties Chaplin had to pay was the ridiculing of his failures as a husband and lover. Stan Laurel had an opinion on Chaplin's love life:

On the big subject of Charlie and the ladies, I don't think the entire truth will be known until Oona tells of his confidences to her—if ever he tells her, if ever she tells us. Maybe they've never even talked about it. About his love life I'll make an educated guess. Charlie as I knew him, and as a lot of our mutual friends knew him, was impossibly, childishly romantic. I liked that about him. Always, from childhood on, always expecting to meet the beautiful princess who would fall in love with him as deeply as he fell in love with her, and then they'd live happily ever after. When he met Hetty, she was from all I've heard a girl who looked just like a little fairy princess, and when that didn't work out, he went out looking for another like her. Notice that he steered away at least in marriage from mature women like Edna who could really help him and be "good" for him. Instead he'd go for these little fairy-princess-looking types—Mildred and Lita and even Paulette with that gamine quality of hers. The trouble with Mildred and Lita and Paulette was that they only *looked* like fairy princesses. Charlie never gave up. He finally found her when he was fifty. Oona was a fairy princess come true—type-casting right out of Disney, young, beautiful, adoring, innocent—and it didn't make one tiny teeny little damn that they were so far apart in years. You also have to remember that Charlie even with white hair never looked his age because he never was his age. Charlie just never grew up. He was always young, always Jimmy the Fearless, always the handsome young prince, and a hell of a rare one who could break your heart and make you yell with laughter at the same time. And at the last he got his fairy princess and they sure as hell lived happily ever after. I think it's one of the great love stories of history.

22
FINAL FILMS

On settling in to Swiss life, the Chaplins found living in Corsier comforting, with one exception. Close to the Manoir de Bain was a national shooting range where Swiss army reservists were required to engage in rifle practice on a continuing basis. Chaplin, who, in his 1922 book, *My Trip Abroad*, praised silence as "that universal grace, how few of us know how to enjoy it!" was devastated. He protested that the gunfire was nerve-shattering and kept protesting until the authorities compromised on the duration and frequency of the firing sessions. After that Chaplin was able to relax and concentrate on his script writing, which was now his principal occupation. Oona for her part proved a most efficient housekeeper. She kept in functioning order the seventeen servants, including a chauffeur and gardeners, who staffed Manoir de Bain.

A friend of the Chaplins said three adjectives best suited Oona: serene, beautiful, maternal. In addition to the four Chaplin children born in the United States there came along in Corsier Eugene, 1953; Jane, 1958; Annette, 1960 and Christopher, 1962. The children were raised with much love and a great deal of discipline. When Harold Clurman visited the Chaplins in 1962 he was told by his host: "Oh, I wouldn't ever send my children to an American school. They're too easy. French schools are tough. My children will have enough money to paper the walls with. They must be prepared for life by some form of hardship. They must learn discipline of some kind. French schools make the children really study."

One at least of the Chaplin children rebelled at the regimen of
French schools. Michael decamped and left Switzerland for a
singing-acting career in London.

Sydney and Charlie Chaplin, Jr., visited their father a number
of times at Corsier. Charlie, Jr., concerned with his father's reputation in the United States, asked him why during the days of sensitivity over the Korean conflict he had invited Chou En-lai to
dinner. Chaplin replied that, although he did not agree with most
of the Chinese leader's policies, he was curious about what "made
him tick." His son was apprehensive about reaction in the States,
and it soon came. In 1954 the *Saturday Evening Post* in all
seriousness said that, after forty years' residence in the United
States, "Chaplin has openly joined our enemy, the Soviet slave
masters." Their documentation for this grave charge was Chaplin's dinner with Chou En-lai.

The *Post* also viewed in strident alarm Chaplin's support of a
passport for Paul Robeson and his acceptance of the Communist-
sponsored World Peace Council's annual prize. The latter may
well have been, as the New York *Times* said, an example of
Chaplin's being used by a Communist unit for propaganda purposes. But Chaplin at least knew what to do with the money: he
donated it to the poor of France through Abbé Pierre, the "rag-
picker priest" of Paris.

It would have given the *Post*'s editors terminal apoplexy to have
seen Chaplin later on a London visit going to a Soviet reception
at Claridge's at the request of visiting nabobs Khrushchev and Bul-
ganin. Chaplin was very pleased with Khrushchev for having given
a recent good will speech that seemed to lighten world tensions.
Chaplin told him as much and Khrushchev pumped his hand,
called him a genius, and said, "They repudiate you but we recognize you. You're the best-known man in Russia." Chaplin was flattered but this was an old tune. The Russian Embassy in Switzerland was in the habit of inviting him to formal parties, during
which an embassy official would always sound Chaplin out on
showing his films in Russia. Briskly Chaplin would inquire about
the financial arrangements. That ended the discussion until the
next party and a similar roundelay.

In any context, Chaplin's radicalism was a myth. "All his life,"
says Alistair Cooke, "[Chaplin's] much abused 'radical philoso-

phy' was no more than an automatic theme song in favor of peace, humanity, 'the little man,' and other desirable abstractions —as humdrum politicians come out for mother love and lower taxes."

Chaplin's business perceptions did not diminish through the years. He realized that his films and much unused comedy footage edited from released material were worth millions. He cabled Rollie Totheroh early in 1954 to empty the La Brea studio's vaults and ship all the Chaplin film to Corsier where special adjustable-temperature bins had been built. Totheroh personally took to Switzerland another precious consignment—Charlie's cane, derby, and pants in a specially constructed bag. The professionally blasé London customs men goggled at these relics.

Totheroh was asked if he would like to continue as Chaplin's cameraman in Europe but he could not for family reasons. Chaplin gave him a generous bonus and so came to an end one of the most fruitful creative partnerships in the history of films—almost forty bountiful years. Rollie Totheroh died in 1967, intensely proud of his years with Chaplin.

Chaplin ended another relationship in his early Corsier years. In February 1955 he called the majority stockholder of United Artists to say that he would sell the Chaplin stock (twenty-five per cent of the company) for $1.1 million cash if the deal could be consummated within five days. Done, and done.

It was inevitable that inaction should wear on Chaplin. His next film, understandably, was stimulated by concerns at hand, deriving from three sources: his exile from America, a consideration of the drama inherent in the atom bomb, and the activities of dethroned royalty in Switzerland. Exile was a bitter fact of life for Chaplin, and he began to craft the story, with a semimessianic flavor of a king who, hoping to use atomic power for the betterment of his people, is deposed by greedy members of his government. Eight miles from Chaplin's home is Lausanne-Ouchy, the residence of several exiled monarchs. There Chaplin visited the ex-Queen of Spain and discussed his scenario, she commenting helpfully on royal etiquette. Chaplin also dined with Princess Marie-José of Italy at her home in Geneva.

By mid-1956 Chaplin began filming A King in New York at Shepperton Studios in England. His leading lady was Dawn

Addams, an English girl married to an Italian prince, Vittorio Massimo. Chaplin had met her when she was making *The Moon Is Blue* in Hollywood, and later when he saw her in a Vittorio De Sica film he was taken with her beauty and intense femininity.

Miss Addams noticed that Chaplin directed the film as a musical conductor would. Having composed the score, she said, he will hum the music to the actors or "he will suddenly become a saxophone or a violin to give one the mood of the scene as the spectator will watch it." She also noticed that if Chaplin had nothing to do there was tension. The actors finally arranged for a piano on the set so he could occupy himself profitably between scenes. Perhaps he knew his script was very slight. Miss Addams seemed to put her finger indirectly on the basic flaw in *A King in New York* when she said (unaware of possible ambiguities), "If I had read the script before he acted it for me, it would hardly have seemed funny at all." Unfortunately Chaplin was not available to act all the roles.

King Shahdov of Estrovia, fleeing a revolution in his country, arrives in New York to take up a fortune banked there which he hopes to spend on beneficent uses of atomic energy. He has also banked special plans for this project. While he is being fingerprinted by an immigration officer he tells a reporter that he is deeply moved by the United States' warm friendship and hospitality. Shahdov is shocked to find his conniving prime minister has stolen the atomic energy funds, and the king is faced with the need to make a living. His faithful ambassador to the United States, Jaumé (Oliver Johnston), introduces His Majesty to the pulsing life of New York. Loud noises and discordant music seem to characterize much of it as they walk down Broadway, and in seeking escape at a nearby theatre, they are overwhelmed by a rock-and-roll stage show that makes Broadway quiet by comparison.

Film previews flash on announcing a gangster film (*A Killer With a Soul*), a drama about sexual identity (*Man or Woman?*), and a Western (the villain's gun fires thirteen times rapidly). Shahdov and Jaumé escape to a restaurant where the raucous orchestra makes communication with the waiter impossible. Shahdov brilliantly mimes his order: caviar—a sturgeon gulping, hauled up and belly contents slapped on toast; and turtle soup—a plate inverted over his walking hand.

Shahdov and Jaumé are forced to live in a hotel. Queen Irene (Maxine Audley) arrives to learn from her husband that he thinks their state-arranged marriage should end. He doesn't want her to suffer it any more, and she says sadly she will do what he wishes. Shahdov is intrigued by Ann Kay (Dawn Addams), a beautiful girl living in the room next to his. She talks him into attending a dinner party given by wealthy Mrs. Cromwell (Joan Ingram), who has been trying to lionize Shahdov. Ann hides a television camera at the dinner table with her hostess' connivance, and during the evening Shahdov becomes an unwitting partner to Ann's conversationally forthright plugs for a deodorant and a toothpaste. Ann talks Shahdov (who has dabbled theatrically) into reciting the "To be or not to be" soliloquy, which he does amiably and abominably, getting the text wrong into the bargain. The television camera catches this too. Shahdov becomes a hit with the vast television audience, for reasons that defy analysis.

Although angered by Ann's trick, and unable to reach the Atomic Energy Commission with his plans for atomic progress, Shahdov realizes that he might as well take financial advantage of his new popularity and he agrees to do commercials.

On a tour of a progressive school he meets a moody young boy, Rupert McAbee (Michael Chaplin), reading Marx. Asked if he is a Communist (obvious shades of a much-asked question), Rupert asks if one has to be a Communist to read Marx. Rupert hurls hearty animadversions against passports and lack of travel freedom. Shahdov *likes* the boy. "Obnoxious, offensive—but a genius," he characterizes the lad.

Shahdov, in doing a whiskey commercial, chokes when drinking it on the air. But Ann congratulates him on being a great comedian; she also encourages him for the sake of his new-found career to have his face lifted. He agrees but the operation leaves him with a varnish-like skin, and he is under strict orders for a time not to move his muscles, not even to smile. Relaxing with Ann at a night club, Shahdov cannot join in the hearty laughter greeting a slapstick comedy act. Strenuously he resists laughing but finally succumbs, only to grab his face, shouting, "I've come undone! It's all slipped!" The plastic surgeon restores him to his former self.

Shahdov befriends Rupert, who has run away from school because the government wants to question him about his Communist parents. ("I'm so sick and tired of people asking me if I'm this, if I'm that!" says Rupert in another heartfelt Chaplin line.) When Shahdov goes out to his bank to get his atomic energy plans, members of the Atomic Energy Commission show up in his rooms. Thinking Rupert to be the king's nephew, they are cordial until he rambles on with a speech learned from his father about those in the United States who are condemned without trial. Shahdov returns but the commission men say they have plans similar to his.

At a congressional committee session Rupert's father admits to having been a Communist but says he resigned from the Party five years ago. Asked to name those who had been in the Party with him, McAbee refuses to answer and is cited for contempt of Congress. Rupert is torn by this. He is taken into government custody in the hope he will talk about his father's past associates. Shahdov falls under suspicion and is subpoenaed to appear before the congressional committee.

In an elevator on his way to the congressional building, Shahdov idly inserts his finger in a fire hose and cannot get it free. He is forced to take the long hose with him across town and into the very committee room itself, the hose end trailing off down the hall. A guard, seeing the hose, thinks there is a fire, connects the hose to an outlet, turns it on. Shahdov, unable to control the surging hose as it pours forth, inundates the committee.

Shahdov proves to be a friendly witness and is cleared of Communism. He and Ann say mutually affectionate good-bys as he prepares to leave for his restored throne in Estrovia. Ann says the American turmoil is all a passing phase. "Quite so," says Shahdov. "In the meantime, I'll sit it out in Europe." Ann says the committee has made him the most popular man in America. A wire comes from the queen saying she has decided against a divorce. Shahdov visits Rupert, who sobbingly confesses that to free his folks he revealed the names of their Communist associates. Shahdov tells the boy to cheer up—that when all the hysteria is over he will have Rupert and his family as his guests in Estrovia. There is, he assures the boy, nothing to worry about.

If *A King in New York* does not sound funny in the telling, it must be said it is not very funny in the viewing. There are some marvelous moments: Shahdov miming his dinner order to the waiter and trying to preserve his face lift, among the few. But the writing is perfunctory ("To part is to die a little") and the physical production is at times dowdy or inappropriate. To instance the last, in the New York theatre the king visits, a door to the orchestra seats is marked "Stalls," the British usage, and similarly an elevator is identified as "Lift." The Washington street scenes are clearly London. The poverty of the directing is epitomized in a fairly long scene between Shahdov and the queen sitting on a sofa. At one point Shahdov, for no other reason than to break up the monotony of their position, gets up for a drink of water.

Seventeen years later, Chaplin said that in retrospect he was a little uneasy and disappointed with the film. He wanted it to be very modern but "perhaps I didn't quite understand it. It started out to be very good and then it got complicated and a little heavy-handed."

A King in New York, in spite of its failings, must be seen—at least once. The parallel, says Stanley Kauffmann, is to a Beethoven lover who knows he must hear the Triple Concerto once before he dies, no matter what he thinks of it.

Chaplin was just beginning to shoot A King in New York when his brother Sydney died on April 16, 1956, in Nice. The loss was the likely impetus for Chaplin's writing his autobiography. When the brothers saw each other in the years after Sydney's retirement there was a special joy in their reunions. Sydney had shared Chaplin's deepest distresses, had given him guidance and encouragement and, above all, had helped him to financial freedom.

In June 1962, Oxford University announced that it had offered an honorary doctorate of letters to Chaplin and he had accepted, with the intention of receiving the honor at the upcoming commencement. H. Trevor-Roper, the distinguished historian and Oxford don, was horrified at the idea. He stated publicly that for an actor, and particularly a comedian, to be so honored by Oxford was a ghastly error, a scandal. "We might as well be honoring a circus clown," he said.

Chaplin got what there was of his Irish up. "That made me mad," he said. "Damned mad." As he took the train to Oxford, he was uncertain what to do about Trevor-Roper's statement. He did not know whether he would be called on to speak; he decided in any case he would write out nothing beforehand. At Oxford he was given the traditional doctoral robes and joined in the academic proceedings. Although hampered by bronchitis, he decided that if called on he would say just a few words. Before conferral he was told he might say something if he liked.

Chaplin rose, faced the distinguished body of scholars, and noticed Trevor-Roper sitting right before him. Softly, and without looking at the haughty don, Chaplin said that he understood some astonishment, even indignation, had been expressed that a mere comedian should be named a doctor of letters. He admitted he was no man of letters and in any case that title was ambiguous. "Man of letters" could mean a variety of things—including a postman. Chaplin admitted he could not compete with that august assemblage on matters of knowledge or morality, but he rather thought he was qualified to talk about beauty because that was a matter of individual taste and preference. Chaplin considered everybody equal on that subject.

Beauty, he said, could be found in the oddest places—a garbage can, viewed in a certain way, might be considered beautiful. Or it could be found in a rose—and at this, Chaplin bent over the podium, opening his hand as if to release the bud—it could be found in a rose floating down a gutter. "Or even," Chaplin said, "even in the antics of a clown."

He looked directly at Trevor-Roper as he said it, and then nodded to his audience in thanks for their overwhelmingly warm applause.

Before Chaplin's *My Autobiography* was published in 1964 there had been great anticipation. In publishing circles the rumors were that Chaplin was going to tell all, and in a way that is what happened. He told all that was truly interesting to *him*—his boyhood and inceptive years and his triumphs, primarily social, among the great ones of the world. Perhaps he cannot be greatly faulted for that in view of where and how he began and where he ended on the heights of accomplishment. But details of his working life were conspicuously lacking, especially any meaningful account of his working with Stan Laurel, Rollie Totheroh, Mack Swain, Eric Campbell, Albert Austin, Henry Bergman, and others. One gets no real flavor of life in the Chaplin Studios. The errors in the book, like those listed in earlier chapters in the present pages, are not vital ones but they should not be there. For instance, he speaks of meeting the impresario Diaghilev in Los Angeles when Diaghilev was not traveling with the ballet company Chaplin saw, was not even in the United States. Yet Chaplin doubtless met Diaghilev somewhere.

The title puzzles. Why the redundant My? Who else's autobiography would Chaplin be writing? Parker Tyler makes the interesting point that the "My" is present "as much to dissociate its subject from the films' various characters, or masks, as from the biographic portraits made of him by others. . . ." Either that, or an editor at Chaplin's publishing house was too timid to discuss the error with him.

The reviewers almost without exception loved the first third of the book and were wearied by the rest. Most, like Arthur Knight, complained of the incessant name-dropping, and some, like Brendan Gill, were appalled. Gill, a complete Charlie devotee, was revolted by the book and its essential irrelevancy. He could not account for the "discrepancy between the fame- and money-loving man who wrote it and the incorruptible artist whose career it fails to describe. . . ." Malcolm Muggeridge also spoke of Chaplin's galloping self-pity and his "everlasting pre-occupation with money." (Muggeridge would have been interested to know that when the Soviets requested reprint rights Chaplin sold Izvestia one thousand words from the book for nine pounds of the best caviar.)

As a book, then, My Autobiography may not be much. It may even be a bad book, but it is all we have of Chaplin speaking in old age, that and his My Life in Pictures, the large and fascinating picture book published in 1974. Budd Schulberg, who did not care for the autobiography very much, ended his review, "After all, Charlie is not a writer, he is our only genius of the motion picture. Do you expect a butterfly to sing?"

"Neither the autobiography nor any book," said Stan Laurel, "ever conveyed a couple of minor but interesting things about Charlie, like his tininess, for instance. He really is a very little man, which used to surprise some people when they first met him. And the curious shape of him. Mary Pickford said he once told her, 'My head's too big for my body, my arms are too short for my body, and my hands are too small for my arms.' He was quite right. As far as I know only Charlie, Jr., ever talked about his dad's real hates. Charlie hated, and I mean hated, telephones—just couldn't abide them. He hated open windows too, and he especially hated anyone failing to knock before coming into a room he was in. This last was a carry-over from his days of poverty when privacy didn't exist for him.

"There was another carry-over from his early days, and that was a passion of his. What you'd call a really grand passion—for high buttoned shoes. What in England we called boots—buttoned shoes coming over the ankles. For Charlie this was the greatest sign of success. This was a childhood dream come true because when we were kids all the great actor-managers wore these hand-crafted high buttoned shoes, all the great successful men in the Edwardian theatre wore them. So when Charlie was able to afford shoes like that, he could never get over it. That meant he was really at the top. He first started to have those shoes made during World War I, and for years after. When he met Paulette she tried to tell him in a very nice way that in 1938 those shoes weren't quite the style any more. Charlie didn't give a damn. He wore them anyway. I think it was the only thing they ever quarreled over. For me, the real proof that Charlie loved Oona above all women on earth was that after they were married he gave up those shoes for her."

On a trip to London at the time *My Autobiography* was published, Chaplin saw Sophia Loren in the film *Yesterday, Today and Tomorrow*. He was enchanted—and interested. For over thirty years he had been reworking the story of a beautiful countess who stows away in the cabin of an American diplomat on a liner outward bound from Hong Kong. He offered the role to Sophia, who took it gladly. Working with Chaplin was a height she wanted to climb.

Marlon Brando, whose respect for Chaplin was vast, accepted the role of the diplomat. Shooting on *A Countess from Hong Kong* began at Pinewood Studios near London on January 24, 1966, and ended five months later. Joseph Morgenstern of *Newsweek* watched part of the filming and was intrigued by Chaplin's boundless enthusiasm and creative energy at seventy-six. Why was he still working at his age? Two reasons: he always needed something to do, and making movies was a lot of fun. Confirming rumors about the film, Chaplin admitted it was old-fashioned, and he confessed to nostalgia. When Morgenstern suggested that nostalgia was another word for love of one's former self, Chaplin said, "Perhaps it is. I wouldn't want to go through all the suffering, the unhappiness again, yet I wouldn't have lived any other way."

Penelope Gilliatt also visited the *Countess* set and marveled at Brando's total attention to Chaplin's sometimes overly detailed instructions on reading a line or doing a bit of business. This form of directing was the opposite of the kind Brando preferred and had worked under his entire career. One day on the set Brando, in keeping with his training, went to Chaplin and said he did not understand the character's motive at that point. Chaplin replied that he didn't know the character's motive either but if he did it wouldn't be very much. He told Brando precisely how to play it, saying in that way it would come off. Brando never asked Chaplin anything again.

Given the director and author, the stars and the cast, the film might have been bad but interesting. *A Countess from Hong Kong* is simply bad.

A very brief synopsis of the film will perfectly suit its arid *longueurs*. A wealthy U.S. diplomat, Ogden Mears (Marlon Brando), is returning home from Hong Kong. When he is in port he spends a hilariously alcoholic evening with a White Russian countess, Natascha (Sophia Loren), who contrives to smuggle herself aboard Mears's ship and stow away in his cabin. Next morning he is appalled to find her there but agrees to help her reach the United States. Mears is hard put to it to keep Natascha from the prying eyes of ship's personnel and also realizes that to get through American immigration the countess must marry someone who will give her American nationality. He persuades his austere and sexless valet, Hudson (Patrick Cargill), to marry the lady for this purpose. Mears and Natascha fall in love and are satisfactorily united.

Chaplin makes a cameo appearance in the film as a steward. In his last scene, seasick, he does not say a word. Chaplin left films as he had entered them, Denis Gifford observes, in silence.

A Countess from Hong Kong got a very bad press, and small wonder. Even allowing for the failure of some critics to realize that this was not essentially comedy but a romantic comedy, one can only watch it with a mixture of boredom, hope, and impatience. One endlessly repeated gag typifies the film's sterility: when Natascha is hiding in Mears's cabin, the door buzzer sounds frequently, causing either or both of them to scatter to the other bedroom. After a bit this simply wears the viewer down.

One very small moment in A Countess from Hong Kong may perhaps serve as emblem for the difference between the early Chaplin and the very late Chaplin, and it is a moment the earlier Chaplin would not have countenanced. Chaplin told Eddie Sutherland that although he did not mind coincidence in his films he could not abide coincidence that was convenient. At one point the countess is hitchhiking, and a huge truck carrying heavy equipment comes along immediately and gives her a ride in the back. Fine. No one in his right mind is going to turn down a hitchhiker like Sophia Loren. Perfectly viable, her getting a ride instantly. But as she swings up on the hard, dirty floor of the truck, by a convenient coincidence, there just happens to be placed there a soft pallet—several blankets—to keep the cold, dirty steel from that lovely body. It won't do.

Chaplin was hurt by the generally disastrous notices the film received. Perhaps because he had so much fun making the film, the cold reception it got was all the more disturbing. It was in the main a happy company. Sophia Loren loved Chaplin and tried to put that love into her work. She felt something less for Brando. One afternoon as she was walking by him, he kiddingly slapped her on the derrière. She was not kidded. "Don't ever do that again," she said, grabbing his arm. "I am not the sort of woman who is flattered by it."

Brando's performance, perhaps because of his need to accommodate to a style of creativity not his own, seems almost muffled, as if he were annoyed or bored, or both.

One of the weightier sorrows of Chaplin's life occurred on March 20, 1968, with the death by heart attack in Beverly Hills of Charlie Chaplin, Jr. Young Charlie's life had been full of stresses. Charming and sentimental by nature, he lacked the extroverted nature of his brother Sydney, and in consequence took life's pains very much to heart. In the title of his autobiography, My Father, Charlie Chaplin (1960), young Charlie revealed not only his life obsession but indirectly how the struggle to be his own man traumatized him into two failed marriages and a drinking problem. All his life he wanted to be recognized as an actor but his name haunted him. Once when he got an interview with a prominent theatrical producer young Charlie, after a long wait, went eagerly into the man's office only to find him reading a newspaper. Ignoring the young man, the producer read for a few moments, then without lowering the paper, said, "Are you as great as *he* is?" Young Charlie turned and walked out. At his son's birth, Chaplin had argued bitterly that it was an imposition on the boy's future to call him Charlie Chaplin, Jr. Chaplin was proved right but it was cruel vindication.

By 1971, Chaplin was working alternately on two scripts. One, *The Freak*, written for his two daughters, Josephine and Victoria, was a circus side-show story about an angel who comes down to earth. The second script, written with son Sydney in mind, was a black comedy about a condemned man in a Kansas jail. The latter more or less died on the vine; *The Freak* was not produced because daughter Victoria left home to get married.

At the Twenty-fifth Cannes Film Festival in 1971 Chaplin accepted a special award for his films and received the rank of commander of the Legion of Honor. Interviewed at the time, he confessed to distaste for most modern films, especially the sensational ones which he regarded as a passing vogue. About his own work, he said:

"Intellectuals have claimed that my films are intellectual. I don't think they are. My ambition has always been to be an artist, not an intellectual. Above all, I wanted to entertain. I still want to."

Meanwhile in the United States both the Academy of Motion Picture Arts and Sciences and the Film Society of Lincoln Center were hoping that Chaplin would accept a shared invitation to visit them. Legally there was no reason why he should not. The McGranery injunction had lapsed long before. The only thing preventing Chaplin's return to the United States was Chaplin. There was no hesitation. He would come.

He and Oona arrived in New York on April 3, 1972, and were greeted by over a hundred newspeople and photographers. They were taken to their suite at the Hotel Plaza where they rested before going to a dinner given by Oona's girlhood friend, Gloria

Vanderbilt Cooper. The next evening was the feature presentation of the New York visit, a black-tie champagne reception at $100 and $250 a head at Philharmonic Hall for the benefit of the Lincoln Center Film Society.

Prior to the reception Chaplin and an audience of fifteen hundred watched a showing of *The Idle Class* and *The Kid*. When Chaplin appeared in his box the applause began resoundingly, interspersed with bravos until everyone stood and the chant, "*Char-lie! Charlie!*" rolled through the hall. The shouting and the applause continued and continued. Chaplin kept bowing and blowing kisses. The applause would not stop. Inspired, he did the things they had grown to love him for—the gestures, shrugs, and moues of Charlie. Each brought forth a roar of recognition and affection. Many, like Norman Mailer, wept. After *The Kid* was shown, the applause stormed again and he said a few words of thanks, ending with "This is my renaissance. I'm born again."

Candice Bergen, on an assignment from *Life*, was moved by his essential shyness and simplicity as well as the depth of the Chaplins' feelings for each other:

> The Chaplins were conspicuous in their simplicity, their absence of props, the lack of preoccupation with fashion. With his small hands and feet and ample middle, Charlie looks the same no matter what he wears: padded—a silhouette forsaken for the love of vanilla ice cream.

On the flight to Los Angeles, Chaplin was asked by a television reporter if he thought "the audience of today" would "understand" his films, then appearing in revival across the country. Properly taken aback by the question, Chaplin rallied and said yes. "I understand them, and God knows I'm no intellectual." As the plane crossed the Grand Canyon he looked out and remembered that Douglas Fairbanks had once told him he did a handstand on the very brink. As the plane got closer to Los Angeles, Chaplin became increasingly nervous, surer and surer that he should not have accepted the invitation. But he calmed down after a bit, trying to convince himself that the place wasn't too bad. "After all, I met Oona there."

In the twenty years since he had seen Los Angeles it had altered drastically. Driving through it, Chaplin said, "It's nothing but

banks, banks, banks." The reception for him by the assembled
Academy of Motion Picture Arts and Sciences the evening of
April 10 rivaled the one at Lincoln Center. Chaplin had been so
badly hurt by the events of twenty years before that he really
feared some members of the audience would hiss. Instead he received another tumultuous welcome, a standing ovation that
lasted long minutes. Close to tears, he accepted his Oscar, blowing
kisses incessantly. Later he said simply, "It surpasses everything."

Returning briefly to New York, he told Richard Meryman how
difficult it was to relate the present to the past, that time
progresses in spite of everything, in spite of oneself. "It's mystic:
to have lived before, yet you are not the same person. But you *were*
the same person."

The same person Chaplin was, fashioned in a Dickensian London, living into an age increasingly too complex for his tastes and
interests, found that his late films, the ones made accommodating
the modern world, did no such thing, that he was indeed a child
of his times and happiest artistically only to be there. Otis Ferguson, as far back as *Modern Times*, made the point that if
Chaplin "keeps on refusing to learn any more than he learned
when the movies themselves were just learning, each successive
picture he makes will seem, on release, to fall short of what went
before." So it duly proved.

Chaplin did not keep up for one thing because Charlie was a
creature of silent film. Yet what does a great actor do when his
supreme impersonation is shunted aside—virtually destroyed—by
inescapable technology? Andrew Sarris says that, "for Chaplin, his
other self on the screen has always been the supreme subject of
contemplation." Exactly. And if Charlie must go, Chaplin tries to
reach us with Verdoux, Calvero, and Shahdov, who may be the
darker, weaker side of Charlie—or of himself—or of both.

Richard Schickel sees surfacing in Chaplin's last films "the increasingly shrill egoism of the artist, a quality transcending mere
self-consciousness, and preventing those of us who were not part
of the first, uncomplicated love affair between Chaplin and the
public from surrendering to his insistent demand for a con-
tinuance of that affair in the old simple terms." This egoism is another hue in the varicolored complexity of Chaplin's personality.

That personality has been the topic of at least minor controversy through the years. The face he has presented to many is one "egotistical, avaricious, opinionated and disorderly," to cite Brooks Atkinson's description. But Atkinson, who loves Charlie, has said the public obloquy Chaplin suffered in the years just prior to the McGranery affair, although unmerited, was inevitable in view of Chaplin's public self as mirrored in the press. How close was the public self to the private self? Who *is* the private Charlie Chaplin?

Of those who have tried to answer that question responsibly perhaps Max Eastman spoke with fullest authority. Eastman, a devoted Socialist when he met Chaplin early in his career and subsequently a militant conservative, was as close a friend as Chaplin ever had, Douglas Fairbanks excluded. Eastman wrote in depth about his friend over the years, and in his view Chaplin's essentially dramatic genius made him impossible to understand fully.

In fact, there is no single character there to analyze but a bewildering and frequently contradictory variety of them. Once when Chaplin approached Eastman about writing a film, Mrs. Eastman grew very excited at the idea but Eastman gently discouraged her enthusiasm. He knew his man. As he told his wife, "Enjoy any Charlie Chaplin you have the good luck of a chance to. But don't try to link them up into anything you can grasp. There are too many of them."

Chaplin was once given a personality-probe test by a psychologist friend of Eastman's. The findings were, at least on the face of it, contradictory:

Emotional Instability:	*Very high*
Self-sufficiency:	*Very high*
Introversion:	*Very high*
Dominance vs. Submission:	*Very submissive*
Self-confidence:	*Very, very low*

How can such contrarieties cohere in the same person, obviously a very intelligent person? The one element Eastman found particularly baffling in the Chaplin profile was the submissive. Chaplin submissive? It then occurred to Eastman that there are two kinds of dominance: dominance as an ultimate fact and dominance as an immediate social attitude—and that "shy and diffident" people like Chaplin "often have a sovereign confidence in their own judgment." As Chaplin's work amply showed.

As to the extremely low self-confidence, it is the present writer's conviction that because this was the spirit in which Chaplin began life, and the spirit in which he lived his first twelve years, so was he formed. Almost anyone's first decade determines who one is going to be. Very bravely all his life he continually outfaced his low self-confidence, conquering it unendingly.

Charlie Chaplin, the deathly shy, undersized, lower-class boy, born into a society that seemed to despise these things, dreamed he would overcome his handicaps, even preposterously dreamed he would go out and conquer the world. Put quite simply, he did. Jimmy the Fearless made his dreams his life.

"AS OF THIS WRITING . . . BY
JIMMY THE FEARLESS."

Queen Elizabeth II knighted Chaplin on January 2, 1975. The Cockney street boy became a Knight Commander of the British Empire. Yet another height reached by Jimmy the Fearless.

Charles Spencer Chaplin died at 4 A.M. on Christmas Day, 1977. "He left us peacefully," said the family doctor, "dying in his sleep —from old age."

The universality of the appreciative affection for him that poured out across the world was dramatized by two of the many statements made. Tass, the Soviet news agency, paid its respects by giving him high praise for his "profound humanism." Vatican Radio spoke of the "unsurpassable heights as an artist, creator, and director" Chaplin had reached, adding: "The little man with the cane and bowler hat was and will remain in the hearts of all. . . . Nobody, as he did, knew how to enter the hidden recesses of the human heart with a simplicity and popularity which became legendary, succeeding in causing laughter by weeping and weeping by laughter."

Chaplin was buried two days after Christmas in the tiny cemetery at Corsier attended by the family doctor, the Anglican clergyman who conducted the service, members of the household, the children, and Oona. Chaplin had made a specific request that no crowds be allowed at his funeral.

Most of the Chaplin children have begun their adult lives in a variety of places. Sydney, after a successful Broadway career as a leading man, moved to Paris and became a successful businessman with occasional appearances in films and television. Geraldine became a sought-after film actress and now lives in Spain with film director Carlos Saura, father of her three-year-old son, Shane Chaplin. Michael Chaplin continues in London, and others of the children have made tentative stabs at show business careers.

* * *

As for Charlie.

Charlie, a radiant Don Quixote in the mean garments of Sancho Panza, ultimately merits John Dryden's definition of the perfect clown:

Legion's his name, a people in a man.

Perhaps he means so much to us because he is each of us as we want to be—a votary of independence, defying the routine and the dull. We are totally captivated by Charlie's cocking his snook, by his standing up so forthrightly to the unreasoning dominance we take for granted so many times in life. He is our happily indomitable surrogate.

Perhaps we don't like this bloodless and enchanting gamin nearly as much as we like ourselves *in* him. That is the lasting triumph of Charlie Chaplin. Better than any artist in this jaded century, he became us as we wanted to be.

SELECT BIBLIOGRAPHY

BOOKS

Adeler, Edwin, and West, Con. *Remember Fred Karno?* London: Long Publishers Ltd., 1939.

Agate, James. *Alarums and Excursions*. London: Grant Richards Ltd., 1922.

Agee, James. *Agee on Film*. New York: McDowell Obolensky, 1958.

Asplund, Uno. *Chaplin's Films*. New York: A. S. Barnes & Co., 1971.

Balio, Tino. *United Artists*. Madison, Wis.: University of Wisconsin Press, 1976.

Behlmer, Rudy, ed. *Memo from David O. Selznick*. New York: Viking Press, 1972.

Bessy, Maurice, and Florey, Robert. *Monsieur Chaplin*. Paris: Jacques Damase, 1953.

Bowman, W. Dodgson. *Charlie Chaplin: His Life and Art*. New York: John Day Co., 1931.

Brownlow, Kevin. *The Parade's Gone By*. New York: Alfred A. Knopf, 1968.

Chaplin, Charles. *Charlie Chaplin's Own Story*. Indianapolis: Bobbs-Merrill Co., Inc., 1916.

——. *My Autobiography*. New York: Simon and Schuster, Inc., 1964.

——. *My Life in Pictures*. London: The Bodley Head, 1974.

——. *My Trip Abroad*. New York: Harper & Bros., 1922.

Chaplin, Charles, Jr. *My Father, Charlie Chaplin*. (With N. and M. Rau.) New York: Random House, 1960.

Chaplin, Lita Grey. *My Life With Chaplin*. New York: Bernard Geis Associates, 1966.

Chaplin, Michael. *I Couldn't Smoke the Grass on My Father's Lawn*. New York: G. P. Putnam's Sons, 1966.

Cooke, Alistair. *Six Men.* New York: Alfred A. Knopf, 1977.

Cotes, Peter, and Niklaus, Thelma. *The Little Fellow.* Secaucus, N.J.: Citadel Press, 1965.

Davies, Marion. *The Times We Had.* Indianapolis: Bobbs-Merrill Co., Inc., 1975.

Delluc, Louis. *Charlie Chaplin.* (Trans. Hamish Miles.) London: The Bodley Head, 1922.

Durgnat, Raymond. *The Crazy Mirror.* New York: Horizon Press, 1969.

Eastman, Max. *Great Companions.* New York: Farrar, Straus and Cudahy, 1959.

Eells, George. *Hedda and Louella.* New York: G. P. Putnam's Sons, 1972.

Eisenstein, Sergei. *Notes of a Film Director.* London: Lawrence & Wisehart, 1959.

Ferguson, Otis. *The Film Criticism of Otis Ferguson.* Philadelphia: Temple University Press, 1971.

Fowler, Gene. *Father Goose.* New York: Covici Friede, 1934.

Gallagher, J. P. *Fred Karno: Master of Mirth and Tears.* London: Robert Hale, 1971.

Giesler, Jerry. *The Jerry Giesler Story.* (As Told to Pete Martin.) New York: Simon & Schuster, Inc., 1960.

Gifford, Denis. *Chaplin.* New York: Doubleday & Co., Inc., 1974.

Gilliatt, Penelope. *Unholy Fools.* New York: Viking Press, Inc., 1973.

Goldwyn, Samuel. *Behind the Screen.* New York: G. H. Doran Co., 1923.

Guiles, Fred Lawrence. *Marion Davies.* New York: McGraw-Hill Book Co., 1972.

Huff, Theodore. *Charlie Chaplin.* New York: Henry Schuman, Inc., 1951.

Kauffmann, Stanley. *Living Images: Film Comment and Criticism.* New York: Harper & Row, Publishers, Inc., 1973.

Kerr, Walter. *The Silent Clowns.* New York: Alfred A. Knopf, 1975.

La Hue, Kalton, and Gill, Sam. *Clown Princes and Jesters.* New York: A. S. Barnes & Co., 1971.

Leprohon, Pierre. *Charles Chaplin.* Paris: Nouvelles Editions Debresse, 1957.

Leslie, Anita. *Clare Sheridan.* New York: Doubleday & Co., Inc., 1977.

McCaffrey, Donald W., ed. *Focus on Chaplin.* Englewood Cliffs, N.J.: Prentice-Hall, Inc., 1971.

Macdonald, Dwight. *On Movies.* Englewood Cliffs, N.J.: Prentice-Hall, Inc., 1969.

McDonald, Gerald D., Conway, Michael, and Ricci, Mark. *The Films of Charlie Chaplin*. New York: Bonanza Books, 1965.

Manvell, Roger. *Chaplin*. London: Hutchinson Ltd., 1974.

Mast, Gerald. *The Comic Mind*. Indianapolis: Bobbs-Merrill Co., Inc., 1973.

Menjou, Adolphe. *It Took Nine Tailors*. New York: McGraw-Hill Book Co., 1948.

Minney, R. J. *Chaplin, the Immortal Tramp*. London: Newnes Ltd., 1954.

Montagu, Ivor. *With Eisenstein in Hollywood*. New York: International Publishers, 1969.

Moore, Colleen. *Silent Star*. New York: Doubleday & Co., Inc., 1968.

Negri, Pola. *Memoirs of a Star*. New York: Doubleday & Co., Inc., 1970.

Parrish, Robert. *Growing Up in Hollywood*. New York: Harcourt Brace Jovanovich, 1976.

Payne, Robert. *The Great Charlie*. (In U.S., *The Great God Pan*.) London: Andre Deutsch, 1952.

Pickford, Mary. *Sunshine and Shadow*. London: William Heineman Ltd., 1956.

Pratt, George C. *Spellbound in Darkness*. 2 vols. Rochester, N.Y.: University of Rochester Press, 1966.

Quigly, Isabel. *Charlie Chaplin: Early Comedies*. London: Studio Vista Ltd., 1968.

Ragan, David. *Who's Who in Hollywood*. New Rochelle, N.Y.: Arlington House, 1976.

Robinson, Carlyle R. "The Private Life of Charlie Chaplin," *Great Stars of Hollywood's Golden Age*. New York: New American Library, Inc., 1966.

Robinson, David. *The Great Funnies*. New York: E. P. Dutton & Co., 1969.

Sadoul, Georges. *Charlie Chaplin, Vie de Charlot: ses films et son temps*. Paris: Les Editeurs Français Réunis, 1957.

Sennett, Mack. *King of Comedy*. (With Cameron Shipp.) New York: Doubleday & Co., Inc., 1954.

Sheridan, Clare. *Naked Truth*. New York: Harper & Bros., 1928.

Spears, Jack. *Hollywood: The Golden Era*. New York: A. S. Barnes & Co., 1971.

Truitt, Evelyn Mack. *Who Was Who on the Screen*. New York: R. R. Bowker & Co., 1974.

Tully, Jim. *A Dozen and One*. New York: Ambassador Books, 1943.

Tyler, Parker. *Chaplin, Last of the Clowns*. New York: Horizon Press, 1972.

————. *Sex Psyche Etcetera in the Film.* Baltimore, Md.: Penguin
    Books, 1969.
Tynan, Kenneth. *Right and Left.* New York: Atheneum Publishers,
    1967.
Von Sternberg, Josef. *Fun in a Chinese Laundry.* New York: The
    Macmillan Co., 1965.
Von Ulm, Gerith. *Charlie Chaplin: King of Tragedy.* Caldwell, Ida.:
    Caxton Printers Ltd., 1940.
Warshow, Robert. *The Immediate Experience.* New York: Doubleday
    & Co., Inc., 1962.
Woollcott, Alexander. *While Rome Burns.* New York: Viking Press,
    1934.
Zec, Donald. *Sophia.* New York: David Mackay Co., Inc., 1975.

ARTICLES

To help those working in sequential approach to Chaplin studies,
these references are in chronological order. Happily, only a few of
the following could come under the heading "Articles Consulted and
Ostentatiously Ignored" or "References Not to Be Referred To," but
one can learn negatively, I've discovered. I cite them all because most
of these articles, reviews, and monographs were written out of love,
and despite inaccuracies and what I consider unwarranted conclusions,
they deserve note from serious Chaplin scholars. And to the latter:
anyone wanting citation of a specific source for any part of this book
is welcome to write me: Box 363, Mackinac Island, Michigan 49757.
The most complete Chaplin bibliography to date is the extensive
Chaplin: A Reference Guide by Timothy J. Lyons to be published
by G. K. Hall (Boston, 1978)—a work unfinished before my publishing deadline and hence unavailable for my purposes.

"Fred Karno," New York *Morning Telegraph,* Oct. 7, 1906.
"Fred Karno Company," *Variety,* Oct. 8, 1910.
"Karno's Comedians," Brooklyn *Eagle,* Oct. 18, 1910.
"Fred Karno's London Comedians," *Show World,* Feb. 4, 1911.
"Fred Karno Company," Vancouver *Press,* Apr. 12, 1912.
"Karno's English Company," New York *Dramatic Mirror,* Nov. 19,
    1913.
MacDonald, Margaret I. "His New Job," *Moving Picture World,* Feb.
    20, 1915.

"Chaplin with Marie Dressler," Fort Wayne *Journal*, Feb. 22, 1915.

Eubank, Victor. "The Funniest Man on the Screen," *Motion Picture*, Mar. 1915.

"Work," *Dramatic Mirror*, June 30, 1915.

"Charlie Chaplin's Own Story (As Narrated by Mr. Chaplin Himself)," *Photoplay*, July 1915, Sept. 1915, Oct. 1915.

"Some Expressions of Charlie Chaplin," *McClure's*, July 1915.

Chaplin, Charles. "What I Am and What I Was," *Filmland*, July 4, 11, 18, 25, Aug. 1, 8, 15, 1915.

Dale, Alan. "On the Movie Situation," Toledo *Blade*, July 17, 1915.

"Chaplinitis," *Motion Picture*, Aug. 1915.

Chaplin, Charles. "How I Made My Success," *Theatre*, Sept. 1915.

"Have You the Chaplinoia?" Kansas City *Star*, Sept. 3, 1915.

Braley, Berton. "Satiety," *Green Book*, Nov. 1915.

"Mack Sennett," *Triangle*, Nov. 6, 1915.

Hirsch, J. B. "The New Charlie Chaplin," *Motion Pictures*, Jan. 1916.

Gaddis, Ivan. "Secret Griefs and Cankers in the Bosom," *Motion Pictures*, Apr. 1916.

Fiske, Minnie Maddern. "The Art of Charles Chaplin," *Harper's Weekly*, May 6, 1916.

Smith, E. H. "Charlie Chaplin's Million Dollar Walk," *McClure's*, July 1916.

"Witty, Wistful, Serious Is the Real Charlie Chaplin," Los Angeles *Sunday Times*, Aug. 20, 1916.

"A Day in 'The Pawn Shop,'" *Motion Picture Classic*, Nov. 1916.

O'Higgins, Harvey. "Charlie Chaplin's Art," *New Republic*, Feb. 3, 1917.

Johnson, Julian. "The Shadow Stage," *Photoplay*, Sept. 1917.

Hilbert, James E. "A Day With Charlie Chaplin on Location," *Motion Picture*, Nov. 1917.

Wagner, Rob. "Charles Spencer Chaplin: The Man You Don't Know," *Ladies' Home Journal*, Aug. 1918.

Chaplin, Charles. "What People Laugh At," *American*, Nov. 1918.

Biby, E. A. "How Pictures Found Charlie Chaplin," *Photoplay*, Apr. 1919.

"Charlie Chaplin Says Laughs Are Produced by Rules," *Literary Digest*, May 3, 1919.

Farmer, Harcourt. "Is the Chaplin Vogue Passing?" *Theatre*, Oct. 1919.

"The Art of Charlie Chaplin," *Nation* (London), July 3, 1920.

"Charlie Chaplin Is Too Tragic to Play Hamlet," *Current Opinion*, Feb. 1921.

Ervine, St. John. "Mr. Charlie Chaplin," *Living Age*, Apr. 9, 1921.

Sandburg, Carl. "Charlie Chaplin," Chicago *Daily News*, Apr. 16, 1921.

Jordan, Joan. "Mother o' Mine," *Photoplay*, July 1921.

"Charlie," *Nation and Athenaeum* (London), Sept. 10, 1921.

"Charlie Chaplin: A Doubt," *New Statesman* (London), Sept. 17, 1921.

"Charlie Chaplin's Art Dissected," *Literary Digest*, Oct. 8, 1921.

Burke, Thomas. "The Tragic Comedian," *Outlook* (London), Jan. 18, 1922.

"Science and Charlie Chaplin," *Literary Digest*, Jan. 28, 1922.

"Chaplin as a Comedian Contemplates Suicide," *Current Opinion*, Feb. 1922.

Delluc, Louis. "How Charlie Chaplin Does It," *World's Work*, Feb. 1922.

Young, Stark. "Dear Mr. Chaplin," *New Republic*, Aug. 23, 1922.

Chaplin, Charles. "We Have Come to Stay," *Ladies' Home Journal*, Oct. 1922.

Chaplin, Charles. "In Defence of Myself," *Collier's*, Nov. 11, 1922.

St. Johns, Adela Rogers. "The Loves of Charlie Chaplin," *Photoplay*, Feb. 1923.

"Charlie Chaplin," *Sunset* (Boston), July 1923.

Higgins, Bertram. "Charles Chaplin's Comedy of Shyness," *Spectator* (London), Sept. 8, 1923.

MacCarthy, Desmond. "Charlie's Cane," *New Statesman* (London), Sept. 8, 1923.

Young, Stark. "A Woman of Paris," *New Republic*, Nov. 7, 1923.

Wood, C. W. "With the Bunk Left Out," *Collier's*, Nov. 17, 1923.

Chaplin, Charles. "Does the Public Know What It Wants?" *Adelphi* (London), Jan. 1924.

"How Much of Chaplin Does Charlie Own?" *Literary Digest*, Feb. 2, 1924.

York, Cal. "Charlie's Unromantic Wedding," *Photoplay*, Feb. 1925.

Bercovici, Konrad. "Charlie Chaplin—An Authorized Interview," *Collier's*, Aug. 15, 1925.

Wilson, Edmund. "The New Chaplin Comedy," *New Republic*, Sept. 2, 1925.

"Two English Views of Chaplin," *Living Age*, Nov. 14, 1925.

Woollcott, Alexander. "Sandman's Magic," *Collier's*, Jan. 30, 1926.

St. Johns, Ivan. "Everything's Rosy at Chaplin's," *Photoplay*, Feb. 1926.

Young, Stark. "Charlot in Rome," *New Republic*, Oct. 13, 1926.

Tully, Jim. "Charlie Chaplin—His Real Life Story," *Pictorial Review*, Jan., Feb., Mar., Apr. 1927.

De Beauplan, Robert. "From Charlot to Chaplin," *Living Age*, Aug. 15, 1927.

Bakshy, Alexander. "Charlie Chaplin," *Nation*, Feb. 1928.

Young, Stark. "Charlie Chaplin," *New Republic*, Feb. 8, 1928.

Seldes, Gilbert. "The Circus," *Dial*, Mar. 1928.

"Charlie Chaplin," *New Statesman* (London), Mar. 24, 1928.

"Bonnie Prince Charlie of the Custard Pies," *Literary Digest*, Mar. 29, 1928.

"Chaplin as Puck," *Bookman*, Apr. 1928.

Ockham, David. "Everyman on the Screen," *Outlook* (London), Apr. 21, 1928.

Hollriegel, Arnold. "Charles Chaplin at Home," *Living Age*, July 1928.

Bercovici, Konrad. "A Day With Charlie Chaplin," *Harper's*, Dec. 1928.

Frank, Waldo. "Charles Chaplin," *Scribner's*, Sept. 1929.

Kisch, E. E. "I Work With Charlie Chaplin," *Living Age*, Oct. 15, 1929.

"Silence Is Requested," *North American Review*, July 1930.

Stevenson, Robert. "The Silence of Mr. Chaplin," *Nation and Athenaeum* (London), July 19, 1930.

Braver-Mann, Barnet G. "Charlie: A Close Up," *Theatre Guild*, Sept. 1930.

Bercovici, Konrad. "My Friend, Charlie Chaplin," *Delineator*, Dec. 1930.

Chaplin, Charles. "Pantomime and Comedy," New York *Times*, Jan. 25, 1931.

"Charlie Chaplin Defies the Talkies," *Literary Digest*, Feb. 28, 1931.

Wettach, Adrian (Grock). "My Colleague, Charlie Chaplin," *Living Age*, Mar. 1931.

"Charlie Chaplin Falters," *Nation*, Mar. 4, 1931.

"City Lights," *Spectator* (London), Mar. 7, 1931.

Forrest, Mark. "City Lights," *Saturday Review* (London), Mar. 7, 1931.

"Chaplin in England," New York *Times*, Mar. 29, 1931.

Fergusson, F. "City Lights," *Bookman*, Apr. 1931.

"In the Driftway," *Nation*, May 27, 1931.

Cami. "The Perfume That Vanquished Charlie Chaplin," *Millgate* (Manchester), Aug. 1931.

Bartlett, A. C. "Charlie Chaplin's No-Man," *American*, Oct. 1931.

Chaplin, Charles. "A Comedian Sees the World," *Woman's Home Companion,* Sept., Oct., Nov., Dec. 1933, Jan. 1934.

Rozas, Lorenzo T. "Charlie Chaplin's Decline," *Living Age,* June 1934.

Churchill, Winston. "Everybody's Language," *Collier's,* Oct. 26, 1935.

"Chaplin: Machine Age Don Quixote," *Literary Digest,* Nov. 2, 1935.

Atkinson, Brooks. "Beloved Vagabond," New York *Times,* Feb. 16, 1936.

Forrest, Mark. "Charlie Chaplin Again," *Saturday Review* (London), Feb. 22, 1936.

"Two Birthdays," *Spectator* (London), Apr. 21, 1939.

Churchill, Douglas W. "At 50 Chaplin Begins to Talk," New York *Times Magazine,* July 30, 1939.

Cooke, Alistair. "Charlie Chaplin," *Atlantic Monthly,* Aug. 1939.

"Scripteaser," *Time,* Aug. 7, 1939.

Crichton, Kyle. "Ride 'Em, Charlie," *Collier's,* Mar. 16, 1940.

"Comedy Has Its Limits," *Christian Century,* June 26, 1940.

Pringle, Henry F. "The Story of Two Moustaches," *Ladies' Home Journal,* July 1940.

Daugherty, Frank. "Two Millions' Worth of Laughter," *Christian Science Monitor,* Sept. 7, 1940.

Van Gelder, Robert. "Chaplin Draws a Keen Weapon," New York *Times Magazine,* Sept. 8, 1940.

Gardiner, Reginald. "The Pleasure of Meeting a Dictator," New York *Herald Tribune,* Sept. 16, 1940.

Chaplin, Charles. "Mr. Chaplin Answers His Critics," New York *Times,* Oct. 27, 1940.

Wright, Basil. "The Great Dictator," *Spectator* (London), Dec. 13, 1940.

Whitebait, William. "The Two Charlies," *New Statesman and Nation* (London), Dec. 21, 1940.

Frye, Northrop. "The Great Charlie," *Canadian Forum,* Aug. 1941.

Schreiber, Flora R. "Bergson and Charlie Chaplin," *French Forum,* Christmas, 1941.

"Chaplin Salutes Karno," *Variety,* Jan. 7, 1942.

"The Gold Rush," *Variety,* Mar. 4, 1942.

Farber, Manny. "The Little Fellow," *New Republic,* May 4, 1942.

Hirschfeld, Al. "Man With Both Feet in the Clouds," New York *Times,* July 26, 1942.

Pegler, Westbrook. "Fair Enough," New York *World Telegram,* Dec. 21, 1942.

Brown, John Mason. "Charlie into Charles," *Saturday Review of Literature*, May 3, 1947.

Pegler, Westbrook. "Some Errors in Chaplin Attitude Toward U.S.," *King Features Syndicate*, May 14, 1947.

Lewis, Robert. "Charlie's Whole Shoe," *Theatre Arts*, June 1947.

Renoir, Jean. "Chaplin Among the Immortals," *Screen Writer*, July 1947.

Dent, Alan. "Charlie Still My Darling!" *Illustrated London News*, Dec. 6, 1947.

"Soviet Magazine Raps Chaplin's Latest Film," *Los Angeles Times*, Jan. 13, 1948.

Capp, Al. "The Comedy of Charlie Chaplin," *Atlantic Monthly*, Feb. 1950.

"Feeling Lost," *The New Yorker*, Feb. 25, 1950.

Tyler, Parker. "Kafka's and Chaplin's Amerika," *Sewanee Review*, Apr. 1950.

Crisler, B. R. "Ageless and Enduring Clown," *Christian Science Monitor*, Apr. 29, 1950.

Brown, John Mason. "Charlie the First and Only," *Saturday Review of Literature*, May 6, 1950.

Lauterbach, Richard E. "The Whys of Chaplin's Appeal," New York *Sunday Times*, May 21, 1950.

Pryor, Thomas M. "How Mr. Chaplin Makes a Movie," New York *Times Magazine*, Feb. 17, 1952.

"Chaplin at Work," *Life*, Mar. 17, 1952.

Knight, Arthur. "Charlie Chaplin and the Dance," *Dance*, May 1952.

Grace, Harry A. "Charlie Chaplin's Films and American Culture Patterns," *Journal of Aesthetics and Art Criticism*, June 1952.

Greene, Graham. "Dear Mr. Chaplin," *New Statesman and Nation* (London), Sept. 27, 1952. (Also in *New Republic*, Oct. 13, 1952.)

"Charlie Chaplin," *Nation*, Oct. 4, 1952.

Barrett, William. "Chaplin as Chaplin—Death of a Clown," *American Mercury*, Nov. 1952.

Bentley, Eric. "Chaplin's Mea Culpa," *New Republic*, Nov. 17, 1952.

Huie, William Bradford. "Mr. Chaplin and the Four Freedoms," *American Mercury*, Nov. 1952.

Kerr, Walter. "The Lineage of *Limelight*," *Theatre Arts Monthly*, Nov. 1952.

Miller, Edwin. "*Limelight*: A Great Comedian Sums Up His Life," *Theatre Arts Monthly*, Nov. 1952.

"The Laugh's On Us," *Nation*, Nov. 15, 1952.

"Unrehearsed Chaplin Comedy," *Life*, Nov. 17, 1952.

Daugherty, Frank. "The Cutting Room Floor," *Films in Review*, Dec. 1952.

"Heretics or Conspirators," *Life*, Dec. 22, 1952.

"New Information on *Limelight*," *Reporter*, Jan. 6, 1953.

"Mr. Ferrer and Mr. Chaplin," *Nation*, Jan. 31, 1953.

Tallenay, J. L. "The Tragic Vision of Charlie Chaplin," *Commonweal*, Feb. 6, 1953.

"The Process of Dissolution," *Commonweal*, Feb. 6, 1953.

Glick, Nathan. "Chaplin's Film Romance," *Commentary*, Mar. 1953.

Murray, William. "*Limelight*, Chaplin and His Censors," *Nation*, May 21, 1953.

Micha, René. "Chaplin as Don Juan," *Sight and Sound*, Jan.–Mar. 1954.

"Double Play: Chaplin to Robeson to Malenkov," *Saturday Evening Post*, Sept. 4, 1954.

"Vodka Brawl," *Time*, May 7, 1956.

"Chaplin Spins the Political Roulette," *Films and Filming*, July 1956.

Callenbach, Ernest. "The Great Charlie Chaplin Chase," *Nation*, Aug. 4, 1956.

Halle, Louis J. "Foreign Relations and Domestic Behavior," *Saturday Review of Literature*, Oct. 13, 1956.

Lane, John Francis. Interview with Dawn Addams, "My Life as Chaplin's Leading Lady," *Films and Filming*, Aug. 1957.

Hinxman, Margaret. "An Interview With Charlie Chaplin," *Sight and Sound*, Autumn 1957.

Houston, Penelope. "A King in New York," *Sight and Sound*, Autumn 1957.

"Unfunny Charlie Chaplin," *Newsweek*, Sept. 9, 1957.

"The Unfunny Comic," *Time*, Sept. 23, 1957.

Kaufman, Wolfe. "A King in New York," *Saturday Review of Literature*, Sept. 28, 1957.

Lee, Paul. "Whither Chaplin?" *America*, Oct. 5, 1957.

"Chaplin in Decline," *New Republic*, Oct. 7, 1957.

Parkinson, Thomas. "A King in New York," *Nation*, Nov. 2, 1957.

O'Donnell, James P. "Charlie Chaplin's Stormy Exile," *Saturday Evening Post*, Mar. 8, 15, 22, 1958.

"Why Chaplin Paid Up?" *Newsweek*, Jan. 12, 1959.

Callenbach, Ernest. "The Gold Rush," *Film Quarterly*, Fall 1959.

Beaumont, Charles. "Chaplin, the Chronicle of a Man and His Genius," *Playboy*, Mar. 1960.

Hurley, Neil. "The Social Philosophy of Charlie Chaplin," *Studies* (Dublin), Autumn 1960.

Crowther, Bosley. "The Modern—Mellower—Times of Mr. Chaplin," New York *Times*, Nov. 6, 1960.

Spears, Jack. "Chaplin Collaborators," *Films in Review*, Jan. 1962.

Clurman, Harold. "Talking to Chaplin," London *Sunday Times*, Dec. 9, 1962.

Steffens, Peter. "The Victorian Tramp," *Ramparts*, Mar. 1964.

Hatch, Robert. "Dapper Wayfarer," *Harper's*, Oct. 1964.

Pritchett, V. A. "Charlie," *New Statesman* (London), Oct. 2, 1964.

Kauffmann, Stanley. "A Man Named Chaffin," *New Republic*, Oct. 3, 1964.

Knight, Arthur. "Travels with Charlie and Friends," *Saturday Review of Literature*, Oct. 10, 1964.

Houseman, John. Review of *My Autobiography*, *Nation*, Oct. 12, 1964.

"The Chaplin Story," London *Times Literary Supplement*, Oct. 15, 1964.

Junker, Howard. "Real Life of the Tramp," *Commonweal*, Oct. 16, 1964.

Russell, Francis. "Only the Little Tramp Matters," *National Review*, Dec. 1, 1964.

Gill, Brendan. Review of *My Autobiography*, *The New Yorker*, Dec. 12, 1964.

Muggeridge, Malcolm. Review of *My Autobiography*, *Esquire*, Feb. 1965.

Tracy, Robert. Review of *My Autobiography*, *Ramparts*, Mar. 1965.

Frank, Gerold. "Charlie Chaplin and His Children," *Ladies' Home Journal*, May 1965.

Robinson, David. "Chaplin Meets the Press," *Sight and Sound*, Winter 1965/66.

Brooks, Louise. "Charlie Chaplin Remembered," *Film Culture*, #40, 1966.

Morgenstern, Joseph. Interview with Chaplin, *Newsweek*, June 6, 1966.

Meyerhold, Vsevelod. "Chaplin and Chaplinism," *Tulane Drama Review*, Fall 1966.

Meryman, Richard. "Chaplin," *Life*, Mar. 10, 1967.

Rosen, Philip G. "The Chaplin World-View," *Cinema Journal*, Fall 1969.

Hickey, Terry. "Accusations Against Charles Chaplin for Political and Moral Offenses," *Film Comment*, Winter 1969.

Wallach, George. "Charlie Chaplin's *Monsieur Verdoux* Press Conference," *Film Comment*, Winter 1969.

Curtiss, Thomas Quinn. "Charlie Chaplin at 82," *International Herald-Tribune*, May 15, 1971.

Reed, Rex. "Chaplin in Cannes," New York *Sunday News*, May 23, 1971.

"Chaplin," *Life*, Dec. 3, 1971.

Phillips, Gene D., S.J. "Charlie Chaplin Revisits Us," *America*, Mar. 11, 1972.

De Lucovich, Jean-Pierre. "Charlie Chaplin Comes Home—But Is Everybody Cheering?" *Harper's Bazaar*, Apr. 1972.

Lyons, Timothy J. "Roland H. Totheroh Interviewed," *Film Culture*, Spring 1972.

Crocker, Harry. "A Tribute to Charlie," "Henry Bergman," *Academy Leader* (Los Angeles), Apr. 1972.

Schickel, Richard. "Hail Chaplin—The Early Chaplin," New York *Times Magazine*, Apr. 2, 1972.

Kanfer, Stefan. "Re-Enter Charlie Chaplin, Smiling and Waving," *Time*, Apr. 10, 1972.

Green, Abel. "Chaplin Returns," *Variety*, Apr. 12, 1972.

"Reborn," *The New Yorker*, Apr. 15, 1972.

"Charlie Comes Home," *Newsweek*, Apr. 17, 1972.

"Like Old Times," *Time*, Apr. 17, 1972.

Bergen, Candice. "I Thought They Might Hiss," *Life*, Apr. 21, 1972.

"Modern Times," *Nation*, Apr. 24, 1972.

Knight, Arthur. "One Man's Movie," *Saturday Review*, May 6, 1972.

Dunne, George H., S.J. "I Remember Chaplin," *Commonweal*, June 2, 1972.

Essays by Charles Silver, Gilberto Perez Guillermo, Gary Carey, William K. Everson, William Paul, Stanley Kauffmann, David Denby, Stephen Harvey, Foster Hirsch, Emily Sieger, David Robinson, and Michael Kerbel. "Charlie Chaplin: Faces and Facets," *Film Comment*, Sept./Oct. 1972.

Sarris, Andrew. "Charles Spencer Chaplin, I," *Village Voice*, Dec. 7, 1972.

——. "Charles Spencer Chaplin, II," *Village Voice*, Apr. 12, 1973.

——. "A King in New York," *Village Voice*, Dec. 6, 1973.

Schickel, Richard. "Deposed Monarch," *Time*, Feb. 4, 1974.

MacKnight, F. C. "Collecting Chaplin," *Classic Film Collector*, Numbers 44, 45, 46, 47, 49. 1974–76.

Roemer, Michael. "Chaplin: Charles and Charlie," *Yale Review*, Dec. 1974.

Rubin, Jay. "Jay Rubin Interviews Jackie Coogan," *Classic Film Collector,* Summer 1976.

Kroll, Jack. "Voluptuous Silence," *Newsweek,* Jan. 10, 1977.

Brakhage, Stan. "Charlie Chaplin," n.d., Unpublished Lecture. Film Study Center, Museum of Modern Art, New York.

ACKNOWLEDGMENTS

I am especially grateful to the following for help:

Larry Ashmead, who first encouraged me in this work; Richard Bann
for continuing help; Blackhawk Films, Davenport, Iowa, and there—to
Kent Eastin, Bill Linholm, and particularly David Shephard for letting
me view much of Chaplin in genuine comfort; James Cagney for some
thoughts on Chaplin; John Carroll for essential irrelevancies; Patrice
Chaplin for special kindness; Tim Clott of rbc films of Los Angeles for
the rare opportunity to see all the mature Chaplin films; Booth Col-
man for aid; Lisa Drew for some good advice; Dick Feiner for encouragement; Denis Gifford for some ideas; Marcia Grimes for unflagging
help in gathering my sources; Bob Haynie of New American Library
for aid in finding the lost; the staff of the Margaret Herrick Library of
the Academy of Motion Picture Arts and Sciences, and in particular
Sam Gill; Stanley Kauffmann for permission to quote from his splendid article on *The Gold Rush*; Jean and Walter Kerr for *Sunnyside*
and for easing the journey and Walter Kerr for permission to quote
from his book, *The Silent Clowns* (Alfred A. Knopf, 1975); Al Kilgore
for being Al Kilgore; Lake Superior State College Library; Herb Levin
for helping me track down the trackless; Timothy J. Lyons for permission to quote from his Rollie Totheroh interview; Linny McCabe,
whose genuine skill as a projectionist makes me even prouder to be his
father; Deirdre, Sean, and Rosalie T. McCabe for editorial assistance;
Donald W. McCaffrey for some tips; Roger Manvell for permission to
quote from his *Chaplin* (Hutchinson Ltd., London, 1974), a very
wise book; Paul Myers and Monty Arnold of the Library of Performing Arts, Lincoln Center, for some active clues; George C. Pratt of

Eastman House for suggestions; Bill Rabe for the usual et ceteras; Louis A. Rachow of the Walter Hampden Memorial Library of The Players for some detective work; Anne G. Schlosser of the Charles K. Feldman Library of the American Film Institute Center for Advanced Film Studies; Tom Sefton for help on the legal aspects of Chaplin's life; Charles Silver and Emily Sieger of the Film Study Center, Museum of Modern Art, for gracious aid; Jack Totheroh for delightful hospitality and insightful views of his dad. And last, to dear Stan— God bless.

PHOTOGRAPHIC CREDITS

Pictures number 11, 12, 13, 14, 16, 17, 22, 23, 24 through courtesy of Roland Jack Totheroh, number 13 originally a Max Munn Autrey photograph, and number 23 originally a William Wallace Photo; pictures number 2, 4, 5, 9, 10, 15, 18, 19, 20, 21, 26, 27, and 28 through courtesy of Richard W. Bann, number 15 originally World-Wide Photo; picture number 6 courtesy of Museum of Modern Art; picture number 25, courtesy of Culver Pictures; pictures number 1, 3, 7, and 8, personal collection, John McCabe.

CHAPLIN FILMOGRAPHY
BY DENIS GIFFORD

1914

MAKING A LIVING   Feb. 2 (1030 ft.): Keystone   *Producer* Mack Sennett   *Director* Henry Lehrman   *Screenplay* Reed Heustis   *Photography* E. J. Vallejo   *Cast* Charles Chaplin (Sharper), Virginia Kirtley (Girl), Henry Lehrman (Reporter), Alice Davenport (Mother), Chester Conklin (Cop), Minta Durfee (Girl)

KID AUTO RACES AT VENICE   Feb. 7 (572 ft.): Keystone   *Producer* Mack Sennett   *Director* Henry Lehrman   *Photography* Frank D. Williams   *Screenplay* Henry Lehrman   *Cast* Charles Chaplin (Tramp), Henry Lehrman (Director), Frank D. Williams (Cameraman), Gordon Griffith (Boy), Paul Jacobs (Boy), Charlotte Fitzpatrick (Girl), Thelma Salter (Girl)

MABEL'S STRANGE PREDICAMENT   Feb. 9 (1016 ft.): Keystone   *Producer* Mack Sennett   *Directors* Mack Sennett, Henry Lehrman   *Screenplay* Reed Heustis   *Cast* Mabel Normand (Mabel), Charles Chaplin (Drunk), Chester Conklin (Husband), Alice Davenport (Wife), Harry McCoy (Admirer), Hank Mann, Al St. John

BETWEEN SHOWERS   Feb. 28 (1020 ft.): Keystone   *Producer* Mack Sennett   *Director* Henry Lehrman   *Screenplay* Henry Lehrman   *Cast* Ford Sterling (Masher), Charles Chaplin (Masher), Emma Clifton (Girl), Chester Conklin (Cop), Sadie Lampe (Girl)

A FILM JOHNNIE   Mar. 2 (1020 ft.): Keystone   *Producer* Mack Sennett   *Director* George Nichols   *Screenplay* Craig Hutchinson   *Cast* Charles Chaplin (The Johnnie), Roscoe Arbuckle (Fatty), Virginia

Kirtley (Keystone Girl), Minta Durfee (Actress), Mabel Normand (Herself), Ford Sterling (Himself), Mack Sennett (Himself)

TANGO TANGLES   Mar. 9 (734 ft.): Keystone   *Producer* Mack Sennett   *Director* Mack Sennett   *Screenplay* Mack Sennett   *Cast* Charles Chaplin (Drunk), Ford Sterling (Bandleader), Roscoe Arbuckle (Clarinetist), Minta Durfee (Cloakroom Girl), Chester Conklin (Dancer)

HIS FAVORITE PASTIME   Mar. 16 (1009 ft.): Keystone   *Producer* Mack Sennett   *Director* George Nichols   *Screenplay* Craig Hutchinson   *Cast* Charles Chaplin (Drunk), Roscoe Arbuckle (Drunk), Peggy Pearce (Wife)

CRUEL, CRUEL LOVE   Mar. 26 (1035 ft.): Keystone   *Producer* Mack Sennett   *Director* George Nichols   *Screenplay* Craig Hutchinson   *Cast* Charles Chaplin (Mr. Dovey), Minta Durfee (Girl), Chester Conklin (Butler), Alice Davenport (Maid)

THE STAR BOARDER   Apr. 4 (1020 ft.): Keystone   *Producer* Mack Sennett   *Director* George Nichols   *Screenplay* Craig Hutchinson   *Cast* Charles Chaplin (Boarder), Minta Durfee (Landlady), Edgar Kennedy (Landlord), Gordon Griffith (Son)

MABEL AT THE WHEEL   Apr. 18 (1900 ft.): Keystone   *Producer* Mack Sennett   *Directors* Mack Sennett, Mabel Normand   *Cast* Mabel Normand (Mabel), Charles Chaplin (Villain), Harry McCoy (Boy Friend), Chester Conklin (Father), Mack Sennett (Rube), Al St. John (Henchman), William Seiter (Henchman)

TWENTY MINUTES OF LOVE   Apr. 20 (1009 ft.): Keystone   *Producer* Mack Sennett   *Director* Joseph Maddern   *Story/Screenplay* Charles Chaplin   *Cast* Charles Chaplin (Man), Minta Durfee (Girl), Edgar Kennedy (Boy Friend), Gordon Griffith (Boy), Chester Conklin (Thief), Joseph Swickard (Victim)

CAUGHT IN A CABARET   Apr. 27 (2053 ft.): Keystone   *Producer* Mack Sennett   *Directors* Mabel Normand, Charles Chaplin   *Story/ Screenplay* Charles Chaplin   *Cast* Charles Chaplin (Waiter), Mabel Normand (Girl), Harry McCoy (Fiancé), Chester Conklin (Waiter), Edgar Kennedy (Proprietor), Minta Durfee (Entertainer), Phyllis Allen (Entertainer), Alice Davenport (Mother), Joseph Swickard (Father), Gordon Griffith (Boy), Alice Howell, Hank Mann, Wallace MacDonald

CAUGHT IN THE RAIN May 4 (1015 ft.): Keystone *Producer*
Mack Sennett *Director* Charles Chaplin *Story/Screenplay* Charles
Chaplin *Cast* Charles Chaplin (Flirt), Alice Davenport (Wife),
Mack Swain (Husband), Alice Howell (Girl)

A BUSY DAY May 7 (441 ft.): Keystone *Producer* Mack Sennett
Director Charles Chaplin *Story/Screenplay* Charles Chaplin *Cast*
Charles Chaplin (Wife), Mack Swain (Husband)

THE FATAL MALLET June 1 (1120 ft.): Keystone *Producer*
Mack Sennett *Director* Mack Sennett *Cast* Mabel Normand (The
Girl), Charles Chaplin (The Eccentric Rival), Mack Sennett (Her
Adored One), Mack Swain (The Third Man)

HER FRIEND THE BANDIT June 4 (1000 ft.): Keystone *Pro-
ducer* Mack Sennett *Directors* Mabel Normand, Charles Chaplin *Cast*
Mabel Normand (Miss De Rock), Charles Chaplin (The Bandit),
Charles Murray (Count De Beans)

THE KNOCKOUT June 11 (1960 ft.): Keystone *Producer* Mack
Sennett *Director* Charles Avery *Cast* Roscoe Arbuckle (Fatty),
Minta Durfee (Girl), Edgar Kennedy (Cyclone Flynn), Charles Chap-
lin (Referee), Mack Swain (Spectator), Alice Howell (Spectator),
Al St. John, Hank Mann (Boxers), Mack Sennett (Spectator), George
Summerville, Charles Parrott (Cop), Joe Bordeaux (Cop), Edward
Cline (Cop)

MABEL'S BUSY DAY June 13 (998 ft.): Keystone *Producer* Mack
Sennett *Directors* Mabel Normand, Charles Chaplin *Cast* Mabel Normand (Mabel), Charles Chaplin (The Knut), Chester Conklin (Sergeant), Harry McCoy, Billie Bennett (Girl), George Summerville
(Cop), Wallace MacDonald

MABEL'S MARRIED LIFE June 20 (1015 ft.): Keystone *Pro-
ducer* Mack Sennett *Directors* Mabel Normand, Charles Chaplin *Cast*
Mabel Normand (Mabel), Charles Chaplin (Husband), Mack Swain
(Sportsman), Charles Murray (Man at Bar), Harry McCoy (Man at
Bar), Alice Howell (Sportsman's Wife), Hank Mann (Friend), Alice
Davenport (Neighbor), Al St. John (Delivery Man), Wallace Mac
Donald (Delivery Man)

LAUGHING GAS July 9 (1020 ft.): Keystone *Producer* Mack Sennett *Director* Charles Chaplin *Story/Screenplay* Charles Chaplin
Cast Charles Chaplin (Assistant), Fritz Schade (Dr. Pain), Alice

Howell (Mrs. Pain), Mack Swain (Bystander), George Summerville (Patient), Joseph Swickard (Patient), Edward Sutherland (Assistant)

THE PROPERTY MAN   Aug. 1 (2118 ft.): Keystone   *Producer* Mack Sennett   *Director* Charles Chaplin   *Story/Screenplay* Charles Chaplin   *Cast* Charles Chaplin (Props), Fritz Schade (Garlico), Phyllis Allen (Hamlena Fat), Alice Davenport (Actress), Charles Bennett (Actor), Mack Sennett (Man in Audience), Harry McCoy, Lee Morris

THE FACE ON THE BAR-ROOM FLOOR   Aug. 10 (1020 ft.): Keystone   *Producer* Mack Sennett   *Director* Charles Chaplin   *Story/Screenplay* Charles Chaplin   *from the poem by* Hugh Antoine D'Arcy   *Cast* Charles Chaplin (Artist), Cecile Arnold (Madeleine), Fritz Schade (Client), Chester Conklin (Man), Vivian Edwards (Girl), Harry McCoy (Drinker)

RECREATION   Aug. 13 (462 ft.): Keystone   *Producer* Mack Sennett   *Director* Charles Chaplin   *Story/Screenplay* Charles Chaplin   *Cast* Charles Chaplin (Tramp), Alice Davenport (Woman), Rhea Mitchell (Girl)

THE MASQUERADER   Aug. 27 (1030 ft.): Keystone   *Producer* Mack Sennett   *Director* Charles Chaplin   *Story/Screenplay* Charles Chaplin   *Cast* Charles Chaplin (Himself), Roscoe Arbuckle (Himself), Charles Murray (The Director), Chester Conklin (Himself), Fritz Schade (Villain), Minta Durfee (Heroine), Cecile Arnold (Actress), Vivian Edwards (Actress), Harry McCoy (Actor), Charles Parrott (Actor)

HIS NEW PROFESSION   Aug. 31 (1015 ft.): Keystone   *Producer* Mack Sennett   *Director* Charles Chaplin   *Story/Screenplay* Charles Chaplin   *Cast* Charles Chaplin (Charlie), Minta Durfee (Girl), Fritz Schade (Uncle), Charles Parrott (Nephew), Cecile Arnold (Girl), Harry McCoy (Cop)

THE ROUNDERS   Sept. 5 (1010 ft.): Keystone   *Producer* Mack Sennett   *Director* Charles Chaplin   *Story/Screenplay* Charles Chaplin   *Cast* Charles Chaplin (Mr. Full), Roscoe Arbuckle (Mr. Fuller), Phyllis Allen (Mrs. Full), Minta Durfee (Mrs. Fuller), Fritz Schade (Diner), Al St. John (Bellhop), Charles Parrott (Diner), Wallace MacDonald (Diner)

THE NEW JANITOR   Sept. 24 (1020 ft.): Keystone   *Producer* Mack Sennett   *Director* Charles Chaplin   *Story/Screenplay* Charles

Chaplin *Cast* Charles Chaplin (Janitor), Fritz Schade (President), Minta Durfee (Stenographer), Jack Dillon (Clerk), Al St. John (Elevator Operator)

THOSE LOVE PANGS Oct. 10 (1010 ft.): Keystone *Producer* Mack Sennett *Director* Charles Chaplin *Story/Screenplay* Charles Chaplin *Cast* Charles Chaplin (The Flirt), Chester Conklin (Rival), Cecile Arnold (Girl), Vivian Edwards (Girl), Edgar Kennedy (Man), Norma Nichols (Landlady), Harry McCoy (Cop)

DOUGH AND DYNAMITE Oct. 26 (2000 ft.): Keystone *Producer* Mack Sennett *Directors* Charles Chaplin, Mack Sennett *Story/ Screenplay* Charles Chaplin *Cast* Charles Chaplin (Pierre), Chester Conklin (Jacques), Fritz Schade (Monsieur La Vie), Cecile Arnold (Waitress), Vivian Edwards (Waitress), Phyllis Allen (Customer), Edgar Kennedy (Baker), Charles Parrott (Baker), George Summerville (Baker), Norma Nichols (Madame La Vie), Wallace MacDonald (Baker), Jack Dillon (Customer)

GENTLEMEN OF NERVE Oct. 29 (1030 ft.): Keystone *Producer* Mack Sennett *Director* Charles Chaplin *Story/Screenplay* Charles Chaplin *Cast* Charles Chaplin (Mr. Wow-wow), Mabel Normand (Mabel), Mack Swain (Ambrose), Chester Conklin (Walrus), Phyllis Allen (Wife), Edgar Kennedy (Cop), Charles Parrott (Spectator), George Summerville (Spectator), Alice Davenport (Waitress)

HIS MUSICAL CAREER Nov. 7 (1025 ft.): Keystone *Producer* Mack Sennett *Director* Charles Chaplin *Story/Screenplay* Charles Chaplin *Cast* Charles Chaplin (Tom), Mack Swain (Ambrose), Fritz Schade (Mr. Rich), Alice Howell (Mrs. Rich), Charles Parrott (Manager), Joe Bordeaux (Mr. Poor), Norma Nichols (Mrs. Poor)

HIS TRYSTING PLACE Nov. 9 (2000 ft.): Keystone *Producer* Mack Sennett *Director* Charles Chaplin *Story/Screenplay* Charles Chaplin *Cast* Charles Chaplin (Clarence), Mabel Normand (Mabel), Mack Swain (Ambrose), Phyllis Allen (Mrs. Ambrose)

TILLIE'S PUNCTURED ROMANCE Nov. 14 (6000 ft.): Keystone *Producer* Mack Sennett *Director* Mack Sennett *Screenplay* Hampton Del Ruth *from the play* Tillie's Nightmare by Edgar Smith *Cast* Marie Dressler (Tillie Banks), Charles Chaplin (Charlie), Mabel Normand (Mabel), Mack Swain (John Banks), Charles Bennett (Douglas Banks), Charles Murray (Detective), Chester Conklin (Guest), Charles Parrott (Detective), Edgar Kennedy (Proprietor), Harry McCoy (Pianist), Minta Durfee (Maid), Phyllis Allen (Wardress), Alice Davenport (Guest), Alice Howell (Guest), George Summerville (Cop), Al St. John (Cop), Wallace MacDonald (Cop), Hank Mann (Cop), Edward Sutherland (Cop), Joe Bordeaux (Cop), Gordon Griffith (Newsboy), Billie Bennett (Girl), G. G. Ligon (Cop), Rev. D. Simpson (Himself)

GETTING ACQUAINTED   Dec. 5 (1025 ft.): Keystone   *Producer* Mack Sennett   *Director* Charles Chaplin   *Story/Screenplay* Charles Chaplin   *Cast* Charles Chaplin (Mr. Sniffles), Mabel Normand (Mrs. Ambrose), Mack Swain (Ambrose), Phyllis Allen (Mrs. Sniffles), Harry McCoy (Cop), Edgar Kennedy (Turk), Cecile Arnold (Girl)

HIS PREHISTORIC PAST   Dec. 7 (2000 ft.): Keystone   *Producer* Mack Sennett   *Director* Charles Chaplin   *Story/Screenplay* Charles Chaplin   *Cast* Charles Chaplin (Weakchin), Mack Swain (King Lowbrow), Fritz Schade (Cleo), Gene Marsh (Favorite Wife), Cecile Arnold (Cavegirl), Al St. John (Caveman)

1915

HIS NEW JOB   Feb. 1 (2000 ft.): Essanay   *Producer* Jess Robbins *Director* Charles Chaplin   *Story/Screenplay* Charles Chaplin   *Photography* Roland Totheroh   *Cast* Charles Chaplin (Himself), Ben Turpin (Himself), Charlotte Mineau (Actress), Charles Insley (Director), Leo White (Actor), Frank J. Coleman (Manager), Gloria Swanson (Stenographer), Agnes Ayres (Stenographer)

A NIGHT OUT   Feb. 10 (2000 ft.): Essanay   *Producer* Jess Robbins *Director* Charles Chaplin   *Story/Screenplay* Charles Chaplin   *Photography* Roland Totheroh, Harry Ensign   *Assistant Director* Ernest Van Pelt   *Cast* Charles Chaplin (Drunk), Ben Turpin (Drunk), Leo White (Count), Bud Jamison (Waiter), Edna Purviance (Wife), Fred Goodwins (Man)

THE CHAMPION   Mar. 5 (2000 ft.): Essanay   *Producer* Jess Robbins   *Director* Charles Chaplin   *Story/Screenplay* Charles Chaplin   *Photography* Roland Totheroh, Harry Ensign   *Assistant Director* Ernest Van Pelt   *Cast* Charles Chaplin (Tramp), Edna Purviance (Girl), Bud Jamison (Champion), Leo White (Count), Billy Armstrong (Sparring Partner), Paddy McGuire (Sparring Partner), Carl Stockdale (Sparring Partner), Lloyd Bacon (Spike Dugan), Ben Turpin (Salesman), G. M. Anderson (Spectator)

IN THE PARK Mar. 12 (1000 ft.): Essanay *Producer* Jess Robbins *Director* Charles Chaplin *Story/Screenplay* Charles Chaplin *Photography* Roland Totheroh, Harry Ensign *Assistant Director* Ernest Van Pelt *Cast* Charles Chaplin (Flirt), Edna Purviance (Nursemaid), Leo White (Count), Lloyd Bacon (Tramp), Bud Jamison (Boy Friend), Billy Armstrong (Man), Margie Reiger (Girl), Ernest Van Pelt (Cop)

A JITNEY ELOPEMENT Mar. 23 (2000 ft.): Essanay *Producer* Jess Robbins *Director* Charles Chaplin *Story/Screenplay* Charles Chaplin *Photography* Roland Totheroh, Harry Ensign *Assistant Director* Ernest Van Pelt *Cast* Charles Chaplin (Tramp), Edna Purviance (Girl), Leo White (Count De Haha), Paddy McGuire (Old Servant/Cop), Lloyd Bacon (Footman), Bud Jamison (Cop), Ernest Van Pelt (Cop)

THE TRAMP Apr. 7 (2000 ft.): Essanay *Producer* Jess Robbins *Director* Charles Chaplin *Story/Screenplay* Charles Chaplin *Photography* Roland Totheroh, Harry Ensign *Assistant Director* Ernest Van Pelt *Cast* Charles Chaplin (Tramp), Edna Purviance (Girl), Leo White (Tramp), Fred Goodwins (Farmer), Bud Jamison (Tramp), Lloyd Bacon (Sweetheart), Paddy McGuire (Farmhand), Ernest Van Pelt (Tramp), Billy Armstrong (Poet)

BY THE SEA Apr. 26 (1000 ft.): Essanay *Producer* Jess Robbins *Director* Charles Chaplin *Story/Screenplay* Charles Chaplin *Photography* Roland Totheroh, Harry Ensign *Assistant Director* Ernest Van Pelt *Cast* Charles Chaplin (Man), Edna Purviance (Girl), Billy Armstrong (Other Man), Bud Jamison (Dandy), Margie Reiger (Girl), Paddy McGuire (Cop)

HIS REGENERATION May 3 (963 ft.): Essanay *Producer* G. M. Anderson *Cast* G. M. Anderson, Lee Willard, Marguerite Clayton, Hazel Applegate, Charles Chaplin

WORK June 2 (2000 ft.): Essanay *Producer* Jess Robbins *Director* Charles Chaplin *Story/Screenplay* Charles Chaplin *Photography* Roland Totheroh, Harry Ensign *Assistant Director* Ernest Van Pelt *Scenic Artist* E. T. Mazy *Cast* Charles Chaplin (Assistant), Edna Purviance (Maid), Charles Insley (Paperhanger), Billy Armstrong (Husband), Marta Golden (Wife), Leo White (Lover), Paddy McGuire (Hod Carrier)

A WOMAN July 7 (2000 ft.): Essanay *Producer* Jess Robbins *Director* Charles Chaplin *Story/Screenplay* Charles Chaplin *Photog-*

raphy Roland Totheroh, Harry Ensign *Assistant Director* Ernest Van Pelt *Scenic Artist* E. T. Mazy *Cast* Charles Chaplin (Tramp), Edna Purviance (Girl), Charles Insley (Father), Marta Golden (Mother), Billy Armstrong (Suitor), Margie Reiger (Flirt), Leo White (Gentleman)

THE BANK Aug. 9 (2000 ft.): Essanay *Producer* Jess Robbins *Director* Charles Chaplin *Story/Screenplay* Charles Chaplin *Photography* Roland Totheroh, Harry Ensign *Assistant Director* Ernest Van Pelt *Scenic Artist* E. T. Mazy *Cast* Charles Chaplin (Charlie the Janitor), Edna Purviance (Edna), Carl Stockdale (Charlie the Cashier), Billy Armstrong (Janitor), Charles Insley (Manager), John Rand (Salesman), Leo White (Officer), Fred Goodwins (Thief), Frank J. Coleman (Thief), Wesley Ruggles (Thief), Paddy McGuire, Lloyd Bacon

SHANGHAIED Sept. 27 (2000 ft.): Essanay *Producer* Jess Robbins *Director* Charles Chaplin *Story/Screenplay* Charles Chaplin *Photography* Roland Totheroh, Harry Ensign *Assistant Director* Ernest Van Pelt *Scenic Artist* E. T. Mazy *Cast* Charles Chaplin (Tramp), Edna Purviance (Edna), Wesley Ruggles (Owner), John Rand (Captain), Bud Jamison (Mate), Lawrence A. Bowes (Cook), Billy Armstrong (Seaman), Paddy McGuire (Seaman), Leo White (Seaman), Fred Goodwins (Seaman)

A NIGHT IN THE SHOW Nov. 2 (2000 ft.): Essanay *Producer* Jess Robbins *Director* Charles Chaplin *Story/Screenplay* Charles Chaplin *Photography* Roland Totheroh *Assistant Director* Ernest Van Pelt *Scenic Artist* E. T. Mazy *Cast* Charles Chaplin (Mr. Pest / Mr. Rowdy), Edna Purviance (Lady), Leo White (Count / Prof. Nix), John Rand (Conductor), Bud Jamison (Dot), James T. Kelley (Dash), Dee Lampton (Fat Boy), May White (La Belle Wienerwurst), Paddy McGuire (Trombonist), Fred Goodwins (Tuba Player), Carrie Clarke Ward (Woman)

CHARLIE CHAPLIN'S BURLESQUE ON CARMEN Dec.–Apr. 3, 1916 (4000 ft.): Essanay *Producer* Jess Robbins *Director* Charles Chaplin *Screenplay* Charles Chaplin *from the story by* Prosper Mérimée *and the opera by* H. Meilhac, L. Halévy, Georges Bizet *Photography* Roland Totheroh *Assistant Director* Ernest Van Pelt *Scenic Artist* E. T. Mazy *Cast* Charles Chaplin (Darn Hosiery), Edna Purviance (Carmen), Ben Turpin (Don Remendado), Leo White (Morales), John Rand (Escamillo), Jack Henderson (Lilias Pasta), May

White (Frasquita), Bud Jamison (Soldier), Wesley Ruggles (Tramp), Lawrence A. Bowes, Frank J. Coleman

1916

POLICE Mar. 27 (2000 ft.): Essanay *Producer* Jess Robbins *Director* Charles Chaplin *Story* Charles Chaplin, Vincent Bryan *Screenplay* Charles Chaplin *Photography* Roland Totheroh *Assistant Director* Ernest Van Pelt *Scenic Artist* E. T. Mazy *Cast* Charles Chaplin (Convict 999), Edna Purviance (Girl), Wesley Ruggles (Crook), Billy Armstrong (Crook), John Rand (Cop), Leo White (Lodging House Keeper / Vendor / Cop), James T. Kelley (Drunk / Tramp), Fred Goodwins (Cop / Pastor), Bud Jamison (Cop), Frank J. Coleman (Cop)

THE FLOORWALKER May 15 (1734 ft.): Lone Star-Mutual *Producer/Director* Charles Chaplin *Story* Charles Chaplin, Vincent Bryan *Screenplay* Charles Chaplin *Photography* Roland Totheroh, William C. Foster *Scenic Artist* E. T. Mazy *Cast* Charles Chaplin (The Floorwalker), Edna Purviance (Secretary), Eric Campbell (George Brush), Lloyd Bacon (Assistant), Albert Austin (Clerk), Leo White (Count), Charlotte Mineau (Detective), Tom Nelson (Detective), Henry Bergman (Old Man), James T. Kelley (Elevator Operator), Bud Jamison, Stanley Sanford, Frank J. Coleman

THE FIREMAN June 12 (1921 ft.): Lone Star-Mutual *Producer/Director* Charles Chaplin *Story* Charles Chaplin, Vincent Bryan *Screenplay* Charles Chaplin *Photography* Roland Totheroh, William C. Foster *Scenic Artist* E. T. Mazy *Cast* Charles Chaplin (The Fireman), Edna Purviance (Edna), Eric Campbell (Captain), Lloyd Bacon (Father), Leo White (Householder), John Rand (Fireman), Albert Austin (Fireman), James T. Kelley (Fireman), Frank J. Coleman (Fireman), Charlotte Mineau (Mother)

THE VAGABOND July 10 (1956 ft.): Lone Star-Mutual *Producer/Director* Charles Chaplin *Story* Charles Chaplin, Vincent Bryan *Screenplay* Charles Chaplin *Photography* Roland Totheroh, William C. Foster *Cast* Charles Chaplin (The Vagabond), Edna Purviance (Girl), Eric Campbell (Gypsy Chief), Leo White (Gypsy Hag / Jew), Lloyd Bacon (Artist), Charlotte Mineau (Mother), Phyllis Allen (Woman), John Rand (Trumpeter), Albert Austin (Trombonist), James T. Kelley (Bandsman), Frank J. Coleman (Bandsman)

ONE A.M.   Aug. 7 (2000 ft.): Lone Star-Mutual *Producer/Director* Charles Chaplin *Story/Screenplay* Charles Chaplin *Photography* Roland Totheroh, William C. Foster *Scenic Artist* E. T. Mazy *Cast* Charles Chaplin (The Drunk), Albert Austin (Taxi Driver)

THE COUNT   Sept. 4 (2000 ft.): Lone Star-Mutual *Producer/Director* Charles Chaplin *Story/Screenplay* Charles Chaplin *Photography* Roland Totheroh, William C. Foster *Cast* Charles Chaplin (Assistant), Edna Purviance (Edna Moneybags), Eric Campbell (Buttinsky), Leo White (Count Broko), Charlotte Mineau (Mrs. Moneybags), James T. Kelley (Butler), Albert Austin (Guest), Frank J. Coleman (Cop), John Rand (Guest), May White (Ima Pipp), Stanley Sanford (Guest), Leota Bryan (Girl), Eva Thatcher (Flirtitia Doughbelle), Loyal Underwood (Small Man)

THE PAWNSHOP   Oct. 2 (1940 ft.): Lone Star-Mutual *Producer/Director* Charles Chaplin *Story/Screenplay* Charles Chaplin *Photography* Roland Totheroh, William C. Foster *Cast* Charles Chaplin (Assistant), Edna Purviance (Daughter), Henry Bergman (Pawn Broker), John Rand (Clerk), Eric Campbell (Thief), Albert Austin (Customer), Frank J. Coleman (Cop), James T. Kelley (Customer)

BEHIND THE SCREEN   Nov. 13 (1796 ft.): Lone Star-Mutual *Producer/Director* Charles Chaplin *Story/Screenplay* Charles Chaplin *Photography* Roland Totheroh, William C. Foster *Cast* Charles Chaplin (David), Edna Purviance (Country Girl), Eric Campbell (Goliath), Henry Bergman (Director), Lloyd Bacon (Director), Albert Austin (Stage Hand), Frank J. Coleman (Assistant Director), Charlotte Mineau (Actress), John Rand (Stage Hand), James T. Kelley (Cameraman)

THE RINK   Dec. 4 (1881 ft.): Lone Star-Mutual *Producer/Director* Charles Chaplin *Story/Screenplay* Charles Chaplin *Photography* Roland Totheroh, William C. Foster *Cast* Charles Chaplin (Waiter), Edna Purviance (Edna Loneleigh), Eric Campbell (Mr. Stout), Henry Bergman (Mrs. Stout), Frank J. Coleman (Mr. Loneleigh), Charlotte Mineau (Friend), Albert Austin (Cook / Skater), James T. Kelley (Cook), John Rand (Fritz), Lloyd Bacon (Customer)

1917

EASY STREET   Jan. 22 (1757 ft.): Lone Star-Mutual *Producer/Director* Charles Chaplin *Story/Screenplay* Charles Chaplin *Photog-*

raphy Roland Totheroh, William C. Foster *Cast* Charles Chaplin (Tramp), Edna Purviance (Missioner), Eric Campbell (Big Eric), Henry Bergman (Anarchist), Albert Austin (Minister / Cop), James T. Kelley (Missioner / Cop), John Rand (Tramp / Cop), Frank J. Coleman (Cop), Leo White (Cop), Charlotte Mineau (Wife), Lloyd Bacon (Drug Addict), Janet Miller Sully (Mother), Loyal Underwood (Police Chief / Father)

THE CURE Apr. 16 (1834 ft.): Lone Star-Mutual *Producer/Director* Charles Chaplin *Story/Screenplay* Charles Chaplin *Photography* Roland Totheroh, William C. Foster *Cast* Charles Chaplin (Drunk), Edna Purviance (Girl), Eric Campbell (Patient), Henry Bergman (Masseur), John Rand (Attendant), Albert Austin (Attendant), Frank J. Coleman (Proprietor), James T. Kelley (Bell Hop), Leota Bryan (Nurse), Janet Miller Sully (Woman), Loyal Underwood (Patient), Tom Wood (Patient)

THE IMMIGRANT June 17 (1809 ft.): Lone Star-Mutual *Producer/Director* Charles Chaplin *Story/Screenplay* Charles Chaplin *Photography* Roland Totheroh, William C. Foster *Cast* Charles Chaplin (Immigrant), Edna Purviance (Girl), Eric Campbell (Head Waiter), Kitty Bradbury (Mother), Albert Austin (Immigrant / Diner), Henry Bergman (Woman / Artist), James T. Kelley (Tramp / Immigrant), Frank J. Coleman (Proprietor / Official), Stanley Sanford (Gambler), John Rand (Customer), Loyal Underwood (Immigrant)

THE ADVENTURER Oct. 22 (1845 ft.): Lone Star-Mutual *Producer/Director* Charles Chaplin *Story/Screenplay* Charles Chaplin *Photography* Roland Totheroh, William C. Foster *Cast* Charles Chaplin (Convict), Edna Purviance (Girl), Eric Campbell (Suitor), Henry Bergman (Father / Workman), Marta Golden (Mother), Albert Austin (Butler), Frank J. Coleman (Guard), James T. Kelley (Old Man), Phyllis Allen (Governess), Toraichi Kono (Chauffeur), John Rand (Guest), May White (Lady), Loyal Underwood (Guest), Janet Miller Sully (Marie), Monta Bell (Man)

1918

A DOG'S LIFE Apr. 12 (2674 ft.): Chaplin-First National *Producer/Director* Charles Chaplin *Story/Screenplay* Charles Chaplin *Photography* Roland Totheroh *Assistant Director* Charles Riesner *Cast* Charles Chaplin (Tramp), Edna Purviance (Singer), Sydney

Chaplin (Proprietor), Tom Wilson (Cop), Albert Austin (Thief), Henry Bergman (Tramp / Woman), James T. Kelley (Thief), Charles Riesner (Clerk), Billy White (Café Owner), Janet Miller Sully (Singer), Bud Jamison (Client), Loyal Underwood (Client), Park Jones (Waiter), Scraps (The Dog)

TRIPLE TROUBLE   July 23 (2000 ft.) : Essanay   *Producer* Jess Robbins   *Directors* Charles Chaplin, Leo White   *Story/Screenplay* Charles Chaplin, Leo White   *Photography* Roland Totheroh   *Assistant Director* Ernest Van Pelt   *Cast* Charles Chaplin (Janitor), Edna Purviance (Maid), Leo White (Anarchist), Billy Armstrong (Cook / Thief), James T. Kelley (Singer), Bud Jamison (Tramp), Wesley Ruggles (Crook), Albert Austin (Man)

SHOULDER ARMS   Oct. 2 (3142 ft.) : Chaplin-First National   *Producer/Director* Charles Chaplin   *Story/Screenplay* Charles Chaplin   *Photography* Roland Totheroh   *Assistant Director* Charles Riesner   *Cast* Charles Chaplin (Rookie), Edna Purviance (French Girl), Sydney Chaplin (Kaiser Wilhelm / Soldier), Henry Bergman (Hindenburg / Bartender / Officer), Jack Wilson (Crown Prince / Soldier), Albert Austin (Officer / Kaiser's Driver / Rookie), Tom Wilson (Sergeant), John Rand (Soldier), Loyal Underwood (Captain), Park Jones (Soldier)

CHARLES CHAPLIN IN A LIBERTY LOAN APPEAL (THE BOND)   Oct. 4 (500 ft.) Chaplin-Liberty Loan Committee   *Producer/Director* Charles Chaplin   *Story/Screenplay* Charles Chaplin   *Photography* Roland Totheroh   *Cast* Charles Chaplin (Charlie), Sydney Chaplin (The Kaiser), Edna Purviance, Albert Austin

1919

SUNNYSIDE   June 4 (2769 ft.) : Chaplin-First National   *Producer/Director* Charles Chaplin   *Story/Screenplay* Charles Chaplin   *Photography* Roland Totheroh   *Cast* Charles Chaplin (Handyman), Edna Purviance (Girl), Tom Wilson (Boss), Henry Bergman (Father), Albert Austin (Slicker), Loyal Underwood (Old Man), Park Jones (Fat Man), Tom Wood (Peasant), Tom Terriss (City Man)

A DAY'S PLEASURE   Nov. 26 (1714 ft.) : Chaplin-First National   *Producer/Director* Charles Chaplin   *Story/Screenplay* Charles Chaplin   *Photography* Roland Totheroh   *Cast* Charles Chaplin (Father), Edna

Purviance (Mother), Tom Wilson (Cop), Sydney Chaplin (Father), Henry Bergman (Captain), Babe London (Fat Girl), Albert Austin (Trombonist), Loyal Underwood (Musician), Raymond Lee (Boy), Jackie Coogan (Boy)

1921

THE KID Jan. 17 (5300 ft.): Chaplin-First National *Producer/ Director* Charles Chaplin *Story/Screenplay* Charles Chaplin *Photography* Roland Totheroh *Associate Director* Charles Riesner *Cast* Charles Chaplin (Tramp), Edna Purviance (Woman), Jackie Coogan (Kid), Carl Miller (Artist), Tom Wilson (Cop), Charles Riesner (Bully), Henry Bergman (Proprietor), Albert Austin (Crook), Phyllis Allen (Woman), Nelly Bly Baker (Neighbor), Jack Coogan (Man), Monta Bell (Man), Raymond Lee (Boy), Lillita Grey (Angel) .

THE IDLE CLASS Sept. 6 (1916 ft.): Chaplin-First National *Producer/Director* Charles Chaplin *Story/Screenplay* Charles Chaplin *Photography* Roland Totheroh *Cast* Charles Chaplin (Tramp / Husband), Edna Purviance (Wife), Mack Swain (Father), Henry Bergman (Tramp / Cop), Rex Storey (Robber / Guest), John Rand (Tramp / Guest), Allan Garcia (Golfer / Guest), Loyal Underwood (Guest), Lillian McMurray, Lillita McMurray (Maids)

1922

PAY DAY Mar. 13 (1892 ft.): Chaplin-First National *Producer/ Director* Charles Chaplin *Story/Screenplay* Charles Chaplin *Photography* Roland Totheroh *Cast* Charles Chaplin (Worker), Edna Purviance (Daughter), Mack Swain (Foreman), Phyllis Allen (Wife), Sydney Chaplin (Friend / Proprietor), Henry Bergman (Drinker), Allan Garcia (Drinker), Albert Austin (Workman), John Rand, Loyal Underwood (Workmen)

NICE AND FRIENDLY (Non-commercial film) Accidental Film Corporation *Producer/Director* Charles Chaplin *Story/Screenplay* Charles Chaplin *Cast* Charles Chaplin, Lord Louis Mountbatten, Lady Edwina Mountbatten, Jackie Coogan, Col. Robert M. Thompson, Frederick Neilson, Eulalie Neilson

1923

THE PILGRIM Jan. 24 (4300 ft.): Chaplin-First National *Producer/Director* Charles Chaplin *Story/Screenplay* Charles Chaplin *Photography* Roland Totheroh *Associate Director* Charles Riesner *Cast* Charles Chaplin (Pilgrim), Edna Purviance (Edna Brown), Mack Swain (Deacon), Kitty Bradbury (Mrs. Brown), "Dinky Dean" Riesner (Boy), Sydney Chaplin (Father), Mai Wells (Mother), Charles Riesner (Thief), Loyal Underwood (Elder), Tom Murray (Sheriff), Monta Bell (Policeman), Henry Bergman (Traveller), Edith Bostwick (Lady), Florence Latimer (Lady), Phyllis Allen (Lady)

A WOMAN OF PARIS Oct. 1 (7577 ft.): Regent-United Artists *Producer/Director* Charles Chaplin *Story/Screenplay* Charles Chaplin *Photography* Roland Totheroh *Cameraman* Jack Wilson *Assistant Director* Edward Sutherland *Literary Editor* Monta Bell *Art Director* Arthur Stibolt *Research* Jean de Limur, Harry d'Arrast *Cast* Edna Purviance (Marie St. Clair), Adolphe Menjou (Pierre Revel), Carl Miller (Jean Millet), Lydia Knott (Madame Millet), Charles French (Monsieur Millet), Clarence Geldert (Monsieur St. Clair), Betty Morrissey (Fifi), Malvina Polo (Paulette), Karl Gutman (Conductor), Henry Bergman (Maitre d'hotel), Harry Northrup (Valet), Nelly Bly Baker (Masseuse), Charles Chaplin (Porter)

1925

THE GOLD RUSH Aug. 16 (8498 ft.): Chaplin-United Artists *Producer/Director* Charles Chaplin *Story/Screenplay* Charles Chaplin *Photography* Roland Totheroh *Cameraman* Jack Wilson *Technical Director* Charles D. Hall *Associate Directors* Charles Riesner, Henri d'Abbadie d'Arrast *Production Manager* Alfred Reeves *Cast* Charles Chaplin (The Lone Prospector), Georgia Hale (Georgia), Mack Swain (Big Jim McKay), Tom Murray (Black Larson), Malcolm Waite (Jack Cameron), Henry Bergman (Hank Curtis), Betty Morrissey (Betty), John Rand (Prospector), Albert Austin (Prospector), Heinie Conklin (Prospector), Allan Garcia (Prospector), Tom Wood (Prospector)

Reissue with sound track Apr. 18, 1942 (72 mins.) *Music* Charles Chaplin *Narrator* Charles Chaplin

1926

A WOMAN OF THE SEA (length unknown): Chaplin *Producer* Charles Chaplin *Directors* Josef von Sternberg, Charles Chaplin *Story* Charles Chaplin *Screenplay* Josef von Sternberg *Photography* Paul Ivano *Art Director* Charles D. Hall *Cast* Edna Purviance (The Woman), Eve Southern, Gayne Whitman

1928

THE CIRCUS Jan. 6 (6700 ft.): Chaplin-United Artists *Producer/ Director* Charles Chaplin *Story/Screenplay* Charles Chaplin *Photography* Roland Totheroh *Cameramen* Jack Wilson, Mark Marklatt *Assistant Director* Harry Crocker *Art Director* Charles D. Hall *Editor* Charles Chaplin *Laboratory Supervisor* William F.. Hinkley *Cast* Charles Chaplin (The Tramp), Merna Kennedy (The Equestrienne), Betty Morrissey (The Vanishing Lady), Harry Crocker (Rex), Allan Garcia (Proprietor), Henry Bergman (Merry Clown), Stanley J. Sanford (Ringmaster), George Davis (Magician), John Rand (Property Man), Steve Murphy (Pickpocket), Doc Stone (Boxer), Albert Austin, Heinie Conklin

Reissue with sound track 1970 (71 mins.) *Music* Charles Chaplin *Song* Charles Chaplin *Singer* Charles Chaplin

1931

CITY LIGHTS Feb. 1 (87 mins.): Chaplin-United Artists *Producer/Director* Charles Chaplin *Story/Screenplay* Charles Chaplin *Photography* Roland Totheroh *Cameramen* Gordon Pollock, Mark Marklatt *Assistant Directors* Harry Crocker, Henry Bergman, Albert Austin *Art Director* Charles D. Hall *Music* Charles Chaplin; Padilla (La Violetera) *Music Arranger* Arthur Johnson *Music Director* Alfred Newman *Production Manager* Alfred Reeves *Cast* Charles Chaplin (The Tramp), Virginia Cherrill (The Blind Girl), Harry Myers (The Millionaire), Hank Mann (Boxer), Allan Garcia (Butler), Florence Lee (Grandmother), Henry Bergman (Mayor / Janitor), Albert Austin

(Sweeper / Crook), John Rand (Tramp), James Donnelly (Foreman), Robert Parrish (Newsboy), Stanhope Wheatcroft (Man in Cafe), Jean Harlow (Guest)

1936

MODERN TIMES Feb. 5 (85 mins.): Chaplin-United Artists *Producer/Director* Charles Chaplin *Story/Screenplay* Charles Chaplin *Photography* Roland Totheroh, Ira Morgan *Assistant Directors* Carter de Haven, Henry Bergman *Art Directors* Charles D. Hall, J. Russell Spencer *Music* Charles Chaplin; Leo Daniderff (Je Cherche Apres Titine) *Music Arrangers* Edward Powell, David Raskin *Music Director* Alfred Newman *Production Managers* Alfred Reeves, Jack Wilson *Cast* Charles Chaplin (A Worker), Paulette Goddard (A Gamine), Henry Bergman (Proprietor), Stanley J. Sanford (Big Bill), Chester Conklin (Mechanic), Hank Mann (Burglar), Stanley Blystone (Sheriff Couler), Allan Garcia (President), Dick Alexander (Convict), Cecil Reynolds (Chaplain), Myra McKinney (Chaplain's Wife), Lloyd Ingraham (Governor), Louis Natheaux (Addict), Heinie Conklin (Workman), Frank Moran (Convict), Murdoch McQuarrie, Wilfred Lucas, Edward le Saint, Fred Maltesta, Sam Stein, Juana Sutton, Ted Oliver, Edward Kimball, John Rand, Walter James

1940

THE GREAT DICTATOR Oct. 15 (126 mins.): Chaplin-United Artists *Producer/Director* Charles Chaplin *Story/Screenplay* Charles Chaplin *Photography* Roland Totheroh, Karl Struss *Assistant Directors* Daniel James, Wheeler Dryden, Robert Meltzer *Coordinator* Henry Bergman *Art Director* J. Russell Spencer *Editor* Willard Nico *Music* Charles Chaplin; Wagner, Brahms *Music Director* Meredith Willson *Sound* Percy Townsend, Glenn Rominger *Cast* Charles Chaplin (Adenoid Hynkel / The Barber), Paulette Goddard (Hannah), Jack Oakie (Benzino Napoloni), Henry Daniell (Garbitsch), Reginald Gardiner (Schultz), Billy Gilbert (Herring), Maurice Moskovich (Mr. Jaeckel), Emma Dunn (Mrs. Jaeckel), Bernard Gorcey (Mr. Mann), Paul Weigel (Mr. Agar), Grace Hayle (Madame Napoloni), Carter de Haven (Ambassador), Chester Conklin (Customer), Eddie Gribbon (Storm Trooper), Hank Mann (Storm Trooper), Leo White (Barber), Lucian Prival (Officer), Richard Alexander (Storm Trooper), Esther Michelson, Florence Wright, Robert O. David, Eddie Dunn, Peter Lynn Hayes, Nita Pike, Harry Semels, Jack Perrin, Pat Flaherty, John Davidson (Superintendent), Stanley J. Sanford

1947

MONSIEUR VERDOUX Apr. 11 (122 mins.): Chaplin-United Artists *Producer/Director* Charles Chaplin *Story/Screenplay* Charles Chaplin *from an idea by* Orson Welles *Photography* Roland Totheroh, Wallace Chewing *Associate Director* Robert Florey *Artistic Supervisor* Curtis Courant *Assistant Directors* Rex Bailey, Wheeler Dryden *Art Director* John Beckman *Editor* Willard Nico *Music* Charles Chaplin *Music Director* Rudolph Schrager *Sound* James T. Corrigan *Costumes* Drew Tetrick *Narrator* Charles Chaplin *Cast* Charles Chaplin (Henri Verdoux), Martha Raye (Annabella Bonheur), Isobel Elsom (Marie Grosnay), Marilyn Nash (The Girl), Robert Lewis (Maurice Bottello), Mady Correll (Mona Verdoux), Allison Rodell (Peter Verdoux), Audrey Betz (Martha Bottello), Ada-May (Annette), Marjorie Bennett (Maid), Helen Heigh (Yvonne), Margaret Hoffman (Lydia Floray), Irving Bacon (Pierre Couvais), Edwin Mills (Jean Couvais), Virginia Brissac (Carlotta Couvais), Elmira Sessions (Lena Couvais), Eula Morgan (Phoebe Couvais), Bernard J. Nedell (Prefect), Charles Evans (Detective Morron), Arthur Hohl (Estate Agent), John Harmon (Joe Darwin), Vera Marshe (Mrs. Darwin), William Frawley (Jean la Salle), Fritz Lieber (Priest), Barbara Slater (Florist), Fred Karno, Jr. (Mr. Karno), Barry Norton (Guest), Pierre Watkin (Official), Cyril Delavanti (Postman), Charles Wagenheim (Friend), Addison Richards (Manager), James Craven (Friend), Franklin Farnum (Victim), Herb Vigran (Reporter), Boyd Irwin (Official), Paul Newland (Guest), Joseph Crehan (Broker), Wheaton Chambers (Druggist), Frank Reicher (Doctor), Wheeler Dryden (Capt. Brunel), Edna Purviance (Extra), Christine Ell, Lois Conklin, Tom Wilson, Phillips Smalley, Lester Matthews (Prosecutor)

1952

LIMELIGHT Oct. 23 (143 mins.): Celebrated-United Artists *Producer/Director* Charles Chaplin *Story/Screenplay* Charles Chaplin *Associate Director* Robert Aldrich *Assistant Producers* Jerome

Epstein, Wheeler Dryden *Photography* Karl Struss *Photographic Consultant* Roland Totheroh *Art Director* Eugene Lourie *Editor* Joseph Engel *Music* Charles Chaplin *Songs* Charles Chaplin, Ray Rasch *Choreography* Charles Chaplin, Andre Eglevsky, Melissa Hayden *Cast* Charles Chaplin (Calvero), Claire Bloom (Terry-Thereza), Nigel Bruce (Postant), Buster Keaton (Partner), Sydney Chaplin (Neville), Norman Lloyd (Bodalink), Andre Eglevsky (Harlequin), Melissa Hayden (Columbine), Marjorie Bennett (Mrs. Alsop), Wheeler Dryden (Doctor / Clown), Barry Bernard (John Redfern), Leonard Mudie (Doctor), Snub Pollard (Musician), Charles Chaplin, Jr. (Clown), Geraldine Chaplin (Child), Michael Chaplin (Child), Josephine Chaplin (Child), Edna Purviance (Woman), Loyal Underwood, Stapleton Kent, Mollie Blessing, Julian Ludwig

1957

A KING IN NEW YORK Sept. 12 (109 mins.): Attica-Archway *Producer/Director* Charles Chaplin *Story/Screenplay* Charles Chaplin *Photography* Georges Perinal *Art Director* Allan Harris *Editor* John Seabourne *Music* Charles Chaplin *Sound* Spencer Reeves *Cast* Charles Chaplin (King Shahdov), Dawn Addams (Ann Kay), Oliver Johnston (Jaumé), Maxine Audley (Queen Irene), Jerry Desmonde (Prime Minister), Michael Chaplin (Rupert McAbee), Harry Green (Lawyer Green), Phil Brown (Headmaster), John McLaren (McAbee, Sr.), Alan Gifford (School Superintendent), Shani Wallis (Singer), Joy Nichols (Singer), Joan Ingram (Mona Cromwell), Sidney James (Johnson), Robert Arden (Elevator Operator), Nicholas Tannar (Butler), Lauri Lupino Lane (Comedian), George Truzzi (Comedian), George Woodbridge, MacDonald Parke

1966

A COUNTESS FROM HONG KONG Nov. (120 mins.): Universal *Producer* Jerome Epstein *Director* Charles Chaplin *Story/Screenplay* Charles Chaplin *Photography* Arthur Ibbetson *Production Supervisor* Denis Johnson *Production Designer* Don Ashton *Art Director* Robert Cartwright *Set Decorator* Vernon Dixon *Editor* Gordon Hales *Assistant Director* Jack Causey *Music* Charles Chaplin *Music Director* Lambert Williamson *Music Associate* Eric James *Sound* Michael Hopkins *Sound Recording* Bill Daniels, Ken Barker

Titles Gordon Shadrick *Color* Technicolor *Process* Cinemascope *Cast* Marlon Brando (Ogden Mears), Sophia Loren (Countess Natascha Alexandroff), Sydney Chaplin (Harvey Crothers), Tippi Hedren (Martha Mears), Patrick Cargill (Hudson), Margaret Rutherford (Miss Gaulswallow), Michael Medwin (John Felix), Oliver Johnston (Clark), John Paul (Captain), Angela Scoular (Society Girl), Peter Bartlett (Steward), Bill Nagy (Crawford), Dilys Laye (Saleswoman), Angela Pringle (Baroness), Jenny Bridges (Countess), Arthur Gross (Immigration Officer), Balbina (Maid), Anthony Chin (Hawaiian), Jose Sukhum Boonlve (Hawaiian), Geraldine Chaplin (Girl at Dance), Janine Hill (Girl at Dance), Burnell Tucker (Receptionist), Leonard Trolley (Purser), Len Lowe (Electrician), Francis Dux (Head Waiter), Cecil Cheng (Taxi Driver), Ronald Rubin (Sailor), Michael Spice (Sailor), Ray Marlowe (Sailor), Josephine Chaplin (Young Girl), Victoria Chaplin (Young Girl), Kevin Manser (Photographer), Marianne Stone (Reporter), Lew Luton (Reporter), Larry Cross (Reporter), Bill Edwards (Reporter), Drew Russell (Reporter), John Sterland (Reporter), Paul Carson (Reporter), Paul Tamarin (Reporter), Carol Cleveland (Nurse), Charles Chaplin (An Old Steward)

1974

THE GENTLEMAN TRAMP   Released 1975 by rbc films, Los Angeles. (78 mins.)   *Producer* Bert Schneider   *Director/Writer/Editor* Richard Patterson   *Cameraman* Nestor Almendros   *Music* Charles Chaplin   *Narrators* Walter Matthau, Jack Lemmon, Laurence Olivier. A life and career overview of Chaplin with color footage of his life in retirement at Corsier. Won the Emily Award, American Film Festival, 1976.

INDEX